P9-DCX-579

Zingerman's traditional jewish foods

1980

ari and Paul begin a conversation about how ann arbor could use a traditional jewish deli like the ones they grew up with in detroit (Paul) and chicago (ari).

november 1981

Paul finds out that the building on the corner of kingsley and detroit is available. he calls ari to see if he's ready to open the deli that they had talked about.

march 15, 1982

zingerman's opens its doors for the first time. ari, Paul, and 2 staffers are behind the counter making sandwiches and cutting bread and cheeses.

1986

the 700-square-foot addition to the original zingerman's building is completed. the pie-shaped wedge houses the sandwich line and provides expanded room for dry goods.

1988

zingerman's magic brownies are baked for the first time. the recipe was developed courtesy of ms. connie Prigg, a zingerman's staff member who now lives in baltimore.

zingerman's begins a food rescue program to feed the hungry in our community. food gatherers collects nutritious food from shops, restaurants & hotels and quickly delivers it to the people in need in our community.

"founded in 1982, zingerman's is what other gourmet food shops want to be when they grow up."
"toledo blade"

996

zingerman's catering, famous for extraordinary deli trays and for bringing "the zingerman's experience" beyond the deli's doors and into Southeast michigan, is launched.

1997

the new bread bag from zingerman's bakehouse earns national design recognition from "Print" magazine. zing artists become "Print" favorites, receiving similar recognition the next three years in a row for four other zingerman's design projects.

1998

food gatherers delivers over 2,000,000 pounds of food to help feed those in need in washtenaw county. after three years of outstanding effort, jude walton and mo frechette make the jump to full-fledged managing Partners of zingerman's mail order.

Zingerman's

Guide to Good Leading, Part 1

A Lapsed Anarchist's Approach to

BUILDING A GREAT
BUSINESS

Ari Weinzweig

Zingerman's
PRESS
Ann Arbor
2010

Copyright © Ari Weinzweig 2010

All rights reserved
Published in the United States of America by Zingerman's Press
Manufactured in Michigan, United States of America

First Edition, fifth printing

2020 2019 2018 2017   7 6 5

Cover illustration: Ian Nagy
Interior illustrations: Ian Nagy and Ryan Stiner
Text design: Raúl Peña
Cover design: Pete Sickman-Garner

This book may not be transmitted or reproduced in any form or by any means without prior written permission from the publisher. Brief excerpts for review purposes are fine. Requests for permission should be directed to Zingerman's Press, 3756 Plaza Drive, Ann Arbor MI 48108.

ISBN-13: 978-0-964-89568-3
ISBN-10: 0-964-89568-4

www.zingermanspress.com

Printed, bound, and warehoused locally, in southeastern Michigan.

Printed on FSC certified paper with a recycled content of 100% post-consumer waste.

A COUPLE OF CAUTIONS

Jim Northrup, Native American storyteller extraordinaire and one of my favorite writers, always inserts a disclaimer into his pieces. "The views expressed in this column," he always adds in, "belong to the writer alone." Same here. What follows isn't the official, formal, FDA-approved Zingerman's line; this is just my own take on what we do and why we do it. While I'm pretty confident that most everyone here will be in synch on most of the main stuff—vision, mission, values, etc.—it's safe to say that Paul, each of the other partners, and really everyone who works (and has worked) here will have their own strongly held and very personal twist on all this. Which, I think, is a good thing—it's one of the big reasons why what we do works as well as it does. I'm ever more convinced that the seemingly paradoxical statement, "diverse minds really do think alike," is very much at work in our world. Also, I should add, it's safe to say that few others here have studied anarchism as I have—please don't start quizzing someone working behind the counter on what year Emma Goldman came to the U.S. (1885), or where Jo Labadie lived most of his adult life (Detroit).

Actually, as long as I'm writing, I'll up the ante a bit on Jim's admonition. Not only are the views that follow mine alone, they're also, basically, only half-baked. Any other writer, I'm sure, can relate. The great thing about putting out a book is that it's in print for posterity. The parallel problem with a book is, also, that it's in print for posterity. My mind, by contrast (for better or for worse), never stops moving; a piece gets published, the wheels keep turning, and two hours after I turn in the final manuscript I think of 22 things I wanted to do differently. While this book is indeed in finished physical form in your hands (you're not imagining it), in my head, the development of the ideas inside and the dialogue around them will keep going for a long time to come. The point of the work isn't to attain perfection; as much as we've worked on it, the reality is that, as always, flaws, faults, and (minor) foolishness still abound. My hope is really more to get you thinking than it is to get me talking— even I probably won't agree with everything I wrote a couple years from now. So when questions, ideas, insights, or concerns come up, feel free to just email me at ari@zingermans.com and we'll pick up the dialogue whenever you're ready.

Lastly, I'll add that we've set things up so that each of the essays inside can be read as an independent entity, without having to process the whole book in one well-ordered, linear, preface-to-postscript sitting. That said, if you do read straight through from start to finish, you'll probably find a few paragraphs to be a bit repetitious—don't stress, just skip ahead; gotta have 'em in there in order to facilitate the free form, anar-chistic reading option above. In any case, throwing all these cautions to the wind (or, if you'd rather, out the window), what follows is my imperfect, but very real, effort to get some of what has, and still is, happening when it comes to building a business in my head, out into public purview. I hope it gets you and others around you, thinking, questioning, collaborating, learning, laughing, listening, and leading a little bit more effectively, or at the least, more enjoyably. Here's to much more rewarding, sustainable, and interesting imperfect interaction to come.

Ari

CONTENTS

Preface: Do You Wanna Know a Secret?   9

Foreword by Bo Burlingham: Thoughts from the
    Cutting Edge of Capitalism   13

Introduction: Building a Business from (A) to Z   17

A Bit of Zing Background   27

The "Secrets"

1	Twelve Natural Laws of Building a Great Business	47
2	Contrast, Composition, Content	61
3	Creating Recipes for Organizational Success	69
4	The Zingerman's Business Perspective Chart	77
5	Building a Better Mission Statement	85
6	Revisiting the Power of Visioning	95
7	Writing a Vision of Greatness	111
8	Vision Back	125
9	An 8-Step Recipe for Writing a Vision of Greatness	137
10	A Question of Systems	155
11	Writing and Using Guiding Principles	181
12	5 Steps to Building an Organizational Culture	193
13	Creating a Culture of Positive Appreciation	207
14	Why I Want to Finish Third	219
15	Building a Sustainable Business	231
16	28 Years of Buying Local . . .	245
17	A Recipe for Making Something Special	255
18	Finally, Some Food!	263

Epilogue: Afterthoughts on Lapsed Anarchism,
      Motivation, and Eternal Optimism   273

Time to Eat! Ten Recipes to Cook in Your Own Kitchen

Belle and Emma's Potato Latkes   285

Sandwich #23: The Mary's Commute   287

Red Feta Spread   289

Alex's Red Rage Barbecue Sauce   290

A Spicy BLT   292

To Be, or Lablabi?   294

Zingerman's Magic Brownies   296

Hot Cocoa Cake   297

Brown Butter Caramel Sauce   299

Coffee Granita   301

Extra Bonus Stuff

Zingerman's Vision for 2009   305

Zingerman's Vision for 2020   315

Zingerman's Guiding Principles   325

Notes from the Back Dock   333

Zingerman's Timeline   343

Suggested Reading   347

Appreciations   349

Do You Wanna Know a Secret?

Seriously, not a week—often not a day—goes by without someone asking me some version of, "What do you think has made you guys so successful?" The question comes in different forms: "What are the big lessons I should know before I start?" Or, "What are the top three things every business should do to be sure it succeeds?" Or, "If you had one piece of advice for a new business what would it be?" But the spirit is always the same. While I'm all for sharing quick insights, the truth is that if there was one simple secret I could just share to make a business really great, the world would already be overloaded with very special, super successful, incomparably excellent companies. In which case, it's very safe to say, no one would be tracking down a little food business back in Ann Arbor, Michigan, to see what the heck we're doing out here in the middle of nowhere.

Nevertheless, the questions continue to come—in person, on the phone, via email, from friends, family, the press, and business professionals all over the world. The *Zingerman's Guide to Good Leading* series is my "lapsed anarchist's" (more on that in a minute) effort to share our "secrets" more widely. It's not, of course, the only way to find out what we do. If you really want to know our secrets you could just come and work here for a while—for 28 years people have been accessing the answers simply by being here on staff, taking our training classes, and putting our principles and processes into practice every day. After all, we're a very open organization. And one of the really BIG secrets here (don't tell anyone!) is that we actually teach everything we know about business, leadership, finance, service, and food to everyone who works here, regardless of how old they are, how long they've been on staff, or where they are on the org chart. I figure it takes a good two or three years to get a handle on it all, but you would get paid for learning, and I promise you'll eat really well, work hard, meet some great people, and have a fair bit of fun in the process.

Alternatively, you could take a trip to Ann Arbor and spend a couple of days on the "Zingerman's campus" studying the same behind-the-scenes stuff. For more than 15 years now business owners, managers, and prospective entrepreneurs have been coming from all over the world to attend our two-day ZingTrain seminars. What started with a single survey course known as the "Zingerman's Experience Seminar" has grown to include sessions on leadership, training systems, merchandising, service, human resources, and open book finance, plus a (*Bo*-nus!) session based on Bo Burlingham's book, *Small Giants*.

Each ZingTrain seminar encompasses a solid two days of teaching, learning, meeting other interesting businesspeople, and of course lots of good eating! People leave with new ideas, new connections, and new energy that they can carry back and use almost immediately in their own organizations.

The book you're holding in your hands is a third way to learn about what we do and how we do it. While I'm all for you either working here or coming to a ZingTrain seminar it also seemed like I was long overdue to collect all the business-oriented essays I've published over the last 15 years and create a series of books that anyone could pick up and read, cover to cover or one business "secret" at a time. So, after listening to loads of requests to put the essays all in one place, we've finally gathered them up, in the *Zingerman's Guide to Good Leading* series. *Part 1: A Lapsed Anarchist's Approach to Building a Great Business* is the first of five (or maybe six, or seven, or eight) volumes that will make up the series. Each will hold a set of essays on subjects of significance, the stuff we do that makes us . . . well, that makes Zingerman's Zingerman's.

If you've already spent time here as a staff member or a "seminarian," this book will provide intellectual support and additional details and anecdotes to help you put the ideas into practice in your own organization. For those of you who haven't yet been to a seminar or spent time working on the sandwich line at the Deli or at the bench at the Bakehouse (or anywhere else at Zingerman's), what follows will preview what you'll experience when you eventually do arrive.

Although food is, of course, the core of all our efforts, the books in the *Zingerman's Guide to Good Leading* series aren't about slicing corned beef, baking Magic Brownies, grilling burgers, or selling aged balsamic vinegar. Instead, they outline all the stuff that we would do—well, I guess, that we are doing—to build a very special business of any sort.

The concepts that follow are the basic building blocks of the culture and structure we know now as Zingerman's. The approaches are applicable whether you're running a law office, a library, a restaurant, a record label, a software firm, or an organic farm. They're the behind-the-scenes "secret" stuff that goes into making a very special, sustainable business of any kind. You know—the kind that customers actually *want* to buy from, that staff members really *want* to work in, and that owners truly *want* to dedicate their hearts, minds, and money to.

So, yes, it's true—the "secrets" of Zingerman's are all here, laid out in a series of essays that share the ways we approach most everything we teach (and try to live) about building a great business. They range all the way from nurturing an initial business idea to using our "recipes" for:

- putting together a mission statement (that actually means something);
- writing a vision of greatness (and why it isn't the same as a strategic plan);
- creating the kind of organizational culture we can feel good about (and how to make it even better for the future);
- writing guiding principles (and really using them).

The book is designed so that you can either read straight through from introduction to epilogue or, alternatively, pick and choose the essays you're most interested in, in any (anarchistic) order you like. If you read straight through you'll come across some repetitive parts here and there—skip ahead and have fun with the few minutes you've saved!

Looking ahead, the second volume in the *Zingerman's Guide to Good Leading Series* will focus on personal leadership skills: essays on managing yourself, servant leadership, our entrepreneurial approach to management, and other less talked about but I think pretty effective approaches. Parts 3, 4, and 5 will get into open book finance, customer service (the basics of which are already laid out in *Zingerman's Guide to Giving Great Service*), our approach to marketing, and so on.

Throughout, we'll just keep sharing the stuff we do, explaining why and how we do it, offering up oodles of stories of successes, screwups, and belated glimpses of the obvious. Seriously, if you stick with the series, *all the Zingerman's secrets will be revealed!* And if you come up with questions I haven't answered here, or have thoughts, ideas, insights, or experiences you want to share, I'd love to hear them—you can email me at ari@zingermans.com. Better still, come to Ann Arbor and we can say hi at a ZingTrain seminar, over a cup of coffee or a bit of hand-rolled Bakehouse baguette.

The books in this series will, I hope, give you a good sense of our approach to organizational life. The "inside info" is . . . all right inside. All you have to do is read, adapt, apply, and presto—all your problems will be solved!!! Sounds good, doesn't it? Damn. Think how many books we could sell if it were truly that simple. Unfortunately, I can't say that adhering to everything that follows will guarantee you success. Nothing can. But if you do the work that's outlined in these essays, I will absolutely, one hundred percent, definitely certify that you will significantly increase the odds of getting where you want to go, learning more, getting better bottom-line results, and having more fun en route.

Thoughts from the Cutting Edge of Capitalism

I've long believed that good leadership is a little like pornography (in the famous words of Justice Potter Stewart): hard to define, but you know it when you see it. That, of course, hasn't stopped people from offering definitions. The one I've always liked best I heard from my friend and erstwhile co-author, Jack Stack, the co-founder and CEO of SRC Holdings Corp. (formerly Springfield ReManufacturing) and pioneer of open book management. "Leadership," he said, "is the process of teaching people what reality is." That definition certainly captures the essence of Jack's leadership at SRC, although I'm not sure it covers the full range of possibilities.

Lately I've come to believe that there are really just two basic approaches to leadership, at least as practiced in business. The one we're most familiar with is command-and-control, wherein the leader (or, in a business context, the boss) tells the non-leaders (employees) what to do, and the non-leaders follow orders. Not only is this the way most leaders have led since time immemorial, but, more to the point, it has been the standard mode of corporate management since . . . well, since the invention of corporate management in the early 20th century. Command-and-control was once so widely assumed to be the logical, necessary, and inevitable form of leadership that many business experts didn't even see a need to articulate the concept. It was just there—part of the natural order of things. Bosses ran things; employees did as they were told; and that was that.

Command-and-control is still the prevailing philosophy in many parts of the business world. And there's no denying that it can be effective. In fact, in some circumstances it's the only available option. But in the past 30 years or so—the time I've been observing the business landscape from my perch at *Inc.* magazine—I've seen another approach emerge. I call it "trust-and-track."

As the name implies, trust-and-track is based on the premise that you can indeed trust people to do what's best for the company, provided you give them the proper training and tools. Its practitioners will tell you that a management system built around trust is actually the most effective and efficient way to run a business. The key words here are "training," "tools," and "system." You can't practice trust-and-track successfully without all three, and it takes an enormous amount of effort, persistence, and commitment to develop them. Most of the successful practitioners that I know have developed their own systems over a long period of time, sometimes borrowing from one another, but always adapting what they borrow to fit their respective cultures.

The vast majority, moreover, are in small to midsize companies. I'm not exactly sure why. It may simply be that the larger—and more complex and impersonal—an organization is, the harder it is to establish (or maintain) trust throughout the enterprise. Or it may be that entrepreneurs are more open to experimenting with different ways of running a business than are the professional managers in charge of most big companies. Or that closely held and privately owned businesses have more freedom to develop their own organizational structures and management practices than do companies with outside investors. There could be any number of factors at work.

It's hard to overstate how much these two ways of managing and leading differ from one another. Indeed, they are based on fundamentally different assumptions about human nature. When you get right down to it, command-and-control works off the premise that, when left to their own devices, a lot of people—maybe even most people—can't be trusted or expected to do what's best for the company (or the department, or the organization). They have to be told what to do and then held accountable for the results. To the extent that they're given autonomy, it's usually to accomplish goals set by other people higher up the corporate chain. This sometimes takes the form of "management by objectives," or MBO. As originally described by Peter Drucker in his classic *The Practice of Management*, MBO involves participative objective-setting—the theory being that people can be trusted to accomplish goals they themselves were involved in defining. In practice, however, MBO is often just a thinly disguised form of command-and-control.

I don't mean to suggest that leaders practice command-and-control solely because they don't trust those in their charge. They may truly think it's necessary. They may believe it's the best way to achieve results. They may get satisfaction from exercising power, or from having people depend on them. It's not necessarily shameful for a leader to derive some sense of self-worth from telling people what to do, although it can be a significant obstacle if you're trying to switch to trust-and-track.

Trust-and-track has blossomed in the so-called middle market, and its practitioners are among the most celebrated leaders and companies in their industries: Danny Meyer's Union Square Hospitality Group; Chip Conley's Joie de Vivre Hospitality; Jack Stack's Springfield ReManufacturing; Yvon Chouinard's Patagonia; and Gary Erickson's Clif Bar.

No company, however, has done more to develop the theory and practice of trust-and-track than Zingerman's Community of Businesses, and no business leader has better articulated its principles than Zingerman's Co-Founding Partner and CEO Ari Weinzweig. Granted, Ari doesn't use my shorthand term, but I think "trust-and-track" describes pretty well the extraordinary management system that he and his colleagues have invented. From the Zingerman's Training Compact to its Recipe for Bottom-Line Change, to the Huddles and Departmental Operating Reports, to the vast array of handy formulas for doing just about anything (the 3 Steps to Great Service, the 5 Steps for Handling Customer Complaints, the 4 Steps to Order Accuracy, and so on), it's all about giving people the tools they need to do what's best for the business—*on their own*, without having to wait for, or depend on, someone else to tell them.

To hear Ari tell the story, he and his colleagues are simply applying the ideas and principles to business that Emma Goldman, Mikhail Bakunin, Peter Kropotkin, and other anarchist thinkers enunciated in the politic sphere a century or more ago—at about the same time that such captains of capitalism as Alfred P. Sloan, Frederick W. Taylor, Pierre DuPont, and Donaldson Brown were refining the methods of command-and-control. No doubt these two groups would have been shocked and flabbergasted to learn that, a century on, their ideas would come together at a thriving company in Ann Arbor, Michigan. Then again, many of today's businesspeople and anarchists would be equally astonished by the notion. Except, of course, for those practicing trust-and-track.

If you're one of this latter group, prepare to be not only intrigued, but entertained, enlightened, and inspired by Ari's account of the Zingerman's way of running a business in the pages that follow. This book reveals many of the company's most important leadership practices. Having spent a lot of time at the ZCoB (as they call the Zingerman's Community of Businesses) and having gotten to know dozens of Zingernauts, I can assure you that the company is the real deal. No matter what type of business you have, you will come away from reading *Zingerman's Guide to Good Leading* with fresh insights on how to make your company better than it is.

—BO BURLINGHAM
San Francisco, California

Bo Burlingham is the former executive editor and current editor-at-large of Inc. *magazine. He is the author of* Small Giants: Companies That Choose to Be Great Instead of Big. *He also co-authored* The Knack *with veteran entrepreneur and* Inc. *columnist Norm Brodsky, as well as two books with Jack Stack, the pioneer of open book management. Their first book,* The Great Game of Business, *was honored in 2009 as one of the 100 best business books of all time.*

Building a Business

from Ⓐ to Z *and Back Again**

What follows on the next few pages may well fall into the "more than you wanted to know" category of writing, the stuff the big publishing houses persist in editing out in the interest of hitting the mainstream of the market. Since we're publishing this ourselves, we get to leave it in and let you decide whether you want to read it or not. If you aren't up for a bunch of personal background and a mess of references to rather obscure business writers and early 20th-century anarchists just jump over this part and skip to the section on Zingerman's history on page 27 or the essay on Mission Statements on page 85. Hey, as you'll see below, I'm kind of an anarchist, and it's your book now so you can do this any way you want!

On the other hand, if you're intrigued enough to get into all the strange machinations of my business-minded brain then by all means keep reading. Either way, have fun and snack on something good while you're working your way through these pages so I can show you from the get-go that food, fun, freedom, and management philosophy really can go together!

I guess it was doubly, ironically inevitable. First off, that a kid who grew up on Kraft macaroni and cheese, Pop Tarts, Tang, and canned fruit cocktail would end up starting a business that's gone on to be known as one of the country's best sources for traditionally made full flavored foods. And second, that that same kid, by nature a shy introvert of an anarchist, would somehow be leading (along with my co-founder Paul Saginaw and the 15 managing partners of the various Zingerman's businesses) a pretty successful capitalist company that has been featured in *Fortune,* the *New York Times, Business Week, Inc.,* and the *Wall Street Journal.*

What follows is my imperfect, lapsed anarchist's effort to take all the stuff we teach about business here at Zingerman's and put it out into the world

---

* In case this didn't quite register, the Ⓐ is the old anarchist symbol, and the Z stands for Zingerman's.

where others can get at it more easily. I hope it will help you make your life and the lives of everyone in your organization a little better. I know it has worked well for us—what started with two partners (me and Paul Saginaw), two staff members (Ricky Cohen and Marci Fribourg), and two loans ($20,000 from the bank and $2000 more, interest-free, from my grandmother) has grown steadily but sustainably to where we now support a staff of 500 and show annual sales of over $35,000,000.

The story, I suppose, starts with my childhood in Chicago. As a kid I most certainly never intended to become a leader of anything. I was then, and always will be, an introvert, on top of which I was more than just slightly suspicious of authority. Looking back, I think I pretty much resisted most every prescribed way of doing things with which I was confronted. Not only was I not interested in being a leader, I never even joined a single organized group—my high school yearbook entry showed just my photo and my name. Where everyone else's entry listed some sports teams, theater, French club, or the debate society, mine had only white space.

A little later, when I started studying history at the University of Michigan in the late 1970s, my distrust of authority, along with my fascination with obscure thinkers, drove me to spend a fair bit of time in a section of the University's Graduate Library known as the Labadie Collection. Barely remembered today, Jo Labadie (pronounced, Lah-BAH-die), a Detroiter known during his lifetime as "the gentle anarchist," donated his entire collection of political pamphlets—primarily pieces by anarchists like himself—to the U of M in 1911, creating the core of a now world-renowned collection of publications related to radical politics.

I don't remember there ever being a lot of people up in the Labadie; the pamphlets I latched onto were probably of little interest to anyone other than myself and maybe a half-dozen historians of the radical and obscure. After all, most politically minded students of the late '70s were more interested in student strikes and SDS than sitting in the library looking through a bunch of 50-year-old essays by Emma Goldman.

For me, though, those little books were pretty darned fascinating, both for their content and for the grassroots techniques that their authors had used to publish their political points of view. While their names aren't widely known anymore, a hundred years or so ago anarchists like Goldman, Alexander Berkman, Mikhail Bakunin, Prince Peter Kropotkin, Rudolf Rocker, and Nestor Makhno (an anarchist Ukrainian Cossack general, no less!) were on the cutting edge of political philosophy, the subject of op-ed pages and controversy in the U.S., and really all around the world. In many ways they were my people—back in my college days I probably would have said that I actually *was* an anarchist. Today I'd modify that statement. I haven't really forsaken my belief in the idea of anarchism, but I have, I think, adapted its tenets to what I've found to be the realities of the world in which we live, the one in which we operate the ever-growing capitalist venture called the Zingerman's Community of Businesses.

I should back up here and take a minute to explain what anarchism actually is, because, in my experience, it's mostly misunderstood. To this day many people confuse the terms "anarchy" and "anarchism." While the two sound similar, they aren't the same thing. The former refers to a state of leaderless bedlam; the latter is a philosophy based on respect for the individual and freedom from the restrictions of government or external authority. Many people still assume it to be about bomb throwing or other acts of violence committed in the name of creating chaos. Early in the 20th-century politicians and the press whipped up anti-anarchist attitudes to a point of near hysteria—writer Tom Goyens called it "anarchophobia" (not be confused with the 1990 film, *Arachnophobia*). Back then most businesspeople were out to get anarchists the way the McCarthyites would later hunt Communists during the 1950s.

But, while a small minority of anarchists certainly turned to violence over the years, violence is definitely not at the core of the anarchist concept. The bottom line is that you can most certainly be peaceful and an anarchist at the same time. In truth, most anarchists (like me!) were peaceful people. If you read below the headlines you'll discover that anarchism is actually about a very positive perception of humanity, based on the belief that people want to do the right thing and—if unobstructed by self-serving, authoritarian structures—usually will.

My first efforts to introduce anarchist ideas into the business world taught me a great deal—mostly about how to screw up. Early in my management experience I did my best to just leave people alone in the belief that if I did they would likely do the "right thing" and the business would run well. That approach failed me—and them—pretty miserably. My personal resistance to authority had led me to the inaccurate conclusion that people could be productive without much structure or strong leadership. I was wrong as wrong can be on both counts.

Fortunately, I'm fairly good at learning from my mistakes. I gradually gathered insights from my partner, Paul Saginaw, as well as writers like Peter Drucker, Paul Hawken, Ricardo Semler, Robert Greenleaf, and Peter Block, to name a few, about more effective ways to work. I never got an MBA but I've probably read more business books and attended more business seminars and conferences than most humans. By collaborating, learning, making mistakes, and collectively recovering with everyone here at Zingerman's over the years, I've figured out management approaches that provide a whole lot more valuable and purposeful structure than I was able to create during my early years as a naïve and not very effective manager.

While the 19th-century anarchists whose work I read in my student years certainly stayed with me in spirit, I gradually let go of some of the specific content of their beliefs. Over the years I started thinking of myself more as a "lapsed anarchist." Something like what Roger Baldwin, the founder of the American Civil Liberties Union, described when he told historian Paul Avrich that, "I have never considered anarchism as a philosophy that has guided me, but as a philosophy that has elements which appeal to me, above all liberty and voluntary association."

Over time I stopped trying to leave everyone alone and started working with Paul and others to put due process in place. As the late and very great Peter Drucker wrote in *Management Challenges for the 21st Century*, "Someone in the organization must have the authority to make the final decision in a given area." Although 30 years ago I'd never have believed it could be done, I think we've actually arrived at approaches to management and organization—i.e., the ones described in this book—that give significantly more conceptual, usable, and most importantly, *meaningful* structure than people typically get in more formal or seemingly stricter workplaces. This isn't just stuff that sounds good, though. We know it works because we use it every day. There's no question that it's been a critical factor in creating an organization that *Inc.* magazine generously called, "The Coolest Small Company in America."

Although we may come across as "cool," we don't operate in chaos. While we encourage a giving, open, and caring workplace, we definitely are not a democracy: we're very participative but we really never vote on anything. We have an organizational chart, plenty of documented processes, lots of written recipes for both our foods and our leadership, and no shortage of clearly laid out systems.

After all that qualifying, you might think we sound like any other company out there. What's different, I think, is that rather than letting all that structure stamp out individuality and creativity we've actually set up systems that care for and support the progress of the people who make up our organization. We've developed structures and organizational recipes that require positive participation, and created a culture that pushes anyone with a victim's mindset out to the periphery (if not out of the operation altogether). The idea is always to appeal to the intelligence of the individuals who work here, to encourage them to think critically and creatively, and then to get them to take action to do the right thing even when, at times, they have to "break the rules" in order to do what needs to be done.

In hindsight, we've created a workplace that's very much aligned with the anarchist's respect for the individual and free choice. In rereading a lot of the early anarchists recently I've been struck by just how much of our approach is in synch with what they were saying a century ago. Somehow, the similarity had been lost on me over the years, probably because I—like most of the world—had focused on the anarchists' opposition to authority while failing to appreciate the positive aspects of their vision.

Check out, for instance, what Max Baginski and Emma Goldman had to say on the subject of "Individuality, Autonomy and Organization" at the International Anarchist Congress in Amsterdam in 1907:

> There exists an erroneous conviction that organization does not encourage individual freedom and that, on the contrary, it causes a decay of individual personality. The reality is, however, that the true function of organization lies in personal development and growth . . .
>
> An organization . . . must be made up of self-conscious and intelligent persons. In fact, the sum of the possibilities and activities of an organization is represented by the expression of the single energies [of the group].
>
> It follows logically that the greater the number of strong, self-conscious individuals in an organization, the lesser the danger of stagnation and the more intense its vital element . . .
>
> In short, anarchism struggles for a form of social organization that will ensure well-being for all.

Geez. If I had paid better attention to this stuff back in my early days in management I probably could have saved myself and those around me a lot of time and aggravation.

Now, lest you think that this is just me getting all misty-eyed about my college days, take a look at Dean Tucker's 2008 book, *Using the Power of Purpose;*

How to Overcome Bureaucracy and Achieve Extraordinary Business Success! Tucker is a consultant and teacher who has worked with Boeing, IBM, and other big names of the American business world. I really recommend reading the whole book, but one of the main points he makes is that the old industrial-era business model—the very one the anarchists were so ardently opposed to—is dying, and may even be pretty much dead already.

In Tucker's view this old model was mostly about making money for a small clique of owners and managers. Employees were basically treated like unfeeling, unthinking, very much replaceable machine parts. By contrast, the new model, the one best set up for success in the 21st century, is what he calls, "the purpose-driven company." To Tucker, it's a place where people understand what the organization is trying to accomplish and why, and are strongly committed to its success. It's about vision, values, involvement, mutual support, and respect. According to Tucker, the organization of the future is one where relationships are based on trust, not coercion; where the staff "can 'manage' themselves. . . . Everyone on the team," he says, "shares in the responsibility to achieve the team's objectives. With everyone on the team striving to achieve the same team objectives, they are free to organize as they see fit. It is up to them to figure out how to reach the targets . . . They are adults. They can figure it out by themselves."

These two streams of thought, separated by a century, sound surprisingly similar. I happen to like them both—in part, I'm sure, because what they're advocating is pretty much exactly what we do here at Zingerman's. Reading it all at about the same time helped me understand that two concepts I'd thought were completely incongruent—my belief in anarchism and my desire to help run a growing, very much for-profit business—were actually far more compatible than I'd ever imagined. Because what Goldman, Baginski, and Baldwin wrote about—building a great organization using a "minimum of compulsion" and "a maximum of individual freedom"—is, in all seriousness, at the core of what we do. The interesting thing is that here at Zingerman's it's not just a nice philosophy put out in obscure pamphlets; the stuff actually works, to the tune of $35,000,000 a year.

Let me take all this philosophical talk into the very real business world with another reference to Tucker. He writes extensively about how businesses that want to be successful in the coming years must create settings in which Generation X and Y staff members are likely to thrive. They are, after all, going to be the bulk of the workforce for the next few decades. So what do employers need to know about Gen Xers? And what does this have to do with us . . . or with the anarchists? Well, Tucker reports that Gen Xers, "Lack trust in business and government. Judge on merit rather than status. [Are] independent. Function extremely well on teams." And Gen Yers? They want a workplace that will, "Provide challenging work that really matters. Balance clearly delegated assignments with freedom and flexibility. Be treated as colleagues, not as interns or 'teenagers.' Be respectful and call forth respect in return." The lists go on but I'm sure you're getting the point. It's no wonder that the caring, engaged, open, lapsed-anarchist leadership style we've got here is working so well. And, I would guess, is going to work well for, shall we say . . . X + Y years to come.

For me, the blending of these two seemingly incompatible worlds was further affirmed when I recently reread a work by another (unrelated) Tucker. This time it was Benjamin Tucker, a prominent American anarchist of the late 19th and early 20th century. In a little six-page pamphlet from 1934 entitled, "Why I Am an Anarchist," Tucker posits that the "primary and main conditions" of happiness are "liberty and material prosperity." Sounds a lot like our kind of business to me. A hundred years or so ago there were a dozen different camps of anarchist thought: individualist-anarchism (of which Tucker was the leading proponent), pacifist-anarchism, collectivist-anarchism, communist-anarchism, etc. Which got me to thinking that maybe what we do here could, not too inappropriately, if at least to raise a sardonic smile, be called "anarcho-capitalism"?

Bo Burlingham, longtime editor-at-large for *Inc.* magazine and a fellow anarchist in his philosophical roots, told me, "The thing with the anarchists was that they could never figure out how to take their ideas and really make them a reality. You guys have actually figured out how to do that. The anarchists—" he added, "at least the ones you're quoting—had the right yo-yo but they couldn't come up with the right string. That is, they had the right idea, but no venue or mechanisms for applying it. You've figured out the right venue (business) and a whole slew of mechanisms that actually allow you to bring these ideas to reality."

Call our approach whatever you like, but my views on leadership are pretty much in synch with Roger Baldwin, the aforementioned founder of the ACLU, who said, "I have never departed from the general philosophy represented in libertarian literature—that is, in the goal of a society with a minimum of compulsion, a maximum of individual freedom and of voluntary association, and the abolition of exploitation and poverty." Plug in "business" where he says "society" and you get the point.

So, who'd 'a thunk it? An anarchist guide to good management, strange as it sounds, actually seems to make seriously solid business sense as we get going in the 21st-century. While it's not why we put this series of essays in print, I do feel fairly confident that this is probably the only printed matter you'll ever read that praises both Peter Drucker, the guru of modern business management, and Emma Goldman, the "Queen of the Anarchists" in the same book. That little trivia-in-the-making thrill aside, the obvious question is still, "Who the heck needs another management book?" The easy and honest answer is: no one. The better question, though, may be, "Who would benefit from this book?" And the answer to that, I think, is, *anyone who wants to build a great business.*

With that in mind, the stuff in the following pages isn't just a series of impractical ideas emanating from some strategic think tank, nor is it a bunch of abstract approaches from outdated anarchists, nor another collection of management platitudes from out-of-touch (sorry!) business "experts." Instead, it's the very practical, time-tested, product of a dozen and a half partners, 500 current (and about 5000 past) staff members, and countless organizational achievements and errors, all put together over 28 years of trying to figure out how to effectively lead Zingerman's toward greatness.

I will say with all due modesty that the ideas I've written about here really do work, and not just in Ann Arbor. We've seen people adapt our management approaches to almost every industry, from law firms to libraries, and every size and type of organization, from tiny non-profits to huge multinationals. The UK, Mexico, Canada, the Netherlands, and Tunisia are just a few of the countries where this stuff has been put to work.

Mind you, I'm not here to claim that what we do is the "only" way to run a business, or that we have it all down. Please be clear: what we have going here is hardly utopia. We know that everything we do can be improved upon. We screw up most everything regularly. We forget to finish things, we fall short of living our values, we argue, we wrestle with internal cynics, we slip into sarcasm, we struggle with service miscues, we miss some goals, and we've had years with financial shortfalls. Perfect we are not! As Paul always says, "We have the same problems everyone else does. What's different is how we deal with them."

A good bit of what's different is that we involve so many people in most everything we do. To that point, please be clear that while I'm the guy who gets to write all this stuff down I'm hardly the one who invented it all. Although I've undoubtedly contributed a fair bit over the years, I'm only one of many who have helped make Zingerman's happen. The ideas, approaches, and recipes that follow are the products of a LOT of dialogue, discussion, disagreement, and occasional ducking to avoid balled-up papers hurled (caringly, of course) across the table. None of it is perfect, nor was any of it created in some flash of genius. Our business perspective chart (see page 79) took over a year to get straight. Same with our Training Compact (on page 53). The 2020 Vision (get it?—see page 315) took nine months of at times rather heated work by 15 partners just to get to a draft document we agreed on to share with the rest of the organization. And that was followed by six months of gathering and incorporating input from more than 200 front-line staff members before we finalized the document. So please know, this isn't a panacea, nor is it all about sitting harmoniously in a circle singing "Kumbaya."

Damn. I used "Kumbaya" with a touch of sarcasm. But having just looked it up online as I was writing, I realize that I need to set the cynicism aside. Here's what Wikipedia says on the subject: *"Kumbaya" [literally "Come By Here"] is a spiritual song from the 1930s. . . . The song was originally associated with human and spiritual unity, closeness, and compassion, and it still is, but more recently it is also cited or alluded to in satirical, sarcastic, or even cynical ways that suggest blind or false moralizing, hypocrisy, or naively optimistic views of the world and human nature."* Whoops. I certainly screwed up, unwittingly, on the latter. But that first bit really is actually amazingly fitting—please, all sarcasm aside, "come by here" and check out what we do. You probably won't hear much singing, but it's pretty clear that what we do actually does work pretty well. And, I'm confident, it can yield equally excellent results for others that want to adapt and implement them in their own organizations.

Granted, our approaches are a bit different from the way most of the rest of the world works. A management consultant who attended one of our ZingTrain seminars remarked that what we do here taught him a lot about how to effectively work "the soft side" of business without ignoring the need to deliver positive bottom-line results. Still, it's your call on what you do with this stuff. In all seriousness, it's hardly for me as an anarchist (lapsed though I may be) to tell anyone else how to lead. All I can say is that what's written up in this volume has been a great help to us at Zingerman's, and that I personally have put it into practice, if imperfectly, with great passion, pretty much every day for many decades.

And I'm not alone. What follows has been instrumental in building a business that has helped hundreds, maybe even thousands of really great people learn a lot, make a living, and go after their own dreams in a caring and constructive way—one in which both the organization and the individual do well together. If I doubt the veracity of what we do (which on dark days I certainly have), all I really have to do is look around me and read: first, the faces of the people who work here, followed by a quick scan through a stack of financial statements, and my mood will almost always be improved. It's not always pretty but it really does work.

Here's one more quote from Emma Goldman: "[Anarchism's] goal," she wrote in her 1917 essay, "Anarchism," "is the freest possible expression of all the latent powers of the individual. . . . [which is] only possible in a state of society where man is free to choose the mode of work, the conditions of work, and the freedom to work. One to whom the making of a table, the building of a house, or the tilling of the soil, is what the painting is to the artist and the discovery to the scientist—the result of inspiration, of intense longing, and deep interest in work as a creative force." Again, replace the words "anarchism" and "society" with "Zingerman's" or "our organization" and her words pretty much sum up the kind of work experience we're trying to provide here—one where work provides individuals with creative opportunities to learn and grow (not just an onerous way to make a living) while the business makes money and thrives over the long haul.

Or, if you've had enough of those old anarchists, check out this quote from Anne Good, a staff member at the Bakehouse. Being at Zingerman's, Anne wrote me, "has changed the nature of 'work' for me. It's no longer something I have to do to earn an income . . . work is now part of who I am and how I see the world, and, as a result of it, I get to have an income." Just putting those two quotes together inspires me to marvel at how powerful—even life-altering— this approach can be.

With that in mind, I hope that what follows will, at the least, get you thinking in new ways, asking questions you might not have asked, considering answers you might not previously have pondered. Of equal import, it might get you to go back to those really good gut feelings you still carry with you, to bring out beliefs you've long held, but that, you were told by "those in the know," would never work (like anarchism?). Many people leave ZingTrain seminars shaking their heads and smiling, saying stuff like, "I thought I was the only one who thought this way. It's such a relief to know I'm not alone!"

I hope that, through the writing that follows, I can live up to the standard set by Emma Goldman, of whom her colleague Freda Diamond once said, "She opened your mind and made you think about things you never thought about before. That was her outstanding characteristic. She made people think!"

All the best always, in anarchism, business, food, and life.

A Bit of Zing
Background

While this book emphasizes recipes for effective organizational development, the truth is that our original focus at Zingerman's was, and still is, food. Although you don't necessarily need to know all that much about what we actually do every day to apply the information in the essays in this volume, it seems to me that without a good bit of background it's hard to really take this all in context. I'm sure that most everything about us—the food, the service, the leadership, the merchandising, etc.—has been done in one form or another somewhere else. What's weird about it I guess is that we've brought together otherwise unconnected foods, people, and approaches to leadership in a very mindful and anything but matter of fact way, and that we do it all in one slightly odd organization in a smallish town in southeastern Michigan.

So let's see . . . What is Zingerman's anyway? It started with a small deli but it has obviously grown way beyond that. For nearly 30 years now our emphasis on education, flavor, tradition, and the integrity of ingredients has helped create a living culinary laboratory where customers can experience everything from corned beef and noodle kugel to estate-bottled Tuscan olive oil to terrific grits from South Carolina. We sell tons of brisket, thousands of hand shaped traditionally made, boiled and baked-on-boards Bakehouse bagels, and many thousands of Magic Brownies every year. At the Deli and Roadhouse we serve complete meals to customers from all walks of life every week. We're also local artisan producers—Zingerman's Bakehouse makes traditional bread and pastries; the Creamery crafts fresh cheeses; the Coffee Company wholesales carefully roasted beans; and the Candy Manufactory makes some pretty amazing old-fashioned candy bars! And Zingerman's Mail Order ships it all to food lovers across the country. ·

Finding food, though, is hardly all we do here. We don't just stock the stuff; from the start, it's been our sincere hope that Zingerman's will always be a place where people (both customers and staff) who might not know much about great food when they come in for the first time will leave having had a rewarding and really positive experience (regardless of whether that experience starts with eating or employment). The kind of spot where folks who've never heard of hundred-year-old balsamic vinegar, Nashville hot (as in super-spicy) fried chicken, chess pie, Jewish rye, or handmade harissa can come and taste these things for themselves. An organization in which new staff members who might have come to us only moderately familiar with traditional breads, authentic barbecue, and artisan cheeses can, relatively quickly, become veritable experts. Where these newly developed "specialists" can, in turn, have the opportunity to share their experiences with customers who might not have previously experienced any of this stuff either. Whether it's hot corned beef, home-cooked chicken broth, well-aged wheels of mountain Gruyere, or really good loaves of hearth-baked French mountain bread, we want to bring as much traditional food to as many people around here as we possibly can.

While that little snippet might mean something to those who've been here in person, in rereading it I don't think it really gets across the depth and complexity of what we've got going on. It's not all that easy to explain Zingerman's to someone who's never been here, but I don't give up easily. So . . . maybe I can say that I believe our business is about an overall experience more than any particular product or person. We're an ever-growing but still relatively small and locally owned organization in a small town in the American Midwest where you can encounter full-flavored traditional foods from the furthest reaches of the culinary universe. A place where some "kid" who by all rights shouldn't know much of anything about food can talk with you at length about great olive oils and effectively share the story of each one—where it's made, who made it, and how it tastes. A spot where the staff's enthusiasm for the food rivals that usually reserved for football teams or top 10 musical hits. A place where you might come just to grab a quick lunch but end up leaving having unexpectedly made two new friends, experienced three foods you didn't know you wanted, and picked up a handful of newsletters about polenta, pastrami, or handmade pie crust. Where you can find little kids eating great grilled-cheese sandwiches and immigrants reveling in foods they thought they'd left behind forever.

Given all the good press we've had and the number of visitors for whom we've become a destination, I guess it's safe to say that Zingerman's has become an Ann Arbor institution. Our local customers come in regularly—many every day. People who've moved away make return trips just for the Zingerman's experience. Many who've left Michigan will still make meals out of our food by using our catalog-based mail order business or website. Others come back to take classes at BAKE!, or to learn about business approaches in our ZingTrain seminars. Sometimes it scares me how many people we've actually reached: our guests tell us that most anywhere they go, once they tell people they're from Ann Arbor the odds are that the person will respond by talking about one of two landmarks: either the University of Michigan or Zingerman's. And from what they say, we seem to be gaining a bit each year on the Maize and Blue.

History Lesson

The initial idea for what started as Zingerman's Delicatessen came up in casual conversation with my now-partner Paul Saginaw. We were probably out having a beer after work one night—Paul was the general manager of a restaurant where I was washing dishes back in the spring of 1978. Despite the fact that any HR expert would have called us a mismatch because we occupied opposite ends of the org chart when we met, we were actually sort of a match made in . . . if not heaven . . . then at least in the world of food business idealism. We spent many an evening discussing what we would do if we had our own place and weren't weighed down by the less than super-high standards set by the folks for whom we were working. We talked regularly about how we could build a business that would bring potato pancakes, chicken soup, goat cheese, smoked salmon, and other very special foods to a town that really didn't have much of that sort of thing to offer. And of how we could do it in a way that was unique to us, something special and not just one more copycat of a company trying to make as much money as quickly as it could (usually at the expense of its customers or crew), but rather to do something productive for all the people it would impact.

In 1979 Paul left the restaurant where we worked and, along with a partner, Mike Monahan, opened a fish market inside a converted feed and seed store beside what today is the booming Ann Arbor Farmer's Market. He and I continued to share a pretty wide range of food and business fantasies, but the one idea that stuck with us more than any other was to start a delicatessen. We'd both grown up eating Jewish food—he in Detroit, me in Chicago—and we'd been accustomed to enjoying a good corned beef sandwich when we wanted one.

I'm sure we were hardly the only ones to have the idea. And for a long while, it was just that. Meanwhile I kept on in my mainstream management position. It certainly wasn't a bad job, but it was becoming increasingly clear to me that I was giving my all in an organization of folks with more . . . shall we say, modest? . . . visions and values of food and management.

By the time the students came back to campus in the fall of 1981 I knew I was ready to leave the corporate food world. I really didn't know what I was going to do, but I didn't have any kids, I didn't owe any money, and there really wasn't any reason I could think of to stick with a job that felt less and less rewarding with each passing day. So, without a real plan in mind, on November 1, two days before my 25th birthday, I gave a couple months' notice to the restaurant's general manager and started preparing myself for some unknown, but hopefully exciting future.

Then, in one of those coincidences that looks almost starstruck when you view them with the benefit of hindsight and that later make for really romantic (in this case, business) stories, Paul came by a couple days after I'd announced that I was leaving. Opportunity, he believed, was beckoning; a smallish, two-story, red brick building around the corner from the fish market was coming open, and he thought maybe it was time for me to leave the restaurant so we could open the deli he and I had discussed for so long.

The opportunity turned out to be a pretty good birthday gift for me. We started meeting regularly to review menus, business plans, pro-forma financials, and everything else we thought might be relevant. Emma Goldman and Alexander Berkman were pretty far from my mind: instead of anarchism I was actively studying artisan cheese and the art of cooking corned beef. It's actually the only time in my adult life I've been out of a job. Hopefully it's also the last—with a little luck, creating a pretty special, seemingly sustainable business will keep me off the unemployment line for a long time to come.

Given that this is a book about building a business, it's important to know that, while we've since attained great "success," our idea to do a deli didn't initially meet with a huge amount of positive response. In the weeks before we actually opened people were quick to point out that Ann Arbor had always been anathema to delis—literally a dozen had tried and failed during the previous decade. Most locals were lavishly critical of the location: it wasn't considered a great neighborhood ("downright dangerous," a few really dark-minded folks called it); it was a bit off the beaten path; plus it was hard to find and without anywhere near enough parking. And the economy at the time was pretty terrible, with interest rates running at a seemingly insane 18 percent!

Though we listened carefully to all the concerns of our colleagues and prospective customers, no matter how many times we went over things we just couldn't really figure out any reason why a good deli shouldn't do pretty well. It seemed then—and still does now—that if you sold good food, gave good service, and took good care of your crew, customers would keep coming back. And that if you continued to do it all well and consistently over time you could build a pretty great business.

Back then we didn't have the benefit of author Hugh MacLeod's insight from his terrific 2009 book, *Ignore Everybody*. "The better the idea, the more 'out there' it initially will seem to other people," he wrote, "even people you like and respect. So there'll be a time in the beginning when you have to press on, alone, without one tenth the support you probably need. This is normal."

Even without MacLeod's message in mind, we went ahead with our plans.

Deli Days Are Here Again

On March 15, 1982, a ridiculously short four and a half months after Paul called to tell me the building had become available, we opened. When we let the first customer in that first morning we had just two employees on the payroll—one part-time and one full-time. We also had a lot of loyal friends who were willing to make coffee and clear tables while they waited for us to put their sandwiches together. (Two of them—Frank Carollo and Maggie Bayless—have long since moved into more prominent roles as managing partners of the Bakehouse and ZingTrain, respectively!) We had five tile-topped square tables with four seats at each, and four stainless steel stools covered in not-very-cool-looking forest green vinyl anchored into the floor at a counter that ran across the big front window.

Back when we opened we offered a small but meaningful selection of made-to-order deli sandwiches (25 to be exact); a solid selection of much-loved Jewish specialties like chopped liver and chicken soup; a then "big" but now seemingly pretty small couple of refrigerated cases filled with cured meats, traditionally made cheeses, and smoked fish. Up at the register we stacked breads and pastries from various local bakeries. I don't remember how much we took in on that first day. It felt pretty busy at the time, but the Deli crew probably now rings up more in a half hour of a moderately busy weekday lunch rush. It's not just our sales that were smaller—there was definitely less of pretty much everything (other than maybe energy—we were a lot younger!) than there is today. The smoked salmon, salami, corned beef, and pastrami that got us going remain pretty prominent, though we've added a much wider and more interesting selection of traditional pastas, jams, honeys, vinegars, and other great tasting stuff from around the world.

Still, although things have worked out pretty well, please don't think we had everything exactly right when we opened. Our work schedules were pretty stressful—open seven days, we'd start at about 5 a.m., open the doors at 7, close at 8:30 p.m., do the dishes, straighten the shelves in the cooler, go home, sleep a bit (a few times on the living room floor, where I fell asleep out of exhaustion), and then come back and do it all again. At first we closed early on Sundays, but as soon as we figured out that the cafeterias in the U of M dorms were closed on Sunday, leaving scores of near-starving students looking for a good sandwich ... well, let's just say our half a night off per week didn't last too long.

Like every new business we made lots of mistakes and worked hard to correct them as quickly as we could. Fortunately we were able to make things right more often than not. Lo and behold, we actually did pretty well. Of course, it wasn't a cakewalk and we certainly weren't at all cocky. Kind of confident, I suppose, but careful and cautious too—we definitely didn't take anything for granted. Like most new businesses (at least those that survive) we stocked most every item that seemed like it might draw customers, even if we weren't all that certain about our ability to sell it. I'm sure my mother was more than a bit miffed, but next to deli classics like corned beef, herring, chopped liver, rye bread, and Swiss cheese we stocked cheap cigarettes and then-neighborhood favorites like ham hocks, pork rinds, and big bunches of collard greens.

Ironically, the latter are now a staple at Zingerman's Roadhouse, cooked, of course, with lots of bacon and served alongside hundreds of orders of pit-smoked barbecue every week! Speaking of smoking, in those early years we used to let people light up in the store, and each of the tables had a black plastic ashtray on it. I clearly remember our long-time customer, Larry, sputtering with anger that he was never coming back when we decided in the late '80s to remove the ashtrays and limit the smoking to sausage and salmon.

What *Is* Ann Arbor, Anyway?

One could argue that you don't need to know all about our town to get the idea behind all the business building stuff that follows. But the "soil" in which a business is built does make a difference. Just as you can taste the *terroir* of a good wine or food, you can for sure feel the flavor of Ann Arbor in Zingerman's. Located about 45 miles west of Detroit and about 200 miles east of Chicago, it's got a population of just over 100,000. Ann Arbor is probably best known nationally as the home of the University of Michigan, with its top-ranked business school, law school, liberal arts programs, medical center, and, of course, its high-powered college sports (football almost every weekend in the autumn, followed by basketball, baseball, and hockey the other eight months of the year).

Ann Arbor is one of those out-of-the-way college towns where people like me often go to get a degree and then never seem to leave. The presence of a major university brings a level of variety and cultural activity rarely found in Midwest towns of this size. Lots of music, bookstores, foreign films, and plenty of people from otherwise obscure international origins who are interested in discovering and learning about foods from the far reaches of the globe. And anarchists like Jo Labadie who leave collections to the U of M's library.

Labadie was, of course, only one of the thousands of amazing people who have made this town what it is. Given its size and location it's got a pretty impressive level of diversity: we get to work with some incredibly interesting individuals from the far corners of the Earth. The connections they allow us to make are something special. I remember, many years ago, regularly talking about and tasting Spanish sausage and cheese with a customer who I knew only as "Mr. Kish." It turned out he'd acquired his taste for tapas while fighting in the Lincoln Brigade during the Spanish Civil War (whose members, by the way, included a goodly number of anarchists); he later helped found the U of M's famous Institute of Social Research, and had been active in peace movements and social science all over the world. To cite another interesting example, in 2002 we received our first-ever shipment of an excellent organic olive oil from New Zealand. Our connection? An Ann Arbor mathematician who dropped me a note to see if we'd be interested in trying the oil his brother was producing Down Under. The oil—the green-gold Moutere Grove in its now-familiar black bottle—remains one of my favorites to this day.

Encounters like these make me feel so fortunate to do what we do where we do it. Perhaps the connections I value most are the ones that bring people a taste of a past they'd long ago given up for lost. Consider this letter I got back in 1998 from a wonderful woman named Mildred Steinbock, who used to drive up from Toledo to visit us a couple of times a month. It's a long time ago now but the story still sits with me:

> Dear Ari,
>
> I just read your article on the history of the egg cream. I am 80 years old and grew up in the West Bronx. I've been drinking egg creams for over 70 years except for when I moved to Toledo. I haven't seen an egg cream since I left Long Island two and a half years ago. I don't think you were old enough to remember the Depression. In 1930 the two candy stores on 170th St. competed to cut the price of an egg cream. And for a short while, we impoverished children

could buy an egg cream for 3¢. Maybe there was vanilla egg cream in the Bronx at that time but I don't remember hearing of it. I don't get to Ann Arbor very often and when I do I head for Zingerman's the minute I get to Ann Arbor and for a few minutes I relive my life in New York. It's a pleasure to visit your store.

But the town's demographic diversity has also challenged us. It's hard to get away with selling poor-quality cheese when you're waiting on people who grew up in Paris. You can't cut corners with your corned beef and pastrami when every tenth person who comes in used to live in Manhattan, or serve sub-par barbecue when you have customers who were raised on the real thing down South.

But It's So Small

Again . . . I don't know that you absolutely need to know this. But while what we do probably sounds huge, it's important to note that it all started in 1300 oddly shaped (I think it's a "rhomboid") square feet of space. Having heard about us through food-loving friends and all the positive press we've received, people in other cities almost inevitably imagine the Deli to be some massive Midwestern version of Harrod's food halls. Boy, are they surprised the first time they visit. I can't keep track of how many times I've heard something along the lines of, "Wow, it's really a lot smaller than I thought!" Compared to all the enormous upscale "gourmet" supermarkets that have sprung up since then, the Deli is downright miniscule. Which is fine with us. We never wanted to be one of the biggest, only one of the best.

If you come to town, you'll still find the Deli on its original site at the inter-section of Detroit and Kingsley streets, just down the street from the Farmer's Market and about two blocks up from the old train station. The parking is still bad, the location still hard to find (thank goodness for GPS, cell phones, and Mapquest), but the neighborhood is now considered a great place to live. The two-story, orange-brick, main building, with its mere thousand square feet of selling space, has been in the food business its whole life—it was built as a grocery in 1902. Although our European customers can't quite conceive of something so new being considered of historical significance, the building is on the historic register. Its character is enhanced by the fact that the intersection at which it sits is rather unusual. The vertex at which Detroit and Kingsley come together is probably set at something like 130 degrees, and the Deli's walls are adjoined at that same angle as well. An appropriately, atypically shaped space for a very atypical business.

In 1986, when the building was practically bursting at the seams with business, we added an additional 700 square feet onto the main building. This gave us space to make more sandwiches and to redo much of the building's rapidly aging infrastructure. Not surprisingly (at least in hindsight) this still wasn't enough room for us to do what we wanted to do. So in 1991 we renovated the 19th century wood-frame house next door and added an additional 60 or so seats, along with space where we could make espresso, brew pots of specialty coffees and teas, and offer a much-expanded selection of sweets. This space is now known, affectionately and for obvious reasons, as Zingerman's Next Door.

Outside on the patio are nearly 200 more seats. About half of those are under a heated tent that, amazingly, allows us to have outdoor seating in southeastern Michigan almost year round. If all this seems a bit strange and slightly surreal, it is. But that strangeness and in some cases unintentional and very impractical uniqueness is a big part of what makes the Zingerman's Experience so special. It's all kind of wacked, but somehow it works. People who want quick, simple, and cheap are going to be way better off at the McDonalds drive-thru. But if you get into what we do, it's a wonderfully weird and very much one of a kind experience. As we laid out in our original vision, there are many delis but there's still only one Zingerman's. Much the same can be said about each of the other Zingerman's businesses we've opened around Ann Arbor.

In fact, to make the Zingerman's Experience here in town ever-more interesting we've actually started what's come to be called the Tour de Food: a 24 hour "race" that one customer recently told me with a big smile was like going on a "culinary scavenger hunt." If customers visit all the Zingerman's retail locations (right now, the Deli, the Roadhouse, Bakehouse, Creamery, and Coffee) they get a special prize. They also have fun. They get to see some spots in Ann Arbor they might not have visited. And they taste a lot of good food in the process! Which probably begs the question: how did you get from making corned beef sandwiches into all these other businesses? And why haven't you opened in L.A., London, Chicago, and Las Vegas like most everybody else seems to want to do?

The Vision for Zingerman's 2009

Well, the answer to that goes back to the early '90s. One thing we learned long ago is that success brings what we've come to call "better problems." And one problem we encountered back then was that we were sort of stumped about how to continue growing and maturing in a way that provided positive opportunity for our organization, yet still upheld our long-standing commitment to the community and to doing something unique and special. In the American business community the standard growth model is, of course, that when you're successful, you simply open more "units," first locally, then gradually spreading all over the country. At some point you go public. But we were never able to get clear in our heads how we could take a one-of-a-kind business and replicate it without losing the quality of food and service, and in the process its one-of-a-kind personality. As you open more and more places in ever-more distant locations, a business that was once unique becomes ubiquitous.

With that in mind, Paul and I spent a solid year struggling with what our vision of the future might look like. To be honest, we argued about it a lot—it's no small thing to put down on paper what you want to be doing 15 years into the future, especially when you don't really even know if everyone's going to show up for work tomorrow. But after a solid year of scintillating conversation we finally agreed on a long-term vision, set 15 years in the future. We called it "Zingerman's 2009."

Rather than proposing that we go nationwide, "2009" outlined a way forward that we felt would allow us to build on what we'd successfully started while still creating positive growth opportunities for the people within our organization. The vision (reproduced on page 305) called for us to create what we now refer to as the Zingerman's Community of Businesses, which around here we shorten to "ZCoB" (pronounced ZEE-cob). It's a collection of Zingerman's food businesses, each with its own unique specialty, all located in the Ann Arbor area, and each led by a managing partner (or partners) who have the passion and persistence needed to be really good at anything on a day-to-day basis.

In writing our long-term vision we recognized that we were choosing the challenges that would come with creating a series of interconnected, but semi-autonomous businesses that would operate as one organization. This definitely wasn't the easiest approach we could have taken. But we liked it—and still do. The model has allowed for managing partners to focus on their passions, to go after creating something great within their area of focus in the food world, while providing each other with the strength, support, and community that comes from working together. Out of which we embrace the classic (though clearly not very anarchistic at all) American struggle to balance state's rights and federal control. We may not get it exactly right on a given day, but overall

I think we've managed to stay pretty well centered. Lots of freedom but built within an agreed-upon, fairly well-thought-out framework.

This struggle can, of course, be pretty stressful: there are conflicting interests at play at every level and it's not easy to master the paradoxes they pose. To succeed, each of us has to be OK with changing organizational hats all day—within a matter of 15 minutes any one of us might be called on to act as a supplier, then a customer; a few minutes later we might need to be an advocate for our own business, and then five minutes later look out for the ZCoB overall. It's pretty normal here to report to someone "higher" on the org chart and then quickly turn around and give that same person constructive criticism. Sometimes it all happens in one short conversation! But, hey, we like complexity. And in truth, I think all those seemingly conflicting roles exist in any organization—they just aren't always acknowledged as openly, or addressed as effectively (if still imperfectly), as we seem to be able to do.

I should mention here that although our 2009 vision has gotten rave reviews from business writers and professors all over the country, back in the early '90s our model failed to impress most of the attorneys, consultants, accountants, and other paid and unpaid advice-givers we were working with. "Too complicated," "Having partners is nothing but trouble," "It's too risky," "Just open more delis, that's where your core competence is . . ." We weren't exactly hailed as business heroes. As Katie Frank, who came to work with us in the fall of 2005, reminded me with a big smile, "It's a good thing you and Paul didn't need a lot of data to develop 2009 or it never would have happened."

Eight years later, in 2002, while we were well on our way toward making the 2009 vision work, Bo Burlingham came to visit. We knew Bo from his pioneering reporting on Open Book Finance and *The Great Game of Business* book he had co-authored with Jack Stack. We'd heard his presentations and shared thoughts at the annual Gathering of Games conference. When he came to sit in on part of ZingTrain's two-day-long "Leading with Zing" seminar in 2002 his plan was to stay for part of the session to get a sense of what we had to say. But something we were doing piqued his curiosity. He ended up sticking around for the entire seminar, then stayed for a third day in order to interview ZCoB partners and staff about what he'd learned. Over the following months he called to interview all sorts of us by phone.

Six months later his article hit the newsstands and we found ourselves being billed as "The Coolest Small Company in America" on the cover of *Inc.*

magazine. Bo's piece recounted both our successes and our struggles—the ones we'd already faced and the ones he, and we, saw coming. Of course the press covers the press, so the *Inc.* story was followed fairly quickly by local coverage, and before long we were getting kudos all over town on our "brilliant strategy for growth." Much of the praise came from the same experts who'd criticized us so sharply when we first came out with our vision in the early '90s. But that's just how these things go. If you aren't getting flak for what you're doing, you probably aren't doing anything significant, right?

The article also generated a great deal of interest from businesspeople around the country. So much so that Bo started to search for other organizations whose visions for growth, while unique in themselves, resembled ours in the choice to stay off the typical "expand nationally and franchise as fast as you can" path. What he found ended up becoming the basis for his very fine book, *Small Giants: Companies That Choose to Be Great Instead of Big.*

Getting 20–20 on "2020"

Sticking with the principle (see page 54 for more on the subject) that success means you get better problems, by the mid-'00s we found ourselves facing two of the best organizational challenges we could have hoped to hit. First, we were close to achieving the long-term vision that we'd written back in 1994! And, second, we were so close to the year 2009 that we needed to do a NEW vision. These, mind you, are very good problems. Most organizations never even write a 15-year vision, let alone actually achieve it. To not just survive the 15 years but to thrive is, I think, quite a thing. We knew we were far from perfect. We had (and still have) the same problems as everyone else. But we're dealing with them in a positive, performance-oriented, values-driven, mission-focused, caring and giving way—having fun, learning and helping those around us to grow and improve the quality of their lives overall, and their eating in particular. And that's a very good thing.

So in the winter of 2006, I, Paul, and the 15 partners of the ZCoB all got together offsite and started working to develop a new organizational vision for the year 2020. (Doing 15 years again would actually have made it 2021, but the "20–20 vision" thing was too good to pass up.) Despite my impatience to get it done fairly quickly, the process was actually a lot like what Paul and I had gone through back in 1993 and '94 when we worked on Zingerman's 2009. At times it was frustrating and we fought. At other times it was uplifting, marvelously motivating, exciting, and energizing. As in the early '90s our challenges were to stay true to our roots and stick with the stuff we really believed in while also writing a vision that wasn't just some super-safe extension of the status quo. We wanted to challenge ourselves to do more, to contribute more meaningfully to the lives of those around us. You'll find a copy of the resulting 2020 Vision in the back of the book, so you can judge for yourselves. But personally I think we did pretty well.

The process we used to write the vision was basically what we at Zingerman's now call "Bottom Line Change"—involving as many people as possible in the design and implementation of the change, as opposed to the old model where the bosses decide in the back room and emerge later to tell everyone else what to do. (Details on this process will be laid out in *Zingerman's Guide to Good Leading, Part 2.*) We decided early on that the vision would be written by all the partners, not just me and Paul. That we would stick to the consensus model we'd been using to make decisions in our Partners' Group for many years already. That while the partners would be the ultimate decision-makers we would also consult with everyone in the organization as well as people we respected around the community and across the country to get input and help make the vision stronger and more effective. And that, having gathered this input, we'd adjust the vision, formally adopt it, and then get moving toward 2020.

As with 2009, it took us nearly a year to get all the 15 partners into agreement on a draft vision, then another six months to gather input from more than 200 staff members and incorporate much of that into the finished product. We put the document out in the spring of 2007, and it's still going strong today.

How we do en route to 2020 will I'm sure be the subject of future articles, books, and seminars. All I can say right now is that I'm inspired and excited about the opportunity to go after it. I know we'll be relying heavily on the secrets in this book (as well as, I'm sure, on some new lessons yet to be learned) to help us get there. I'm already looking forward to the chance to get together in, say, 2017 to write the next long-term vision.

Zingerman's Today

On any given day, as I write, the Zingerman's Experience is now created and delivered by 16 partners, about 50 or so managers, and more than 500 front-line staff in eight different businesses in addition to the Deli. In keeping with our long-term vision, each of the Zingerman's businesses is led by a managing partner or partners—people who are passionate about what that business does, who've put real cash on the line to own part of it, and who do a ton of work to get great results every day while leading their business toward success for the long term.

As I write this, the ZCoB includes:

ZINGERMAN'S DELICATESSEN

Still on that same spot at the corner of Detroit and Kingsley, still unique, still crowded, still confusing for first timers, still hard to find, still short of parking, and still, I think (biased though I obviously am), pretty special. Now led by a pair of managing partners, Grace Singleton and Rick Strutz, both of whom joined us back in 2002, the Deli continues to deliver all the same sorts of sandwiches, traditional Jewish dishes, artisan cheeses, oils, vinegars, and other great foods from all of the Zingerman's producers (Bakehouse, Creamery, Coffee, and Candy) that it has for nearly three decades—only now, I think, better than ever.

ZINGERMAN'S CATERING AND EVENTS

From the far corners of the Deli kitchens comes catering for all occasions. Corned beef to caviar, potato salad to smoked salmon, business meetings to bar mitzvahs and weddings—delivered down the block on Detroit Street or all the way into downtown Detroit.

ZINGERMAN'S BAKEHOUSE

We started the Bakehouse in 1992 with our partner, Frank Carollo, to finally get bread for the Deli like the stuff I'd been bringing back from Paris and San Francisco for years. Working under the tutelage of master baker Michael London of upstate New York's Rock Hill Bakehouse we learned to craft traditional, hearth-baked breads true to French, Italian, and old Jewish recipes. Later we added a whole range of butter-laden, full-flavored, know-fat (get it?) pastries and baked goods. Amy Emberling, who was one of the original crew of six bakers before she headed off to Denmark and from there to Manhattan (where she earned her MBA), later returned to the Bakehouse as a second managing partner. Today, the Bakehouse sells bread and pastries to more than a hundred different wholesale accounts across the state.

BAKE!

The Bakehouse's much-loved teaching kitchen, offering classes on breads, pastries, cakes, biscuits, croissants, pies, and much, much more. Not to mention the special week long BAKE-cations.

ZINGERMAN'S CREAMERY

Just up the sidewalk from the Bakehouse Ann Arbor's only creamery makes fresh, hand-ladled cream cheese, a variety of fresh goat and cow's milk cheeses, incredible gelato, and more. John Loomis is the longtime cheesemaker and managing partner. The Creamery has one of the country's best little cheese shops on site, as well.

ZINGERMAN'S MAIL ORDER

Ships all those full flavored and traditionally made foods to people like you all over America. Led today by a trio of managing partners—Mo Frechette (the original Mail Order man, who packed boxes in the basement of the Deli nearly 20 years ago), along with Toni Morell and Tom Root (who together led the work to create the first Zingerman's website back in 1999). Check out their work by mail or online at www.zingermans.com.

ZINGTRAIN

Offers training and educational seminars on subjects like those covered in this book, as well as our approach to service, management, merchandising, and other engaging subjects. Oh, yeah: ZingTrain does custom consulting, too. Maggie Bayless is the managing partner who pushed the organizational envelope to create ZingTrain back in 1994. Stas' Kazmierski came on board as a second managing partner in 2000 after 25 years of doing organizational change and design work for Ford and other fine folks.

ZINGERMAN'S ROADHOUSE

A full-service, sit-down restaurant serving really good American food. Alex Young is the (James Beard-nominated) chef and managing partner who does everything from growing the Roadhouse's vegetables at Cornman Farms to working to perfect a menu of ground-fresh-daily burgers, whole hog barbecue, Memphis-style fried chicken, Maryland crabcakes, and a wide selection of American beers, bourbons, wines, and cheese. The Roadhouse is also home to the Roadshow, a 1952 Spartan aircraft aluminum trailer permanently parked out front of the restaurant, where customers can get great drive-up coffee, homemade doughnuts, Bakehouse bread, pastries, and sandwiches.

ZINGERMAN'S COFFEE COMPANY

Roasting really good beans right here in Ann Arbor. You can sip the Coffee

Company's craft roasts at the Deli, Bakehouse, Roadhouse, and Roadshow as well as at other leading cafes, restaurants, and retailers around the country, and now at their new retail space. Allen Leibowitz led the way as managing partner of the coffee company back in 2003, and was joined by co-managing partner Steve Mangigian in 2008.

ZINGERMAN'S CANDY MANUFACTORY

Our most recent arrival, the Manufactory crafts candy bars by hand, as they would have been made in the early days of the last century. Charlie Frank, now the managing partner, started making the amazing Zzang! bars while working as the pastry manager at the Bakehouse and we later spun the idea out into a business all its own. Zzang bars are now sold in specialty shops all over the U.S.

Food Gatherers

Back in 1987 Paul had one of his typically out-of-the-box, sounds-strange-at-the-time-but-turns-out-to-be-brilliant ideas. "Why," he wondered, "couldn't we start up a non-profit program in Ann Arbor to get left-over food from restaurants and food shops like ours to people in need?" All the requests for contributions that came in every week from local non-profits had given him the sense that there were more effective ways to help people than just making random donations. The idea was to take the food that typically was getting tossed—slightly overcooked meat, vegetables that were still tasty but had turned just slightly brown, extra bread, etc.—and get it to people who were going hungry right here in town.

The more we worked on the concept, the less we were able to find any good reason *not* to do something. Similar programs had already been successful in other cities, and the need was just as great in Ann Arbor. So we went for it. We hired one of our sandwich makers to do the initial research and coordinate with the local health department. We set aside enough of the Deli's office space and other resources to create a viable infrastructure. And as Paul's vision blended with the efforts of many folks across our organization and our community, Food Gatherers was born.

Food Gatherers' core mission—then and now—is to fight hunger by making food available to community agencies serving folks in need. It also coordinates with other area hunger relief agencies to develop additional food resources, and partners with more than 100 non-profits countywide who are working on issues from daycare for low-income children to substance abuse. The organization was the first food rescue program in Michigan, and, as far as we know, the first founded by a for-profit business.

Today Food Gatherers is one of the most successful programs of its kind in the country, delivering more than 2,000,000 pounds of food in Washtenaw County last year alone. And it has won awards for efficiency of operations, too: the Food Gatherers crew rescues a pound of food for less than the price of a postage stamp! We've also developed a new Community Kitchen and training program for homeless individuals in our area to help get them safely and successfully back into the workplace. All of which started with that wacky, seemingly impossible, idea that Paul had back in the mid-'80s.

The "Secrets"

The essays that follow aren't really secrets but they are, in essence, the "secrets" that so many folks have been asking for. Most all have been published in at least one form, and often in two or three, over the previous 15 years. We've given them a bit of an edit to minimize repetition and get rid of any ridiculously outdated information. Beyond that we've left them pretty much as they were when they first came out. Amazingly (to me), most of the information has remained remarkably relevant and almost completely current. Thanks to Jim Reische for his insightful editing, and to everyone who has read and helped with the revisions.

taking loaves of bread from the brick-lined oven at the bakehouse

Twelve Natural Laws of Building a Great Business

A More Organic Way to Operate?

I most definitely could not have listed all 12 of these tips anywhere near as clearly back when we opened in '82 as I did when I wrote this piece 25 years later. But the truth is that these "natural laws" really are all things that we did to get going back in the early '80s. I think they're as true now as they were then and will still be true 20, or 220, years hence. They are very much the same sort of behind-the-scenes attitudes and approaches that have guided us over the years. And, although I haven't run any other businesses, I'm pretty confident that every successful organization would likely have followed many of these same approaches. Each organization will, of course, have its own applications, but the laws themselves will, naturally, remain the same.

Two or three times a year we teach the two-day Zingerman's Experience seminar here in Ann Arbor. Twenty-five or so outside businesspeople and a few ZCoB staffers come together to get a sense of what we do differently from standard-issue businesses. After getting the introductions and other preliminaries out of the way we turn things over to Paul, who immediately asks everyone to close their eyes and point in the direction that they believe to be north. He then asks everyone to open their eyes while leaving their hands up in the air. Given that so many of the participants are from out of town it's not surprising that their fingers are pointing in pretty much every direction. Almost everyone laughs. But the organizational point is made.

Paul then takes out his pocket compass and shows everyone where true north actually is. While I guess someone *could* choose to argue, no one ever does. The compass bearing isn't an opinion—no matter how much we might will it to be otherwise, north remains north. It's a natural law.

What follows are what we've come to believe here are the *natural laws of doing business*—the organizational equivalents of "due north." Our experience at Zingerman's (which includes working with hundreds of other organizations through ZingTrain) is that these laws are applicable to any business or non-profit, regardless of size, scale, age, service, or product. They work well for solo operators and big corporations, publicly traded companies and privately held firms, mainstream businesses and mavericks, LLCs, C-Corps, S-Corps, and limited partnerships, too. Just as you're free to ignore Paul's compass and head out in whatever direction you *want* to be north, you can ignore as many of these laws as you like. But like them or not our experience is that they still apply.

So . . . here we go. A dozen natural laws of business. Like I said, some will seem obvious, some less so. But I hope they help you as much as they have us.

1. An inspiring, strategically sound vision leads the way to greatness (especially if you write it down!)

Some people certainly find ways to build successful organizations without ever writing out a clear and explicit vision of greatness. But our experience is that they're a lot more likely to create something special when they've actually written their vision down. And having your vision in writing certainly makes the work it takes to get there a lot more enjoyable, too.

What's a vision? As we define it here, it's a picture of what success looks like at a particular point in the future. If you're starting a business, I'd suggest that you pick a time at least three to five years in the future, and longer might be even better. Your vision will talk about what your business does, and why it's special. How the people who work in the business feel about being part of it. How your business relates to its customers, and about how it fits into the community. It could even detail what you as owner will do, and how much money you want to make. To be effective the vision needs to inspire the people who will be doing the work. It also needs to be strategically sound—i.e., while your goals should be ambitious, you want them to be realistic, too. To that end, the vision should also have some key measurables so that everyone involved has some sense of what you're aspiring to: "As big as we can be as fast as we can get there" is NOT a vision. To be effective the vision also needs to be in writing, so that you and your fellow travelers—business partners, employees, etc.—will be literally and figuratively on the same page. And, lest we forget, you'll need to communicate your vision regularly to the rest of your organization so that people will know where you're going.

Please note, too, that the vision is NOT a strategic plan—the plan is how you intend to get from where you are to the vision. But everyone has to be in agreement on where you're going before you can start mapping out action steps for how to get there.

There are no "right" or "wrong" visions—you can write one that says you want to grow your firm into a $100 billion company operating all over the globe, or one that says you'll be the sole employee. Your goal in either case is simply to provide a clear sense of the scale at which your business will operate. But for reasons both concrete (people work a lot more effectively when they understand how you define success) and spiritual (things just seem to come together better when you've written them out), this vision thing really works.

2. YOU NEED TO GIVE CUSTOMERS REALLY COMPELLING REASONS TO BUY FROM YOU

This seems exceedingly obvious, but I've encountered a lot of businesses that don't get it—they seem to think that people ought to buy from them "just because." But from the day we opened at Zingerman's we've always taken the approach that we need our customers way more than they need us. We've always assumed that we have nothing to offer that anyone really *needs*. And we've worked with the knowledge that we don't sell anything that a hundred (or now, with the web, a hundred thousand) competitors aren't offering some reasonable facsimile of, often with better parking or lower prices. Instead, we've always worked with the belief that we have to give people lots of really good reasons to buy from us.

The answer to the question of what those persuasive reasons are will vary from one business to the next. But if you don't think the reasons your company is offering are all that exciting, they probably aren't. If that's the case, I'd say start working to come up with more as quickly as you can—the risk of offering too many compelling reasons would be what we'd consider a "good problem." (More on that in a minute.)

3. WITHOUT GOOD FINANCE, YOU FAIL

This one is so widely accepted that I almost didn't include it on the list. But you know what happens when you "assume," right? Plus it's quite possible to fulfill most or all of the other natural laws as they're laid out here and still not have a sustainable business from a financial standpoint. Granted, it's way more likely that your finances will be good if you live up to all the other laws on the list, but there are still absolutely no guarantees. Many businesses that are doing special things fail every year because they don't manage their money well.

I'll be brief here because there are a million places for you to learn about business finance. (You may want to start with Karen Berman and Joe Knight's book, *Financial Intelligence*, or come to ZingTrain's Fun, Flavorful Finance seminar.) The bottom line (pun intended) is that you can have all the good intentions and good ideas in the world, but you still have to be profitable in order for the business to survive; you do have to have cash on hand in order to pay the bills; and if you don't pay your taxes properly and on time you'll get in a lot of trouble.

4. PEOPLE DO THEIR BEST WORK WHEN THEY'RE PART OF A REALLY GREAT ORGANIZATION

I suppose there have been times in history, like during the Great Depression, when people would take just about any job they could get. But unless your vision is to be the only person active in your business, you're going to want to provide a really great place for people to work. Why? Because while offering a great, rewarding, spiritually sound workplace won't by itself guarantee success, I can assure you that any business that does so will outperform organizations that follow the other 11 natural laws but ignore this one. In fact, I'll posit that you won't really be able to make many of the other principles work very well for very long without providing a great workplace.

Here at Zingerman's we've always taken the approach that we were going to treat the people who chose to work with us as if they were volunteers. As with our customers, we need our staff way more than they need us. So how rewarding does the workplace have to be? Well, pretty darned rewarding. Please note that we mean "rewarding" in every sense of the word—financially, sure, but also emotionally, intellectually, and physically. We're always working on how to make Zingerman's a more positive place by sharing our vision (see Law #1 above), by involving people in running the business, by creating and promoting processes for organizational change, by practicing open book finance, by offering great training, etc.

Ultimately people want to feel that their work makes a positive difference; that their extra efforts are noticed; that they can improve the quality of their lives and the lives of those around them through their work. When we accomplish this we have more fun, service improves, sales go up, and all those other good things that we like to see, start to happen—and with amazing regularity!

5. IF YOU WANT THE STAFF TO GIVE GREAT SERVICE TO CUSTOMERS, THE LEADERS HAVE TO GIVE GREAT SERVICE TO THE STAFF

This rule is less obvious and probably less widely accepted than some of the others. But it's every bit as important. It's one of the key tenets of Servant Leadership, which is the core of our leadership philosophy here at Zingerman's. (We learned it from Robert Greenleaf's excellent book, *Servant Leadership*.) Here's the deal: *the service that the staff gives to customers is never going to be better than the service that we as leaders provide to the staff.* The tone comes from the top; although exceptional service providers may occasionally crop up on their own, they'll always be the exception. The rest is up to us.

It's pretty easy to determine how well you're doing on this point: I can tell with a very high degree of accuracy how the leaders of one of our businesses or departments are treating their staff simply by watching the way the staff wait on customers.

6. IF YOU WANT GREAT PERFORMANCE FROM YOUR STAFF, YOU HAVE TO GIVE THEM CLEAR EXPECTATIONS AND TRAINING TOOLS

This concept is the core of Zingerman's Training Compact, which we developed under the leadership of Maggie Bayless, managing partner at ZingTrain, back in the mid-'90s. We've been working to live up to it—if imperfectly—ever since. To run a great organization it's very clear that we need to be clear about what we're asking from the folks who work for us. And then we need to effectively teach them how to meet our expectations.

The validity of this natural law was confirmed in Marcus Buckingham and Curt Coffman's book, *First, Break All the Rules,* in which the Gallup Organization surveyed 1,000,000 workers and 80,000 managers to determine which factors were most important for keeping the best workers in their jobs for the longest period of time. Their single most important element? *Clear expectations.* Second most critical? *The tools to do their work,* among which effective training figures at the top of the list.

7. SUCCESSFUL BUSINESSES DO THE THINGS THAT OTHERS KNOW THEY SHOULD DO. . . BUT GENERALLY DON'T

This is a rule that Paul and I learned about 25 years ago from consultant and executive coach Tim Connor. Seriously . . . while business books often focus on some stroke of Steven Jobs-like genius, I think that more often than not the real genius is mostly in doing the sort of drudgerous stuff that anyone who really thinks about it could do, but doesn't. Most people don't do this type of work because it seems too hard, too boring, too unrewarding . . . too something. For whatever reason the best businesses do it anyway, while their (oft-complaining) competitors can't quite muster up the energy to make it happen.

I could tell a thousand stories to illustrate this point but the one that always sticks in my head is about how we got our bread back when we first opened the Deli in the early '80s. We knew that if we wanted to have a great corned beef sandwich (a key part of our vision) we had to build it on great bread. After testing loaves from better than 20 different sources, we settled on the rye bread from a bakery about 45 minutes away, in the Detroit suburbs. Our excitement quickly turned to uncertainty when we went to talk to the owner. He was happy

Zingerman's ®
training compact

trainer agrees to:

trainees agree to:

(1.) document clear performance expectations

(2.) provide training resources

(3.) recognize performance

(4.) reward performance

take responsibility for the effectiveness of their training at zingerman's.

to sell to us but he didn't deliver to Ann Arbor. So working with him meant someone had to leave Ann Arbor early enough to get back with the bread before we opened the doors at 7 a.m. And, mind you, the winters in Michigan make for difficult driving. I think nearly every other bakery was willing to deliver. But we wanted the best bread we could get, and that meant we were going to drive to Detroit every day to get it. Which we did about 3800 times (round trip) until we opened Zingerman's Bakehouse in 1992.

I'm not telling you this story to brag, but merely to illustrate the value of the law. At the time we probably didn't agonize that much over the decision—it just seemed clear to us that it was the right thing to do. Although most everyone would have said it was a good idea to go around and taste all the breads in the area before choosing one, I'd guess that few, if any, of our competitors did so. And if they did, they probably—and very understandably—didn't feel like driving all that way every day to get it. So they settled for something subpar while we kept making that boring, often icy, early morning drive to Detroit and back.

If you look around at the most successful businesses in any industry I bet you'll find that each has a folder full of similar stories. Not only are they an important part of the company's initial success, but the truly great organizations continue to do such things even as they grow and mature. While their competitors cut corners, they just keep doing all those unglamorous little things: they stay open late, they open early, they thank a few more staff and customers, they pay a bit more to get better raw materials, they forgive loyal employees who err, they give a bit more to the community . . .

8. To get to greatness you've got to keep getting better, All the time!

The most successful organizations and individuals understand this. From medicine to the arts, non-profits, or pro sports—the best in any field are all going after improvement all the time. You can call it continuous improvement, *kaizen,* or whatever you like. The reality is that if we're not learning, growing, and improving then the marketplace is going to pass us by.

Early on in my leadership life I used to think we'd get to some point where success would allow us to coast. Man, was I ever wrong on that one. Fortunately I realized the error of my ways in time. In truth, I think running the business well actually gets *harder,* not easier, the longer you go on. But once I made peace with that reality, then living this rule was infinitely less stressful for me.

(By the way, it took me a long time to learn it but this drive for improvement can very much coexist with appreciation for what we've already achieved. See Law #12 below for more on the latter.)

9. Success means you get better problems

Although most of us are raised with the belief that effective work *eliminates* problems, the reality is quite different. We're *always* going to have problems. The key is to pick the problems you want and then appreciate the chance to work on them, all the while working to get better problems still.

Don't believe me? OK, would you rather have too few customers and struggle to make your payroll, or have sales so strong that you have to struggle to keep up? Obviously I like seeing sales levels right "on plan" best of all, but the reality is that generally I'd rather have sales be too high than too low. Similarly, I'd far prefer the problem of having too many good people in the organization and not quite enough opportunity for them all in the moment than to have too few good people.

Quick story to illustrate the point. A customer was having dinner at Zingerman's Roadhouse not long ago. While he and his family were enjoying their evening's experience he shared with his server that the person who had taken their order during a morning visit to the Deli just hadn't been as enthusiastic as our staff usually are. His server that night was on top of things—she apologized (even though she had no idea who it was at the Deli nor any inkling of what had really happened). She took the initiative to buy the family an extra appetizer as a way to help make it right and follow up her verbal apology. And then she shared the story with me to see what else I thought we should do.

As the guest and his family were leaving I stopped him to add to the apologies that the server had already given, to check that his dinner experience was good (it was), and to thank him again for sharing the story so constructively. I asked what else I might do to be of help. He shook his head. "Look," he said with a smile. "I've been a customer of yours for nearly 20 years. We started going to the Deli when we were students here. Now we live in Florida and we're huge fans of everything you do. We buy mail order all the time. And when we come back up to visit we come in to eat every day. We've been in town all weekend and we've had two meals at the Roadhouse, two at the Deli, and we've been out to visit the Bakehouse, too. We love everything you do. It's just that you guys have set the bar SO high that when we got service that would probably be fine most places but just isn't at the standards we know we're gonna get here . . . it just surprised us. It wasn't all that bad really—the woman who waited on us just wasn't very . . . 'Zingy.'"

You've got to love it when your customers have turned your business's name into an adjective that connotes great service. There are a lot of businesses that would kill to have a customer complaint of that kind.

But the truth is that great businesses get complaints like this all the time. By contrast, most of the others have set the bar so low that their customers don't even notice the shortfalls anymore, let alone say anything about them. While the latter is certainly less stressful in the moment it definitely doesn't lead to success. Ignorance only *feels* like bliss; reality remains the same whether anyone tells us the truth or not.

10. WHATEVER YOUR STRENGTHS ARE, THEY WILL LIKELY LEAD STRAIGHT INTO YOUR WEAKNESSES

It took me a really long time to recognize the truth of this law. But having realized the reality of it I can't recall a single time that it hasn't proven true. I can tell you, too, that accepting it has radically reduced my stress level. I used to think there was this big conflict at work between "good" and "bad" qualities, either in me or in the organization overall. But the reality is that pretty much anything we're good at is going to, at some point, be carried a bit too far and become a problem.

To forecast what's likely to come up one has only to look at what's already an organizational or personal strength and then extrapolate from there. So, for instance, I'm personally very focused and I don't let go of something I believe in very easily. Certainly that quality has contributed positively to what I've been able to achieve over the years. But it's sort of inevitable—following this natural law—that sometimes I'm going to stick with something longer than I should. The same holds true organizationally. One of our strengths here at Zingerman's is that we're a very participative workplace. What's the almost inevitable weakness, then? Sometimes we have so many chances for people to participate that things take longer than they might have otherwise.

Embracing the reality of this law makes life far less stressful: instead of fighting our weaknesses we can actually predict them and then plan ways to manage around, or through, them. If we do that well, managers can be more effective and everyone can have more fun at work. And it also gives each of us—as individuals and organizations—the opportunity to understand why we do what we do, and to adjust our behaviors accordingly.

11. IT GENERALLY TAKES A LOT LONGER TO MAKE SOMETHING GREAT HAPPEN THAN PEOPLE THINK

Early on in our work together Paul taught me that, in his view, "Professionalism means sticking with something long after the glamour has worn off." Everything I've seen, heard, and learned since has supported that belief.

While most people seem to think that everyone else's work or life or whatever is glamorous (the grass is always greener and all that), few things are actually very glamorous after the third or fourth day of doing them. Front-line people think it would be great to be the CEO and be in charge of everything; CEOs think about how nice it would be to just be able to go clean the cooler for an hour and not have anyone bother them! And while there are the hole-in-ones of the business world that you can probably point to as exceptions, nearly all great organizations, nearly all long-term, sustainable businesses, take a really, really long time to build. They may seem from the outside like "overnight" successes, but very few of them actually are.

We've all seen or been part of the "flavor of the day" approach to management. You know . . . companies start stuff all the time. But few stick with any change or innovation long enough to really make it work. I don't mean that longevity alone is enough to make something succeed—just that even the best ideas take a long time to really get going.

For instance, we're big proponents of Open Book Finance. We use it religiously and even teach a two-day ZingTrain seminar on the subject. But I'll tell you flat out that for the first five years or so of doing it we were probably mediocre at best in our implementation. It took another three or four years to really get good at it. (One big difference? We started getting a lot better when we finally wrote down our vision for it! See Law #1 above.) Could others have done it more quickly and more effectively? I'm sure many could, and I know some have. And, believe me, I'm not recommending doing it poorly just so you can say you stuck with it. All I'm saying is that, although we eventually arrived at a great result, it took us a really long time to build it into our organizational systems, training, culture, and daily routines. No offense, but most organizations would have given up long before they'd arrived at anything really special. Their loss—Open Book Finance is one of the best things we've ever implemented!

My experience here (this part is anecdotal, not necessarily a natural law) is that it takes about two years for us to achieve some level of equilibrium for any meaningful change or new business. It then takes another year or two to get good. And it's only then—three to four years after we started—that we've got ourselves in position to go after greatness. Getting that greatness, in my experience, generally takes another two years, too. And then, in keeping with Law #7, we just keep working to get better anyway!

All of which reminds me to remind you: one of the most effective ways to increase the odds of getting to where you want to go is to keep bringing out the vision (as in Law #1) so you can remind yourselves, and others in the organization, of what you're collectively trying to achieve. In ain't easy but sticking with stuff works. Let me quote from a 1931 piece by essayist Logan Pearsall Smith: "The test of a vocation is the love of the drudgery it involves." Couldn't agree more!

12. Great organizations are appreciative, and the people in them have more fun

I added this one to the list fairly recently. It's not that having fun is a novel idea—here at Zingerman's we've had it written into our guiding principles for years. But we long ago realized that fun was something we had to actively make happen, not something that would arrive on its own. In fact, we've had fun making things fun, now that I think about it. Over the years we've worked hard to create a culture and systems that are positive and appreciative. And without question it has contributed enormously to us being the organization that we are.

Note that by "having fun" I'm not talking about a bunch of goofy behaviors, making your staff wear funny hats or pins, or telling jokes (although in the right culture any or all of those might work). I'm talking about the quality of the energy in our work environment; about enjoying and appreciating all the really amazing little things that surround us every day but that so many people don't stop to appreciate; about realizing that it's the ride and not the destination that's really the point of things.

Not long ago Amy Emberling, one of the managing partners at the Bakehouse, shared an article, "Manage Your Energy, Not Your Time," by Tony Schwartz and Catherine McCarthy, that pushed me to think about this. The article was about how leaders—or any of us, really—can focus our attentions on building energy instead of managing time. The authors weren't down on the latter, but just acknowledged what we all know to be true: there will never be more time than there is. Personal energy, however, can be expanded very effectively. Schwartz and McCarthy found that successful leaders, regardless of personal style, were generally very energized and excited about their lives and work. The article listed a couple of characteristics that contributed to this increased energy level. One was that energized, high-achieving individuals live in appreciative, positive settings.

I think I can safely say then that this is a natural law: great organizations are appreciative, enjoyable places to be. Lack of fun, conversely, is a sign of impending trouble. Paul Hawken wrote about this in one of the first—and still one of the best—business books I ever read, *Growing a Business*. "Laughter and good humor," he wrote, "are the canaries in the mine of commerce. If employees, customers, and vendors don't laugh and have a good time at your company, something is wrong." You can learn a lot from the style of smile—or lack thereof—that you see backstage.

And before some cynic says something like, "well that's easy for them because they're successful, so of course they're having fun," I'm going to posit that in this case, as in so many other things in life, the behavior actually very often precedes the feeling. Great organizations aren't having fun just because they're great (though it's usually way more fun to work with the problems of success than those of failure); rather, they're great because the people in them are actively appreciative and have learned to enjoy doing whatever it is they need to do to succeed in ethical and caring ways.

This is true, by the way, even when—perhaps, especially when—times are tough. No matter what we're dealing with at Zingerman's, we work hard to be kind to each other, and to recognize that although we'd rather not be struggling, we're glad to be doing it with people we really like.

Chip Conley, the founder and CEO of Joie de Vivre Hospitality, California's largest boutique hotel group, shares a great example of this in his highly recommended book, *Peak: How Great Companies Get Their Mojo from Maslow.* During the depths of the dot-com crash Joie de Vivre was as hard hit as any other Bay Area hotel group. As sales suffered Chip had to go without salary for a number of years. Perhaps harder still, after many years of success he had to approach his investors with a capital call to raise operating cash for the hotels. As part of the call he and his staff designed a T-shirt to send to each investor. On the front it said, "*San Francisco Hotels 2002: The Sky is Falling,*" and on the back, "*Joie de Vivre Hospitality. Strong Enough to Restore the Sky.*" And then, underneath . . . "*I bought a hotel in San Francisco and all I got was this lousy T-shirt?*" A little humor in the face of great financial adversity goes a long way!

The capital call went very smoothly, the company stayed strong, and they're doing well now. Obviously the shirt was not the keystone of the company's recovery. But, hey, the humor helps. After they made it back to equilibrium, one of the company's investors sent Chip back a T-shirt that said, "*Joie de Vivre Hospitality . . . No Bankruptcies, No Defaults, No Salary.*"

I'll close this discussion of the last of the twelve laws with another quote from Logan Pearsall Smith. It's from his 1931 essay, "Life and Human Nature," which I first saw in Chip's book. The piece immediately struck me as being so much in sync with this twelfth rule. "There are two things to aim at in life," Smith wrote. "First, to get what you want; and, after that, to enjoy it. Only the wisest of mankind achieve the second."

Natural Conclusion

So let me end here by appreciating all the amazing people whom I get to work with every day. I feel very fortunate to be in this organization, to be partners with Paul and now 15 others as well, and to work with more than 500 great staff members. I feel the same way about the hundreds of quality-oriented suppliers we buy from, and the thousands of caring supportive customers we have here in what I think is a really great town. And we get to do it all in an industry full of interesting colleagues. That the bar is set so high, I think, is a really good problem. I look forward to the challenge of helping raise it even higher in the years to come.

I hope these natural laws are of some help to you and those you work with. And that they lead to greater success and more rewarding lives for all.

charlie frank, managing partner of zingerman's
candy manufactory, at the mixing bowl

Contrast, Composition, Content

---

*Part Two: Designing a
Great Business from the Inside Out*

The more I work with this 3 C's approach, the more I (a), realize just how different it is from the way that most people do business; and (b), believe in it. Throughout this book you'll find references to "making something special," to doing unique things, to creating a business that's grounded, that's delivering meaningful memories for its customers and for the people who work in it. To my experience, it's just a lot more likely that those things are going to happen when the design of the business comes from the heart, is something the owners really believe in, and then is built up in ways that emanate from there. The alternative is what I would consider an old-school approach in which people try to figure out "what they're supposed do" or "what the market wants" and then back down to what they personally have to do to make that happen, while, they hope, making a lot of money in the process. The results of these two ways of working may look much the same, but are actually likely to yield very, very different businesses.

If you're reading titles closely you could well be looking for Part One of this piece. Don't worry. "Contrast, Composition, and Content, Part One: A Recipe for Good Graphic Design" will show up in another volume of *Zingerman's Guide to Good Leading* (if you can't wait, email me now and I'll send it off *tout de suite*). But, as you already know, I'm a lapsed anarchist, so why can't I opt to put Part Two before Part One if it makes more sense to do it that way? And the thing is, I need Part Two of the piece now, when we're talking about designing a business. So here it is.

The insight that's covered in this essay actually came to me more out of frustration than anything else. I kept thinking about why it was bothering me that people so often wanted to talk to me about this, that, or the other new business "concept." I'm not sure where this interest in concepts—as opposed to content—comes from. It's so antithetical to the way we work that it secretly raises my ire every time someone asks about it. I try to stay calm on the surface; no one means anything bad by it. Plus, Paul long ago taught me the extremely helpful phrase, "When furious, get curious." And so, rather than just raging I reflected—what was it about those questions that was raising my anxiety?

I think it's that these queries miss what I believe is the heart of the matter, the stuff that, to me, is really at the core of making the kind of special, sustainable business we're going after here. I think, too, that my frustration comes because so many of the folks who ask seem to believe that a "good concept" is all you need to create a great business. It's as if they're looking for that one brilliant idea, the supposed "secret" that's going to make them a lot of money.

In truth, I feel the same sort of frustration about the widespread use of the term "brand." I'm regularly approached by people (often, I'm afraid, people with big-time business school backgrounds) who seem more worried about "designing a brand" than they are about what their business is actually going to do every day. They're not slackers: they've done in-depth profiles of their potential clientele; they have a logo, a business name, and a couple of really catchy little tag lines to stick on things. But all too often they seem to have more passion for having a hip idea than for whatever it is that they're going to make or sell.

If I'm honest with myself, and with you, I think this approach to business is totally backward. That's not a value judgment, merely an observation that might be of value to others. I certainly don't begrudge others doing either or both, and I know that there are certainly plenty of instances where that sort of outside-in approach pays off financially. But speaking for myself money's not the be-all end-all. I'm more in line with Alex Wupperworth, aka "Brand Hijack," who once said in an interview, "You can't create cool yourself. You can only follow your own convictions, your own sensibility, to create a world-class design." Which is, quite clearly, what we work hard to be about here at Zingerman's.

Design is, in truth, how I came upon the . . . pardon the use of the term . . . "concept" of Contrast, Composition, and Content in the first place. I was co-teaching our ZingTrain MerchandiZing seminar with Becky Winkler for about the eighteenth time. Becky was doing a segment on signmaking in which she covers the concept of those "3 C's." The way she teaches it is that the consumer is drawn to our work by the contrast—which could be bright colors on a sign, or maybe a strange shape; something that really stands out from everything around it. From there the eye is taken in deeper by the sign's composition—for instance, the name of the product might be the biggest thing on the sign so our eye goes there first. If that works well, then lastly we get to the content—we actually read the copy of the sign, which conveys meaningful bits of information and gives us good reasons to buy the product. So, to the consumer it's contrast, then composition, and only at the end the actual content.

Interestingly, inexperienced artists often design by basically following the same perceptual sequence as the consumer. They start by trying to come up with a cool-looking design (the contrast), then back up from there to things like headlines and hierarchy (the composition), and usually have little true feel for whatever it is that their design is supposed to be selling (the content). The results are rarely, if ever, very effective.

What Becky pointed out in her presentation was that *effective* design work is always done in the *opposite* order. Which means that the most important thing for a great designer to know about is the content, i.e., the actual product. What's so special about the item at hand? Why is it worth buying? What will it do for the customer? What makes it so unique? Only after they know a lot about what it is they're marketing, and have some feeling—or better still, real passion—for it will the effective designer move on to composition. Based on which elements of the content are most important, they organize the sign so that the most critical info reaches the eye most quickly. Only at the end will they get to the thing that the consumer notices first: the colors or visuals or whatever it is that's different enough to get the guest's attention. In other words, the contrast. All three need to be done well, but, again, the marketing work is best done when it begins with understanding and belief in the product, that all-important content.

As I was listening to Becky I was suddenly struck by a big, belated glimpse of the obvious: although she was teaching this recipe to an audience interested in graphic design, the idea was equally applicable to all our other "design" work, whether it was designing a business, a product, or pretty much anything else of consequence.

From the consumer's perspective, in business the 3 C's work this way:

Contrast is how we differentiate our store, catalog, or service from everyone else's. It could be a unique name, a really cool and appealing look and feel, a great staff uniform, a wacky website, a witty tag line, a great ad, our official "colors," catchy names for our products . . . Like a bold color scheme on a poster or a strange shape on a marketing brochure, these are the things that get customers' attention and make them curious to learn more about what we do.

Composition is the way we organize our business to serve our customers. Just like in a good piece of graphic design, effective composition prioritizes what we do in a way that holds the customers' attention. It's the choice we make about which products to put in prime position on our menu, the stuff that gets the best shelf space, what goes into Aisle One, where things go on our website, the way we arrange our cash registers to be more service-oriented, the staff training we invest in to ensure a good customer experience. All of these things are placed in order to get customers to the products and services we want them to buy, and that they might really most want, i.e., our content.

Content is what actually gets people to come back. For us at Zingerman's that means the food and the service. For you it's whatever goods or services you

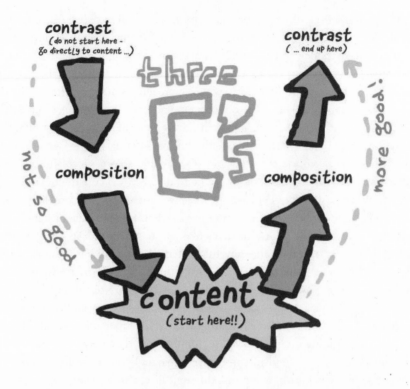

provide. But regardless, it's the main point of the customer's experience. While our "look and feel" may be fun (contrast) and we may have figured out effective ways to organize things (composition), it's what the customers buy and the way we treat them while they're buying it. Cute ads and catchy tag lines may bring people in, but it's the food and service they get when they arrive that bring them back for more. And for us that means that we need to really work at making amazing food and delivering exceptional service, at selling products we really believe in and always working to improve all of them all the time.

So, just to restate, the way I see it, the best, most meaningful, and ultimately most effective work in business, (as in graphic design) comes when we go through the 3 C's in reverse order. We start with the content and build a business we believe in—not a concept that works from the outside in, but something of substance, something special, something close to our hearts. That gives us a good shot at making a great business out of it. Because, to state the almost obvious, when we do something positive and meaningful, it's (duh!) more likely that positive and meaningful things will come from it. And that's I think what business is about. Creating something special that will have a positive impact on those around for a long time to come—not just a quick catchy "concept" that lets you make money and get out quickly before the glitz is gone.

Mind you, I'm not saying that there's something wrong with the latter—it's just not what we do here. I know our approach—starting with content we really care a lot about—isn't the only way to create, or even to run, a successful business. But it is the way we approach things here, and it's the most effective way I know to build a sustainable, sound business that lasts.

Someone asked me the other day if you could start a successful business that was built only on flash, or, in the lingo of this 3 C's construct, "contrast." My answer was, probably. Pet Rocks worked well for a while, and probably made someone some serious money. A cute logo and an eye-catching design might well get people in the door. But that's likely to be the end of it. On the other hand, when we start with meaningful content . . . that's what I think creates loyal customers. It's what gives the staff something to believe in. It's what makes things solid instead of shifty, sustainable instead of short-term.

The marketplace is overfull of businesses that are mostly built around concepts and brands but have little meaningful material at their core—to me, they're like houses that are built on unstable foundations. They may look great from the outside, but they tend to come apart amazingly quickly when the winds of public opinion start blowing in a different direction or when the economic ground they're built on shifts. On the other hand, if you start the design of your business with solid, very special content, you've got a good chance at getting somewhere, of making something meaningful that contributes positively to the lives of all involved: the foundation is solid, the footings deep, the framing likely to hold even under stress.

Paul Hawken wrote about this in his classic book, *Growing a Business.* Touching on the (over-) focus on concepts he said, "The idea itself is the tip of the iceberg. The iceberg is your life. Don't worry about anyone stealing your idea because they can't steal your life." No matter how good the idea, it's still a heck of a lot of work to make it a success. (Overnight successes, while they get much attention in the press, probably hardly ever happen in real life, and even when they do they still take a ton of effort.) Business, in my experience, is way too much work to be doing something you don't feel passionate about. As Mr. Hawken made clear, "business shouldn't be something you do to live, but something you live to do."

All of which explains why I think of the business design process as similar to the process for making posters. The best business builders (or designers) begin with great *content*. What are you trying to do? Why are you doing it? Who are you doing it for? Why are you excited about it? Why is it special? Make it really great and the rest of the work will be a whole lot easier.

From there we move to the *composition*—how will you organize yourself to sell your products and services in a way that makes your customers want to come back? Where will you locate? What hours will you be open? What sorts of services will you provide?

And finally you come to the *contrast:* the brand and the marketing. Figure out a way to present yourself in the marketplace in a way that gets people's attention and draws them to your business so they can experience your service and products. And if the goods and services are good enough they'll come back over and over again for a long time to come.

asa wilson, roasting a batch of beans at zingerman's coffee company

SECRET #3

Creating Recipes for Organizational Success

*How We Apply the Principles
of Good Work at the Stove
to What We Do with the Staff*

The longer we work with our organizational recipes here at Zingerman's the more convinced I am that they've contributed to what we've achieved organizationally. Many of the essays that follow this one—on mission statements, writing visions of greatness, etc.—rely on this concept. The key, as you'll see, is that our recipes have to be clear enough and applicable enough so everyone in our organization can use them, yet flexible enough so they can be adapted to any situation. Plus you and I as leaders need to be stubborn enough to stick with them for long enough (at least two or three years to really get them well-woven into our culture here) so that everyone in the company really gets into using them!

It's almost a given that a lot of us who are strange enough to be drawn to the lively, loveable chaos of the food business also have a bit of an aversion to structure. It's a natural thing—we like the food world because we don't have to sit in offices or deal with large corporate structures. This comfort with chaos and uncertainty can be helpful to those of us who started our own businesses: to make a small startup successful you have to be able to work well on the fly— quickly changing concepts, ideas, and procedures, etc.—in order to adapt to the inevitable, unexpected problems that get thrown at us each day. At the early stages of a startup, that kind of constant change is actually essential.

But when we get past the startup stage we start to grow up. Maturing in business, as in our personal lives, means finding new, more appropriate, and more effective ways to relate to our world. This is where our distaste for systems can become a problem. If we as entrepreneurs see structure as restrictive, our managers and staff are likely to do so as well: after all, they were probably drawn to work with us, in part, for our sense of entrepreneurial freedom. Many of us anarchist types live in near-literal fear of becoming General Motors or some restrictive, rule-laden government agency. We made it early on without writing everything down, and it often just seems like more fun to wing it.

That might well have worked just fine when our businesses were small and we were working there ourselves every day. The problem comes when you want to take a day—let alone a week, or, dare I say it, even a month—off without having everything come apart. Sound familiar? A woman who recently opened a nice new restaurant in town stopped by the Roadhouse for dinner the other day. Unsolicited, she started telling me how incredibly anxious she was because she was going out of town for a weekend for the first time since she'd opened. I reassured her that, 20 years after we opened, I still get a little worried. But I also worry a lot less than I used to, for two reasons: the great people who work with us, and the ever-better organizational recipes we've put in place to keep things running in the right direction.

Building and Using Our Recipe Book for Success

The importance of these recipes was reinforced by one of the most insightful books on organizations and leadership that I've read, Ichak Adizes's *Corporate Lifecycles*. Adizes's theory is that organizations move through their lives like people, developing in stages from "Infants," to "Early Adolescence," to "Adolescence," to "Go-Go" [his equivalent, I think, to the late teen years], and "Prime. . . ." "Prime" is, as the name implies, the best stage at which an organization can be. Basically, it's an effective maturity: still vital and lively, but also organized and systematic. It's the spot where I want our own organization—many years after we've opened—to be.

To quote Adizes, "Prime organizations know what they're doing, where they're going, and how to get there. They make money and are similar in growth characteristics to the Go-Go with one major difference. A Go-Go can tell you why they made money. A Prime can tell you why they are *going to* make money. And they do."

"Prime," he goes on, "does not mean that you have arrived, but that you are still growing. It is a process, not a destination." And, "in a Prime organization there is a climate of repetitive success. Failure is unusual and it gets attention."

As he explains it, an organization that is operating in "Prime":

- has an institutionalized vision and creativity;
- has a results orientation;
- makes plans and then follows those plans;
- predictably excels in performance;
- can afford and benefit from both growth in sales and profitability;
- has functional systems and good organizational structure.

I want to focus here on the last of these characteristics—what we at Zingerman's call our recipes for organizational success. These recipes include "3 Steps to Great Service," "5 Steps to Handling Customer Complaints," "4 Elements of of an Effective Vision," "5 Steps to Effective (Bottom Line) Change," and "3 Steps to Great Finance."

Why do I use the term "recipe"? Because, like good recipes in the kitchen, these management systems:

- provide enough structure for newcomers to really understand what to do, and help them succeed more quickly;
- still leave enough room for skilled "cooks" to adapt and adjust the recipes as appropriate.

Besides which, we're in the food business! So recipes seemed to be an ideal analogy for tying food and management together. Bottom line? Effective recipes for leadership and operation work because they're simple enough for beginners, flexible enough for experts, and very teachable.

Oliver Wendell Holmes once said that, "I would not give a fig for the simplicity this side of complexity, but I would give my life for the simplicity on the other side of complexity." The truth is that as our organizations grow they are going to get more complex. It's impossible not to—the more we grow, the more people we interact with, the more food, customers, product lines, and space we have, the more complex our lives are going to become. Longing for the old days where we just got to "do what we wanted to" is very understandable. But I've come to think that it's really just nostalgia for an era that's over and probably wasn't half as much fun when we were in it as it seems to be in hindsight (think high school). And using the Adizes analogy of organizations maturing, it seems akin to trying to go back to living like an 18-year-old when you're actually already 38—it can be fun for a day or two but it doesn't really work very well for any extended period of time.

To build on this approach I looked to the work of Karl Weick, one of the University of Michigan's best-known business professors. Weick breaks learning and solutions out into three stages of development:

1. Superficial Simplicity
2. Confused Complexity
3. Profound Simplicity

Although it sounds conceited, I've come to believe very strongly that our recipes for success operate at the level of "profound simplicity": that what we've done is develop Justice Holmes's "simplicity on the other side of complexity." We have taken the complex realities of organizational life and framed them into simple, usable, meaningful recipes that help people in our organization succeed, and help us deliver better food and service to our guests.

Of course great people are a critical part of any organization that wants to be successful. But without the recipes, even great staff are likely to be inconsistent. They'll try hard to do the right thing, but mostly what they'll expend their energy on is doing what they personally think is right. Imagine if every cook in your kitchen changed the tomato soup recipe to meet his or her own personal taste. Ten cooks, ten tomato soups. To be successful, people need structure. Only when we have great "cooks" working with great recipes do we achieve the sort of success we're looking for.

Where to Begin

What follows is, basically, a five-part recipe for building an organizational recipe. To test out the concept, pick a process or procedure that's a fairly consistent element of your organizational routine. It could be a broad area like customer service or it could be something more specific, like how to count the cash at the end of the day or how to answer the phone. Once you've identified your area of emphasis, here are the five things to do to make it work:

1. TEACH THE RECIPE

I know that in the theoretical organizational world you have to actually do the second step below—"Define It"—before you can teach it. But I've also learned from 25 years of doing this stuff that if we don't commit to teaching our recipe we'll probably never make the time to define it. So jump in: take out your calendar book and put down a date when you're going to present your first recipe to everyone else you work with. Then go public with it—tell everyone else that you're going to present it. At which point you'll be kind of stuck. But stuck in a good way! Because now you have to figure out what it is you're going to say. And that's when you get down to defining and documenting your recipe.

Of course, teaching the recipe once isn't going to be enough. You'll have to teach and teach and teach it many times if you really want everyone to use it. Teaching can, of course, mean formal classroom training, but it can also mean things like simply talking about the recipe on shift, posting it near work areas, etc. Quite simply, the more we teach the recipe the more effectively we're going to be able to use it.

2. DEFINE IT

Now that you've made your public pronouncement you can start writing the actual recipe. Give yourself a month to get it done. Start by sitting with the people who do the actual work in question. Together, write up the steps that you currently follow to complete the task. Number them as you would when writing an actual recipe in a cookbook. Come up with a name: simple and memorable or nice and catchy usually work best. And there you go—you have your first draft.

Like any recipe it will need to be tested, so have everyone try it for a week. Ask them to take notes on what works and what doesn't. Then get back together. Review things and make adjustments. And then . . . get going. Write up your revised version of the recipe and start using it.

3. LIVE IT

Of course, just having the recipes alone isn't enough. We have to actually use them. And, I've learned (and re-learned more times than I'd like to admit) that if we don't use them . . . drum roll . . . they won't work. This is probably the least glamorous part of the process: the day-to-day task of really doing it—walking the talk, using the recipe, making it a part of every day behavior within the organization.

Emotionally this can be the hardest part of the equation for those of us who started our businesses. We just want to do what we want to do. Rules are for other people. The problem is that our staff are watching us all the time. If we don't follow the recipe, they aren't going to either.

4. MEASURE IT

How do you know if the recipe's working? You need to take measurements. I'd recommend tracking two things: first, whether people in the organization are actually using the recipe. And, second (and more important), the degree to which you're achieving what the recipe is designed to achieve. If you're shooting to reduce mistakes on orders, then track accuracy. If your recipe is targeted at better finance, then track your financials. You get the idea.

While one of these recipes isn't going to single-handedly fix everything that's wrong with our organization, if we get the right people in place and they're using a well-written recipe then we should see meaningful improvement. Make the measurement fun, make it visible, and make sure everyone knows the score on a regular basis.

5. REWARD IT

To make all this work it's imperative that we recognize and reward those who are using the recipe and using it well. Even simple verbal appreciation is important: merely saying something positive to a supporter can make a big difference.

You can also reward people more formally for using the recipe. Better still, reward the improved results that come from using it—that way the individual staff member wins and the organization as a whole wins as well.

Final Thoughts

I'm not suggesting that other organizations should just take the recipes we use at Zingerman's and implement them; we haven't created some new version of the Ten Commandments. But any organization that has successfully gotten past the startup phase will benefit from seeking its own recipes—recipes that can help you and your staff achieve Justice Holmes's goal of "simplicity on the other side of complexity."

Ultimately, the entire organization and its stakeholders can benefit—customers, staff, suppliers, investors, and managers. Everyone's going to win because good people, using well-written recipes, create what, as you already know, author Ichak Adizes describes as an organization operating in "Prime." Recipes help us to more effectively hit our goals, reduce stress, and create a more enjoyable place to work, while improving the quality of our products, our service, and our finance. All of which makes work more fun!

So why wait? Start writing recipes and get "cooking" as soon as you can!

created in 1995, the bPc is the visual representation of how our organization works

The Zingerman's Business Perspective Chart

The Visual Lay of Our Organizational Land

I don't think I'd ever have imagined back in '94 and '95 when we were working on this seemingly silly chart that it would end up being used in every single class we teach and referred to with enormous regularity by folks all over our organization all day, every day. It's anything but a secret—we've actually used and taught our Business Perspective Chart so often that, strange as it might sound, we actually have lots of people from other parts of the country who have been to ZingTrain seminars and now refer to it regularly, as well. Who knows, maybe one day they'll hang it up in Congress as a point of reference to help frame difficult discussions! Seriously, though, this thing really has been a huge help to us. See what you think.

This chart is something we developed in the mid-'90s in an effort to help us get—and keep—our priorities straight. We did the work while we were starting ZingTrain and for whatever reason we had the insight to realize that we would benefit from creating a visual model of how our organization works. In part we needed to get clear in our own minds how training fit at Zingerman's, especially (though certainly not exclusively) because we were about to open our own training business.

In the 15 years since then we've gone over the chart at the beginning of almost every class we've taught—and we teach a lot of classes. The exercise has really helped all of us, both as instructors and as students. Teaching it as often as we do has enabled us to build a common language for everyone in the organization—almost every staff member at every level in every one of our businesses will be able to give you a pretty decent definition of terms like Mission, Vision, Principles, Systems, and Culture. And they'll all be able to tell you about our three bottom lines.

In-depth essays on the elements of the Business Perspective Chart follow. But, for the moment, here's a quick glossary of what the key terms on the chart mean to us. I say "to us" because if you read a hundred business books you're going to get a hundred different definitions. I'm not here to argue about whose is right, but when we use these words at Zingerman's, here's what we mean:

MISSION

The mission is what business we're in. It answers these questions: "What do we do?" "Why do we do it?" "Who are we that are doing it?" and "Who are we doing it for?" Our mission is to bring a great Zingerman's Experience to everyone we

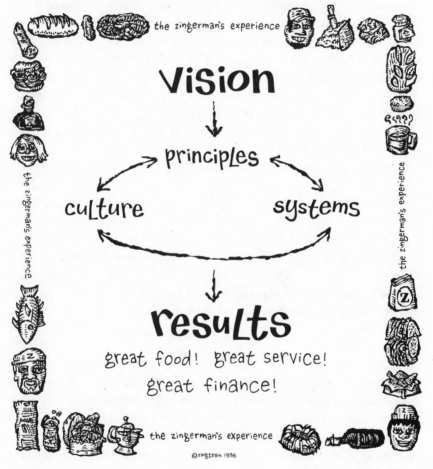

Zingerman's®
business perspective

the zingerman's experience

Vision

↓

→ principles ←

culture   systems

the zingerman's experience

↓

results
great food! great service!
great finance!

the zingerman's experience

©zingtrain 1996

come into contact with. That's our daily work for today, tomorrow, and forever, to bring staff, customers, suppliers, and community members we work with a really positive experience in all that we do.

Vision

Vision is an inspiring and strategically sound picture of your chosen future. Unlike the mission, which is very broad and is probably in place for the rest of your organizational life, the vision has a lot more specifics and, so, may change over time. It addresses what you do, how big you are, how you work together, what your community and customers say about you, and so on. Creating a vision is all about starting with a positive picture of what you want to happen rather than what you don't like about the present. We do visions for our entire organization (Zingerman's 2009 and now Zingerman's 2020), for each of our businesses (say, Zingerman's Bakehouse 2011), for each department within each business, for each product we make, for each job, and even for every shift.

Bottom Lines

We have three bottom lines at Zingerman's—food, service, and finance are all bottom-line issues for us. (Service for us includes service to each other and to our community, as well as to customers.) Which means that we're committed to delivering results in all three areas as ends in themselves, not just as means to some financial goal. We really do measure ourselves on all three dimensions and we really do treat all three with equal gravity.

Systems

Systems are the formal procedures we create and use to accomplish our daily work. They include everything from kitchen recipes to forms for new staff hires to standard operating procedures for our catering and mail order businesses. They aren't an end unto themselves but they are a very important factor in a successful operation: without them we'd basically be back to a state approximating anarchy ☺, with each of us doing our own version of whatever it is we think we should be doing.

Principles

Principles are how we've committed to working with each other while doing what we do. Synonymous with "values" or "ethics," they're an explicit affirmation that the ends don't justify the means for us. Whatever we do we're going to do it in a way that's ethically sound, as difficult as that may be in any given situation.

CULTURE

Culture is the way we live every day—essentially, the personality of the organization. It's where talk becomes walk, where we live—or don't live—our principles, and stick to—or don't stick to—our agreed-upon systems. Most everything else on the Chart starts as a concept or a document. But the culture—flawed and imperfect as it is—is *the way we really work.*

MINDING—AND CLOSING—THE GAPS

So, to sum up these last few points, the systems and principles are the way we *say* we're going to work, and the culture is how we actually *do it* every day. In my fantasy we live our principles perfectly and follow our systems all the time. But in reality we're human and we fall short: Sometimes we don't honor our values as carefully as we should. At other times we fail to follow a system that we've all agreed on. On occasion the entire organization will lose track of something that we've all said we're going to do. I wish that that weren't the case, but rather than dysfunctionally pretending it's not—which would actively devalue everything we say and do—I'd rather deal in the real world.

My point in acknowledging these gaps is that:

a. when they do happen, it's *not* OK;

b. knowing that it's not OK, we have an obligation to get things back into alignment;

c. every member of our organization shares in that obligation;

d. only through the committed effort of everyone here will we get things back in alignment with our mission, vision, bottom-line goals, and guiding principles.

Achieving alignment means making changes. It could mean altering our behavior to help us adhere to our Guiding Principles or systems. It could mean adjusting a system to fit what we actually do in real life every day. In extreme cases it could involve altering our Mission, Vision, Principles, or Bottom Lines (although that would be pretty drastic and I don't think it's ever happened in the many years we've been working with this approach).

One simple example of how we live this struggle every day is on the highway. We all know that the speed limit signs say "70 MPH." But we also know that the "real" speed limit is the one we've absorbed culturally, the one that says that you can go as fast as you want until you see a patrol car parked in the median strip. At which point you quickly brake, your heart starts pounding, and you pray you aren't going to get pulled over (at least that's what I do). We accept this cultural compact so unquestioningly that we even get pissed at the police for enforcing the published, and very well publicized, speed limit. That's how well-established the gap is between the rules and the culture.

My point here is that although we pretty much all participate in this cultural deviancy, it doesn't make us evil terrorists out to take down civilization as we know it. To be clear, the same sort of gap between our systems and our culture that happens on the highway also happens every day in our organizations. How we manage that problem—how well we limit the gaps between our principles and our practice—is up to us as a group. I would suggest very strongly that the more we tolerate gaps between the two, the lower our credibility as leaders and as an organization sinks, and the more likely that we're going to run into even greater gaps down the road. (In case you were wondering, I do still regularly drive over the speed limit.)

In my experience, it's infinitely easier to rewrite a system than to meaningfully change an organizational culture. Rules can be modified with a quick memo, but to actually change the culture takes coherent vision, effective communication, years of stubborn persistence, relentless followup, and more than a little luck. Witness the difficulty we've had eliminating racial discrimination from our society: Congress and the courts passed laws, took action to enforce them, and yet racism persists. When there are gaps like this between our systems and our culture (or between our systems and principles, or principles and culture), we at Zingerman's believe, and actively teach, that it's the responsibility of *everyone* in the organization—not just the formal leaders—to work to bring them back into alignment.

Why does it matter? Ultimately, it's the culture that's the real and meaningful measure of our work—not the stuff we put on paper or bandy around in staff meetings. Anyone can say the right thing. It's the doing part that's so difficult—it's tough to be consistent day in and day out.

Back to Training: Where Is It on the Chart?

Back at the beginning of this essay I mentioned that when we developed the Business Perspective Chart we were trying to figure out where training fit into it all. And if you actually check out the chart closely you'll see that training isn't on there. We decided that although ZingTrain was clearly a business built to provide training, that training was merely a tool to greater ends: ethically sound bottom-line results, to a vision we could agree on and an effective commitment to living our mission. Early on, an insightful staff member (I can't remember who, I'm afraid) theorized that training was represented by the arrows—that good training helped us connect the bigger areas of the chart and get where we needed to go.

Why We Use the Business Perspective Chart

My main point here, I guess, is that we very actively use, teach, and talk about the chart all the time. Any manager or partner at Zingerman's needs to be ready to teach it at any moment. Most should be able to explain it pretty well. In fact, I'll bet that almost anyone at Zingerman's would be able to give you a good presentation on what it means and how it works. Please note that the significance of this latter point is *not* the fact that they can recite it by rote—I sang the *Star Spangled Banner* at school for years before I realized that I didn't even understand what many of the words actually meant. The point is that everyone at Zingerman's shares a common language: that we understand the difference between a Mission and a Vision, know why both are so important, what our bottom lines are, and how our guiding principles fit into it all. As weird as it may sound, people here have near daily dialogues to identify places where we're falling short of aligning our daily work with other pieces of the chart. And you know what? It works.

the olive oil shelves, and a sample set up, at the deli

Building a Better Mission Statement

Setting Out Your Organizational North Star

Twenty years ago or so I was pretty solidly certain that mission statements were little more than a serious waste of time and one more dumb "flavor of the day" thing for businesses to do instead of taking care of their real work. As you'll see when you read this essay, I now believe that my late-'80s cynicism on the subject was dead wrong, and that I've since come to see the creation of our mission statement as one of the most important things we've ever done here. While I would never say that you need to drop everything else you're doing and run home to write one, I think a mission statement can be a very valuable investment of important, if not urgent, time—if you really are going to use what you come up with in your organization. Here at Zingerman's, I can say with confidence, we're radically better off for using ours as actively as we do.

Way back in the spring of 1992 we assembled a work group of managers, staff, and owners and set out to put to paper a statement of what Zingerman's was all about, to write what's referred to in business books as a mission statement. I have to say that at the time I was pretty skeptical. In fact, in hindsight I'm not even sure why I agreed to do it. Probably because Paul was telling me it was a good thing, and he usually ends up being right about this kind of stuff. Maybe also because I'd read some books and articles that made me think we'd be missing the boat if we didn't do it—mission statements were very much in vogue back then.

Still, I was skeptical. We'd already been in business for 10 years, and we'd achieved a fair bit without benefit of one. Mission statements, to me, seemed like little more than lame poetry to be posted near the customer bathroom or employee breakroom and then quickly forgotten. I know I'm not the only one who felt this way. Gauri Thergaonkar, a manager at the Deli who had a great deal of experience in the corporate world before she started working with us, told me she was actually "disappointed, even a little panicked" when she heard we had a mission statement: "I was so burned by the absolute worthlessness of the many visions, missions, and principles I had been exposed to elsewhere," she said, "that I had decided that the very concept was worthless."

I'm happy to say Gauri and I were both dead wrong. By the time our writing exercise was done, about 70 or 80 of our staff members (out of a total of about 100) had gotten involved. Together we came up with the Mission Statement and Guiding Principles that we still use at Zingerman's today. It wasn't a small project, but it was worth every cent we spent. In fact in hindsight it was worth many times what it cost us.

For clarity's sake let me say that I'm talking here about creating a mission statement, not a "vision statement." Pretty much every business book gives a different definition of the two, but I'm not really interested in establishing the superiority of one over another. What's important is to be clear about what we mean by the terms, since at Zingerman's we use the two very differently.

Vision, as I've been saying, is a picture of what things are going to look like when we successfully arrive at where we're going and when things are working really, really well. What will "success" look like for your business five years down the road? What will be happening? How big will your organization be? What will you be known for? What will the community say about you? What will the press be reporting? How will the people who work here be dealing with each other inside the organization?

Mission is altogether different. It's the answer to four basic but incredibly important questions:

- What do we do?
- Why do we do it?
- Who are we that are doing it?
- Who are we doing it for?

When we started our project at Zingerman's I thought these questions seemed simple-minded and even, actually, sort of goofy. Maybe you do, too. But in truth they aren't very easy to answer, especially not when you're committing to living with your answers for the rest of your organizational life.

The first question—What do we do?—proved the most challenging of the four, and probably also the most valuable, as well. We started with the obvious answers, like, "We're a deli—we serve food." But of course, what we were doing at Zingerman's was more than just being a deli. Someone suggested that what we did was "give service," but then others argued that we couldn't exclude the food so that didn't seem like the answer. Someone else offered that maybe Zingerman's was about "education"—granted we did do a lot of educating, but it was hard to claim that it was our entire mission. I mean we are located in Ann Arbor, and we do have a small school here in town that you might have heard of.

After many weeks of meetings and hours of hand wringing, eye rolling, rewriting, and paper shredding, I'm pretty sure it was Paul who suggested that what we really do is deliver an exceptional and unique experience. The group called it the "Zingerman's Experience." And so, we agreed that, when all else was said and done, *we were here to bring the Zingerman's Experience to as many people as possible.* The food, the service, the atmosphere, the staff, the signs, the information, the fun . . . they all went into making the experience of coming to Zingerman's something special.

Once we had that first question answered we went on to the other three:

Why do we do it? Because we believe that if we do our jobs well we can leave our community, our staff, and everyone else we work with a little better off than when we got here. And because it's a rewarding and enjoyable way to make a living.

Who are we? We are the people who work here at Zingerman's. New and old, baker and bread-seller, dishwasher and dreamer, accountant and assistant manager, owner and offsite caterer, sandwich maker and signmaker.

Who are we doing it for? For our guests, for ourselves, for our community, for the folks who make the great foods we work with.

The actual wordsmithing of the Mission Statement came next. It's not the perfect document by any means, but here it is anyway, just so you can see an example of one that's worked out pretty well.

ZINGERMAN'S MISSION STATEMENT

We share the Zingerman's Experience

Selling food that makes you happy

Giving service that makes you smile

In passionate pursuit of our mission

Showing love and care in all our actions

To enrich as many lives as we possibly can.

That's Nice But Who Cares?

"So," you might reasonably wonder, "what difference does it make in your hectic, resource-strapped, crazy day-to-day food business life to know that your mission is to provide people with a Zingerman's Experience?" Actually, it's huge. The Mission Statement does for our organization what the North Star does for travelers (at least in the days before GPS devices and cell phones). No matter how lost or frustrated we may feel on any given day it's always there to give us a sense of direction. No matter how dark, frustrating, or confusing things may seem we can always come back to the idea of the Zingerman's Experience. And if we get lost in the day-to-day details, the Mission Statement helps us to stay focused on the big picture.

What does this look like in practice? Because the Mission Statement trumps any and all of the little details in our various and varied job descriptions, it helps to clarify the true priorities in our work. While we make great products, we also try to give exceptional service, and we do a whole lot of training, tasting, packaging, and cleaning. We do our share of administrative activity, too. In truth, it's remarkably easy to do any or all of that stuff while still falling short of delivering a great overall experience to our customers, staff, and community. But the Mission Statement makes it clear that regardless of the particulars of our day-to-day jobs, *the real assignment for every single one of us who works here is to deliver great Zingerman's Experiences to those around us.*

Our Mission Statement helps us preempt the all-too-common "that's not my job" excuse that you hear in so many organizations. Providing a quality Zingerman's experience is *everyone's* job; age, experience, position, all become completely irrelevant. First day on the job, last day on the job, managing partner or part-time dishwasher, we *all* have the same mission.

So the real question about this or any mission statement is, "Is it meaningful to the people who work in the organization—does it support them in doing a better job, feel better about their work, help themselves as individuals and the business as a whole to succeed?"

The answer, of course, can only come from the people who work here. The above-mentioned manageress, Gauri Thergaonkar, once told me that, "Not only were the vision, mission, and guiding principles here really relevant, they changed how I behaved. They gave me guidance on days when I wasn't sure what I was supposed to do, they explained to me how I played a role in the organization and what my contribution was, what it could be, what it affected." Dan

Satwicz, who worked for many years receiving orders on the back dock at the Deli, shared that, "The mission has been a very big part of why I've been satisfied with my work for the last seven and a half years." Charlie Frank, a manager at the Bakehouse and now managing partner of the Candy Manufactory, told me that, "When I approached Zingerman's about a job a number of years ago, the statement was a signal to me that this was a great fit for me. I still feel that way now many years later."

How Do We Make the Mission Statement Meaningful?

We teach it. Over and over again. I review it in the new staff orientation (which Paul or I still teach even though we have over 500 staff members). We go over it in most every staff training class (and we teach a lot of classes!). We go over it in ZingTrain seminars. It's in our staff handbook and probably about 50 other places I've forgotten about. It's incorporated into job descriptions, service programs, etc., so that each of us sees and thinks about the idea of the Zingerman's Experience most every day.

We talk about it. We've integrated the concept of the Zingerman's Experience into our work so thoroughly that it now comes up in casual business conversations at most every level of the organization. You'll hear it mentioned in planning meetings, in project management, and probably even in breakroom bitch sessions. One manager shared that, "I hear it regularly referred to in discussions, especially the phrases 'passionate pursuit,' 'love and care,' and 'enrich as many lives as we possibly can.'"

We do it. I don't mean that we've completely and perfectly realized our mission. Far from it—I'm always trying to improve my effectiveness at living the mission, and the same can be said for many of those who work with us. But in querying folks throughout our organization about the meaning of the mission statement in their work, it became very clear to me that we really are making it a part of everyday life at Zingerman's. Erin Fairbanks, an assistant manager at the Deli, told me, "I worked with companies that made me memorize their mission statement as part of my training. But the strange thing was, they never really made me actually *learn* it. At Zingerman's, you do see the mission when you start. But it's funny, a few months down the road, when you run into it again in a class or something, you can't help but think to yourself, 'Well, jeez, I do that every day.'"

The great thing about this is that you really need nothing more than to understand the statement and be willing to make it a reality. When I teach the mission, I often tell our staff, "You don't need an MBA. All you have to do is find someone you're working near—a customer, a co-worker, or just a guy walking down the street—and do something nice for them. It could be bringing them a taste of something really good. It could be opening the door for them. It could be walking them to their car. Or it could be sending them a thank you note." The point of all those examples is that the actual work of enhancing people's experience is pretty simple. "Living the mission," I often go on, "isn't rocket science. Nor do you need a seven year residency in neurosurgery to do it well."

Having said something like that about a million times, I once had the memorable experience of having a relatively new staff member repeat those two truisms back to me in a way that still makes me laugh many years later. I really don't know if he meant to say it the way he did or not but I thought it was so brilliant that I still use his phraseology today. Anyway, the story unfolded at the new staff orientation class. I go through this stuff about the mission fairly early on, but it often comes up again as we move through the two hours. On this particular day we got to another manifestation of the mission, and this very nice fellow who had been with us for a couple of months chimed in and said, "Well, it's like you said: 'It's not rocket surgery!'" I loved that. After all, he's right; what we do here is most definitely not even remotely like rocket surgery. So have fun! Live the mission!

Tips for Creating a Mission Statement in Your Organization

1. GET HELP

If you can possibly afford it, get someone from outside the organization to help you manage the process of creating your mission. Having someone who's very good at process work allows you to stay focused and be active in discussions without having to manage group dynamics, timing, etc. I don't want to make this an advertisement but I will say that Stas' Kazmierski, one of the managing partners of ZingTrain, is very, very good at this. We first connected with Stas' back in '92 when we hired him as an outside consultant to guide us through the process of writing our own Mission Statement and Guiding Principles.

2. GET AS MANY PEOPLE INVOLVED AS POSSIBLE

I don't know if I can stress this enough. The more you involve others in your organization, the more effectively they're going to buy into the results. In hindsight probably the most incredible aspect of our own effort was that by getting staff involved we ended up with a mission and principles that really belonged to the entire organization, not just to a select few at the top of the org chart.

Kathi Dvorin, who was part of the mission work group, shared her memories of the experience: "Back then I was a teenager who had been with Zingerman's for less than a year, so I was a little surprised that I was being asked to help. I kept thinking, 'Why does my opinion matter?' Up until Zingerman's, my experience in the workforce had never shown me that the thoughts and ideas from a new person would be welcomed or even considered." Kathi's experience is pretty standard in the work world. But our experience is that truly amazing things can happen when people are given the chance to participate in creating something special. "Later," she said, "it hit me just how incredible it was that my leaders had asked for input from a relatively new front-line employee. Shoulder to shoulder with other front-line employees, managers, partners, and co-founders, we created something really special."

3. DON'T BOTHER DOING ONE IF YOU DON'T REALLY WANT TO USE IT

I don't mean this facetiously. Creating a mission statement and making it meaningful for your organization is not a small project. Nor is it one you should delegate out to a low-level staff member, an operational manager, or an outside consultant. There are a thousand good reasons to not want to do one. So take it from someone who has worked through his own skepticism: it's not worth the aggravation if you're not going to stick with it. *In fact, I'm convinced that it's worse to write a mission statement and not use it well than it is to not write one at all.* If you spend resources and people's time and effort creating a mission statement only to let it languish then you're likely to leave your staff exhausted and down instead of engaged and upbeat.

4. DEMONSTRATE IT DAILY BUT DON'T PUT IT ON DISPLAY

I know this runs counter to convention, but we generally don't post our mission statement anywhere that customers would be likely to see it. Not that we're hiding it from them. It's just that we figure if we deliver a great experience to our guests, they're going to know what we're trying to accomplish. And if we don't . . . who cares if we have a nice mission statement? The proof is in the performance, not a pretty poster.

Conclusions

I don't know if I've convinced you to invest the time and money it will take to create—and *use*—a mission statement for your organization. I can tell you that even the best mission statement (if there is such a thing) is not a panacea that will solve all of your organizational issues. What it is, is a very valuable tool. When designed well and used thoughtfully it really does make a difference. If you're up for the effort I really recommend it!

Shelby Kibler showing a student how to shape loaves in a class at "bake!"

Revisiting the Power of Visioning

Why Positive Futuring Really Works

Secrets 6–9 are all about what we call "visioning"—a planning process that starts with the end in mind. Any of the four essays that follow will be helpful on its own, but I think all four taken together will make for the best balanced "meal." That said, if you want to go straight to taking action, you can flip to page 140 for a series of quick visioning exercises.

I know it's a bit odd to place the piece on "Revisiting the Power of Visioning" before the original "Writing a Vision of Greatness" piece I did on the subject a few years earlier. But, like the 3 C's design essay, this is another case where it seems to work better going in reverse order. So . . . here you go—"revisit" first, then "visit!" Regardless of order, by the time you're done with this and the following three essays, at the least you'll be really clear on how passionately I believe in the positive power of this tool. As you'll see, visioning as we teach it here is actually very simple, but amazingly (or should I say, "ama-Zing-ly?") powerful.

I think it's best to tell you up front that this essay is basically a sales piece. It's not really my style to put the hard sell on anyone, so I'm sort of reluctant to even say it that way. But I really am selling, so why hide it? The good news though is that what I'm selling won't cost you any money; it isn't something that you'll find featured at a trade show, nor is it going to come one case free with ten. You won't find it cheaper online, and there's no charge for shipping no matter how often you use it. It will take a bit of time, some serious, if enjoyable, work, and an open mind. But there's really nothing you have to spend money on to purchase what I'm pushing.

My product here is a belief—a passion, here at Zingerman's, for the effectiveness of visioning work. You might be familiar with the concept, but for those who aren't, in a small, practical nutshell, visioning is the process we use to start any new project—large, small, and everything in between. It's the idea of beginning our work by first figuring out what we want success to look like at a particular point in the future, then working backward to the present. (For comparison's sake, this is totally different than the way most of us have been trained in life, which is to start with the present and then figure out a way to work forward.)

Why sell something that brings me no financial return? Because I've been almost overrun of late with positive examples of how well it works. I've seen the visioning process consistently contribute very tangibly to the organizational and personal lives of those who use it. Without visioning, it's so easy to be dragged down by all the pressures around us, to get overwhelmed by the ever-present problems and roadblocks. But visioning really does lift us up to a more positive level of energy—it's a lot more fun. So here's my sales pitch.

A Look Back

It's probably a good 20 years or more since I first started learning about vision-ing. I don't think it came up in any sort of really formal way—it was likely more just hearing about it from people like my partner Paul and others around me who had some experience working with it. And I can't honestly say I was particularly open to the concept when I heard about it. At best I was probably moderately receptive, and more than likely, almost actively resistant at first.

Having been teaching it for many years now, I know that I'm not the only one who struggled to assimilate this approach. While the idea of visioning—or, as Steven Covey called it, "beginning with the end in mind"—sounds great, the truth of the matter is that it runs almost completely counter to the way I naturally think. On top of which, it's pretty much the opposite of the way most of the world works. So, it's safe to say I wasn't an easy sell on the subject. Fortunately, Paul and others around me were. And I've seen it in action for long enough now that, all these years later, I actually get it. I can say with certainty that I :

a. Fully embrace the idea of visioning

b. Use it all the time in most every part of my life

c. Teach it regularly, and

d. Have actually gotten to be really good at doing it.

It's not just me, either. Visioning work has become almost old hat for us at Zingerman's—so much so that we probably take it for granted. But even so, I've lately received an influx of positive comments about the power of the process, and how it has enriched people's approach to business and life in general.

The latest note I got on the subject is really what triggered my move to do this piece. It came from Jim Mellgren, who's made, sold, and written about specialty food for many years now (and done all of them well). A friend had forwarded him the article I'd written a number of years ago on visioning. After reading it, he wrote to compliment me on the essay and to ask permission to quote from it in one of his upcoming columns. I'm actually embarrassed to reprint what he said because it's not my style to promote my own stuff that way, but in the interest of selling others on the value of visioning I'm going to quote him here. He wrote me that it was a "brilliant essay and quite compelling." And then he went on to say, "You have a nice way of writing these business-oriented essays that make them not only very readable, but they give one the feeling that everything in it could be accomplished and that it would be important to do so."

The reason I'm using his testimonial really is because I think that his last statement is right on—I truly have learned that *anyone who's ready to learn the visioning process can use it.* And I really, really think that visioning is important work of huge value to every one of us. So thanks, Jim, and thanks to everyone reading this, for taking the chance to learn about or share experiences about something small but seriously significant in terms of changing the way I (and so many others) approach our future.

Buying In

In case you didn't read about visioning in one of the earlier essays, *at Zingerman's a vision is a picture of what success looks like for us at a particular point in the future.* That means it's:

1. **Inspiring.** To all who will be involved in implementing it.
2. **Strategically sound.** We actually have a decent shot at making it happen.
3. **Documented.** You really need to write your vision down to make it work.
4. **Communicated.** Yes, if you want your vision to be effective you have to not only document it, but actually tell people about it.

The "Writing a Vision of Greatness" essay that follows gets into much more detail about how to do this. But the key point here is that the work is about agreeing on what success will look like, *not* about what's wrong with life as we currently know it. It's about writing out something that gets us excited, that makes us want to get up each morning and work through the inevitable challenges that come up en route to getting to an inspiring long-term outcome. While most of our day-to-day work may be pretty mundane, the vision is something special—a picture of the beautiful "cathedral" that we're all working together to build.

Remember, a vision (as we define it) is *not* a mission statement. Neither is it a strategic plan. We do those too, but, again, they're totally different. A strategic plan is how you'll get where you want to go. But you can't really plan your trip until you know where you're going, and that's what a vision tells you. Which is why we *always* start with writing the vision, and only then back up to putting together the strategic plan.

Where We Learned It

I'm not an expert on the history of visioning but from what I know it origi-
nated with a guy named Ron Lippitt, who happened to live right here in Ann
Arbor. I guess that gives our town the chance to become the capital of visioning, a chance to be a center for positive futuring and all the good things that
go with it. For me though it's most significant because if he hadn't lived here, it
would have radically reduced the odds of me learning about his work. One of
the people who taught me most about using the technique is Stas' Kazmierski,
now one of the managing partners at ZingTrain, but who, 30 years ago, was a
young Organizational Development consultant living in the Ann Arbor area,
studying what was then (and I guess still is) this pretty radical stuff that Ron
was working on. We used Stas's expertise back in the early '90s to guide us
through the writing of Zingerman's mission statement and guiding principles.
In 2000, he came on as a co-managing partner at ZingTrain. In many ways, he
was the main bridge over which visioning entered our world. I've heard lots of
Ron Lippitt stories from him, and we've adapted what we've learned into what
we now call visioning, as well as into the organizational change process (which
we call "Bottom Line Change") we now use and teach.

Back in the late '50s and early '60s, when he was developing his ideas,
Lippitt called his work "Preferred Futuring." The core insight, the "aha" behind
his approach, came as he sat through dozens of the problem-solving sessions
that were common at most large (and probably small, too) organizations back
then (and still are today). He noticed that these meetings almost always started
out with the attendees going over all of their problems, and then trying, with
increasing frustration, to figure out a fix. As the list of the problems grew, Ron
observed, the energy level in the room declined drastically. When team members did finally arrive at a semblance of a "solution," more often than not they
were simply advocating adaptations of existing practices—people almost never
seemed to arrive at innovative approaches. Their answers were generally reac-
tive efforts to avoid pain, rather than proactive work to move toward something
positive.

Ron's idea was to reverse that entire flow. He found that when the process was shifted from problem solving to "preferred futuring" (or what we now
call visioning), participants' energy levels increased, and their innovative ideas
flowed far more freely. While the people in the room weren't any smarter or
more creative, they consistently came up with more interesting and effective
solutions—visions of the future that they were excited about and eager to go
out and make happen.

Ron Lippitt died in 1987. I'm sorry not to have known him. He was clearly a great guy and an exceptionally innovative thinker. But he left all of us a gift—a simple, usable, intellectually and emotionally satisfying tool that we can use almost every day and in every part of our lives. I feel good that we at Zingerman's have been able to take what Ron was teaching and bring it—through ZingTrain and through our staff members who've moved on—to the business world in very practical and helpful ways. Without question, the increased energy and more creative outcomes that Ron sought to achieve half a century ago are still happening when we use his work today.

Strange—But in a Good Way—True Stories

I'm sure it would be easy to dismiss this stuff as something that we at Zingerman's have taken to some strange corner of the intellectual universe. But there are way too many examples of its effectiveness to write it off as loony. As Ron Lippitt realized 50 years ago, *visioning really does get people focused on the positive things that can be done,* not on what's wrong with what we have today. It really does get people to think outside the norms. It truly does get people to actively go after the future of their choosing, instead of just trying to get away from what they don't like about the present. And—it's wild to me that this is really true, but—because it gets us thinking in such different ways, using the visioning process gives us the power to alter the entire way we work with the world around us.

"I was actually about to quit," recalls Laurey Masterton, owner of Laurey's Catering in Asheville, North Carolina. "I was about to toss it all in. But I attended the Zingerman's Experience seminar and I listened to the part about creating a vision and realized I DID want to keep my business going and that I DID have some ideas about what my vision for the future of my business was. That vision included the look, the feel, the food, the descriptions, the finance piece (sort of), and a pretty complete, sensory description of my deepest thoughts about my creation." So instead of cashing it in, she turned it around—today her store is doing well, a financially viable, sustainable, healthy business with a lot of happy staff and a solid grounding in the community. And as a postscript I should add that Laurey also went on to become president of the Asheville Chamber of Commerce.

Here's another story, from Renee Malone, owner of a consulting company with the great name of Kick the Moon.

> "When I enrolled to attend the ZingTrain Small Giants semi-
> nar two months ago," she wrote me, "I was feeling the weight-

of-a-stalled-dream upon my shoulders. An entire year had passed since I began negotiations with my client—a prospective business 'partner'—to design and facilitate a certification-training program that would become the opportunity of a lifetime. We had invested energy, time, money, and emotion into the project—and we still didn't have a business arrangement! It was during the Visioning exercises at the seminar when it dawned on me that, regardless of how clear I was about my vision for our arrangement, what counts in the end is what my prospective 'partner' sees. I had to work to build his vision of our partnership before any decision would be made. After the course, I put my paradigm shift into action. I worked to build my prospective partner's vision by turning our ideas into evidence so he would see for himself how I could bring solutions to the problems associated with the development of the certification program. In the end, we finalized our business agreement. We have a deal. And this week, I launched my dream, our dream."

Vision and Innovation

Over the last month or so I've been asked to speak to three completely different business groups on the topic of "innovation." I'm sure I was invited because people think—and they're probably right in this case—that Zingerman's has consistently innovated for many years. They want to understand the magic behind what we've done, the secret of staying innovative when most everyone else seems to stick to the status quo. I understand their desire. Like most people in the world, I used to think that innovation was the result of some lightning bolt of brilliance. But I've learned that innovation happens most often when you build in (and regularly use) processes and recipes that encourage it.

One of the biggest contributors to the level of creativity in our organization is the regularity with which we teach, use, and stick to the visioning process. We start pretty much every planning effort with a draft of a positive vision of the future. And we do it at every level of the organization. Whether we're working on visions for a business five years out, a project that will be done in five months, or a dinner special that will be on the menu at 5:00 tonight, we're pretty consistently "beginning with the end in mind." Just as you'd expect from Ron Lippitt's research, our people tend to be more positive and more energized than their counterparts in most other organizational cultures. And that means that the work they do is apt to be more creative and innovative than what their peers—of equal intelligence—are probably doing most everywhere else.

Rob Dube, who attended one of our ZingTrain seminars, wrote me not long afterward to tell me about a project called TonerForAutism.com that he and his partner, Joel Pearlman, launched after attending the Small Giants seminar:

> "It's a new division and the future of our organization. Did you know that 1 in 150 children are diagnosed with autism; and that more children will be diagnosed with autism this year than with AIDS, diabetes, and cancer combined? This issue personally affects my best friend and business partner and we are determined to make a difference. We appreciate your support more than you could imagine."

I think it's a great idea. Check out the website and, if you like it, support their work!

Big Visions: Zingerman's 2020

If you'd like to see what a long-term organizational vision looks like, you can find a complete copy of ours in the back of this book. This is the future we've agreed we're going after here at Zingerman's, one that's inspiring for us and also strategically achievable. But it isn't one anyone else should use—it's just ours!

We haven't completed the strategic plan where we describe exactly how we're going to get to the 2020 Vision. Instead, we have our action steps lined up for the next few years, and each year we'll move those out another couple years. But the point is that by documenting and actively communicating the 2020 Vision we have a clear sense of where we're going as an organization, and a pretty decent sense of what things are going to be like when we get there. And because we know where we're going, it also helps us to know where we aren't going, and hence turn down opportunities that might distract us from our chosen work.

At Zingerman's we also put on what we call *ZAP*, or Zingerman's Annual Planning. We start this annual process by articulating a three-year vision for the whole organization, and work from there toward visions for each business, department, and project. Again, only after we write the visions do we start on our strategic plan. My point isn't to detail our whole planning process, but merely to show you that we always start with a vision and work back from there.

Vision for Projects

At the next level down, we also begin every new project with a vision. A few examples follow. They're not perfect, but it's actually *because* they're not perfect that I'm sharing them. They're just real life, in-the-moment projects of various scopes and sizes, initiated by people at various levels of our organization. I've cleaned out a bit of internal lingo, but other than that they're reproduced here exactly as they were written by our staff and managers. Note that they're always written in the present tense. I can't tell you why that makes a difference, but it does. In fact, we've achieved all of these visions pretty much as they were written.

WESTSIDE FARMER'S MARKET VISION

I'll start with the draft vision for a small Thursday evening farmer's market that we host in the parking lot of Zingerman's Roadhouse, on the west side of Ann Arbor.

It's the longest day of the year; the sun is at its pinnacle of warmth and light. Throngs of people are milling around the Roadhouse parking lot on this Thursday afternoon, amazed and excited at the abundance of locally produced goods and services ranging from several gorgeous varieties of tomatoes to handmade soap and artisan crafts, to herbs and plants, plus a very strong synergy of Zingerman's items—cheese from the Creamery, breads from the Bakehouse, and the ever-energetic Roadshow crew caffeinating all the vendors and customers. Every vendor is selling the best of what there is to offer, growing or producing themselves what they sell. There's a tangible truth patrons have come to trust—that all these products have a story and none of them traveled very far to get here. Tents and awnings cover the stalls, creating a colorful and festive mood. There are 15–20 vendors at the Market, so it's accessible and maintains variety but remains magnetic and welcoming.

The WSFM [West Side Farmer's Market] continues to provide our customers with the best products available and serves as a catalyst for community development by offering an educational component and a local music scene. We have space reserved for weekly scheduled acts, including local musicians, demonstrations, and educational activities. Several people recognize the Roadhouse Chefs selecting vegetables from the Market's vendors for the weekend's menus at the Roadhouse. The market is a family event, where parents bring their children after school and meet to shop for fresh produce. After shopping, families enjoy a snack from the Roadshow at our picnic tables. Guests are thrilled with the produce, the chance to visit with neighbors, and best of all, connect with the farmers who actually grow their food.

This year, the WSFM planning committee is helping to generate interest and support throughout the area business community for the Market. Local businesses hang posters or hand out flyers about the Market and participate in promotions that encourage their customers to visit the Market. These companies recognize the potential for the Market to draw additional patrons to the area and increase business throughout the Westside. These developing relationships with area businesses and the Westside neighborhood at large are enabling the WSFM to become a more self-sustaining entity. While Zingerman's remains an active and essential supporter of the Market, the WSFM is a self-sustaining entity.

The WSFM planning committee operates under an inspiring mission statement and is taking steps toward making the WSFM a fiscally independent operation. Our market manager is working closely with the Zingerman's liaison to ensure organization and success, from honing job descriptions to developing and proposing paid WSFM positions. We have a great group of vendors working together who are already excited to build on these successes for next year. Visions and action steps are laid out for the coming years at our annual WSFM debrief.

This was written in 2005, before the market began. As one example of how accurate it was, I checked with the market manager to see how many vendors we had at the start of the 2010 season. Answer? Twenty.

WEBNESDAY VISION

Here's another one that was written for our *Webnesday* program at Zingerman's (you read that right—it's not a typo), a regimen we set up to help keep websites fresh and alive. It was written in the winter of '08, looking out a year and a few months.

Vision for Webnesday, July 2009

Everyone at Zingerman's knows that Wednesday is Webnesday around these parts. In the same way that Tuesdays have long been known across the organization for bagels and Nashville hot fried chicken, Wednesday is known for being the day that everyone checks the web. All marketing reps spend five to ten minutes checking out their own website and one other ZCoB (Zingerman's Community of Businesses) website. They're looking at things to assess the effectiveness of what's on the site, spot errors or typos, look for missed opportunities to maximize sales or improve service, etc. They send out their observations that day. Each business's web manager makes the call on what changes are going to be made and is responsible for making those changes just as they were before the advent of Webnesday.

As a result of all that attention the websites are way better than ever, front-line staff know about them, in the business promotional work is linked much more quickly and effectively with the websites. As awareness goes up, so too does the percentage of staff using the websites, both for training purposes and to get questions on product info and events.

Like the Farmer's Market the program is working well, and very close to what's written here.

ZINGERMAN'S ROADHOUSE CULTURE CLUB VISION

This one comes from a work group of managers and front-line staff that was created at the Roadhouse to help improve the quality of the work experience. It was written in the fall of 2007.

It is August of 2008 and the Roadhouse Culture Club is going strong! We have only been in existence a year, but we are a club that has made great strides in improving daily life at the Roadhouse. We have a group of people who are committed to creating a positive culture and are vocal in their departments.

Our meetings have fantastic attendance and each member finishes his or her projects on time. The club's goals are discussed at each meeting to see how close the goal is to being completed. Some of the goals we have achieved:

- Sending out birthday cards to staff members
- Awarding the monthly "Guiding Principle Award"
- Helping champion the Culture of Clean in the restaurant
- Helping new staff get through orientation on time by promoting classes and training

The Personal Piece

One thing that I think we do very differently here at Zingerman's is that when we write business visions we always stress the importance of incorporating the author's personal passions and desires into what he or she writes. While the vision—for the whole organization or a particular project—needs to be inspiring and strategically sound, it also can and should include things that will help us as individuals to live our own dreams. So if you own the business and want to travel as part of your work, write a vision of greatness that includes travel. If you want to take long summer vacations with your family, then write that in too. There aren't any "right" or "wrong" things to include—the point is merely to create a future in which you and I as leaders and as writers of the vision will feel fulfilled and rewarded.

Taking Visioning Home—
People Using the Process in All Parts of their Lives

The first section of our 2020 Vision (see page 315) is titled, "Better Tomorrow than Today: Changing Our World." In it we talk about our commitment to leaving everyone we work with—customers, suppliers, community, environment, and staff—a bit better for the interaction. Teaching and using the visioning process have turned out to play a really positive role, to a degree that surprises even me. Although I'd never have expected it 10 years ago, *most all of us who have learned to use visioning at work now use it in our personal lives, as well.* Meaning that, per the 2020 Vision, we've contributed positively to the quality of the lives of the people who work with us, in ways that have nothing directly to do with our work.

This was driven home for me after I asked everyone here for examples of how they've used visioning. About half of the replies talked about applications completely outside of Zingerman's. For example, Charlie Frank and Katie Janky, two of our longtime managers at the Bakehouse, talked about using it for their wedding. "We're doing a lot of the work for the event ourselves," Charlie said. "So we started with a combined, shared vision, then made action steps and timelines. I think it came to us naturally since we're so exposed to it at work." Carlos Souffront, cheese specialist at the Deli, wrote about how he uses visioning in his after-hours life as a professional DJ. The applications are endless: in fact, Bily Charley, who handled purchasing for the Deli, told me he used visioning to keep himself on course toward *any* personal goal he'd committed to reaching.

Staying the Course

Like Bily Charley, I've found that one of visioning's big benefits is that it helps us maintain our course when we—as we always will—start to slide away from what we've committed to going after. Author Rosabeth Moss Kanter has written about what she calls "Kanter's Law," which says that, "everything can look like a failure in the middle." But having a written vision helps overcome that mid-course feeling of impending doom. It's a lot more likely that we're going to stay the course when we've already committed to ourselves and others that we're going to get a successful conclusion, and when we all know what that conclusion (i.e., our vision) is.

Steve Mangigian, co-managing partner at Zingerman's Coffee Company, was using much of this vision stuff even before he joined our organization. Steve shared that, "Only once I have a firm and realistic outcome in mind (one that I can actually 'envision'), then I outline in my mind the steps that need to occur to get to that outcome. As I go through each step, I celebrate a brief victory (helps build confidence and self esteem), but never keep my eye off the outcome. (In other words, I am not satisfied nor is the project complete until the outcome has been achieved.) For me, the absolute bottom line is I must be able to see the end before I begin."

Carlos Souffront, our musically minded cheesemonger (or maybe he's a dairy-loving DJ?) that I mentioned, shared that for every event he works, he starts by basically putting together a vision of what he wants the evening—including the music—to feel like. "When I start playing," he explained, "I'm really nervous and I might falter a couple of times. But I'm already playing records that send a clear message of where I'm trying to go. At first some folks in the room would rather not be along for the ride—I just figure, 'I lost a few, oh well, gives the rest more room to dance and enjoy themselves.'" Fortunately, Carlos has a clear vision that he can stick to instead of panicking. "And then things really start to gel. The audience and I have had some time to warm up and get to know each other and that's when things turn magical. The audience actually triggers the best ideas of how to achieve the sound, ideas I hadn't even thought of. Now it's interactive, and it's a great party!"

Stas' Kazmierski, co-managing partner of ZingTrain, has said that when you actually write down your vision, "the powers of the universe will conspire to make it happen." I don't know how much the powers really conspire, but I do know that it's uncanny how reliably we achieve the visions that we agree on in writing. We may never get 'em perfect, and there are certainly examples where we've failed, fallen a bit behind, or moved slightly off course. But if we have a vision in writing, one that everyone buys into and believes in, and that we've actively and effectively shared . . . we almost always arrive at our destination.

The Power in Practical Terms

I know this will all sound sort of silly and new-agey to people who aren't into hearing it. You're welcome to roll your eyes if you want. I did when I first started learning about it. But there's just no way around it—the power that comes out of this visioning stuff is huge. All I can say is that it has worked well for me personally and has been a big contributor to making our organization what it is today.

Without sounding too circular in my logic, the truth is that if you have a vision of an organization with a culture in which people feel good about their work, take responsibility for what they do, feel like they can make a difference, and believe that their efforts really matter, then putting the visioning process in play will really help you to get where you want to go. Of course, it's only one contributor. I know enough to know that whatever we've created in our culture is the product—as all cultures are—of a million different factors and the sum total of a zillion-point-one different individual actions by thousands of people who've worked here over the last 28 years. But it's pretty clear to me that a big piece of that culture has come to be what it is because of the work we do around visioning.

I'll close with one last testimonial. It comes from Terry Caldwell, who has owned and run Bodywise Therapeutic here in Ann Arbor for more than two decades. I was a bit anxious about putting Terry's story in here because it's very personal, so I emailed her to ask how she felt about the idea. "You may use what I wrote," she sent back, "if you believe it may help someone. I went back and reread it and do not feel that I could write something else that would be as real." I've reread it about 10 times and it still makes me cry every time:

> "Thank you so much for the past couple days. The ZingTrain workshop was wonderful. It really boosted my spirits. I don't know how much you know, but I have had an illness for a year and a half. The past six months so badly I have been unable to do the work I have loved so much for over 20 years. I have seen many specialists, including the Mayo Clinic last summer, and still do not have a diagnosis. The Western medicine folks say I have 'an illness that has not fully disclosed itself yet,' aka, 'we don't know what's going on.' As

you can imagine, this is hard on my family, my staff and, most of all, me, who loves to be busy and involved. This being said, it has been very hard for me to vision as I don't know if I will survive this. Fear has paralyzed me in many ways. That is why I had such a hard time starting my vision draft. Once it was written, though, it brought me so much joy and hope. Every time I read it I believe I can do it. I will survive and thrive to see these things happen. I do not know the 'hows' in-between, but am filled with optimism."

Thanks to Terry, Ron Lippitt, everyone I've quoted above, and a thousand other great folks who've done this work around here or shared stories, I know that I'm filled with optimism as well. And I hope you might be too. Here's to whatever inspiring, strategically sound vision you might have for better tomorrows for you and everyone around you.

P.S. A Vision about Visioning

As I approached the end of this essay, I realized that, although I'm reluctant—I'm nervous about exposing my true feelings; it might not happen; some people won't like it; etc.—the truth is that I actually have a vision about visioning.

My vision—and this is really just a draft, so I'm still working on it—is that 10 years from now, visioning is an intrinsic part of the way that thousands of progressive organizations around the world do their work. These groups write strategic plans as often as they used to, but now they don't start working on a new plan until they've first agreed on their vision of success. And my vision is that Ann Arbor is one of the capitals of visioning work: people come here from all over the world to learn the process and take home the tools they need to put visioning to use in their own lives. My vision is that the Ann Arbor community has developed an inspiring and strategically sound vision for itself. And that the model has been adopted on a national basis, as well—that when people run for office, they don't tell us what's wrong or how they're going to fix things right off. Instead, they start by sharing a meaningful, inspiring, and strategically sound vision for the future. And that as a result, our world is at least slightly better off than it was a decade earlier: that people enjoy their lives more, feel more inspired and able to make a difference, appreciate each other more, are more patient with each other . . . and that a whole lot of lives have been made better in the process.

the black bench out front of the delicatessen

Writing a Vision of Greatness

And Why It's Not the Same as a Strategic Plan!

So, backing up a bit, if I've successfully sold you on the idea of visioning, then let me return now to the basics of the concept. I wrote this piece a long time ago, but it's just as true today as it was 10 years or so ago. Which I guess, in thinking about it, is the sign of a pretty powerful idea—an approach that isn't a product of the times, but rather a timeless concept that is scalable and applicable for most anyone, in any organization and any era. Having used visioning for decades now, I can say with high certainty that this stuff really works. Don't use it at your own risk.

One of the most frequently asked management questions I hear is, "How do you motivate people to work so hard?" Although I wish I could offer some simple answer it's obviously a pretty complex issue. Most of those who ask seem to want to focus on straightforward stuff like pay rates, bonuses, and benefits programs. But, personally, if I were going to recommend one place to begin your motivational efforts, it would be to write a vision of greatness for your business or organization. Imagine going to a website where you could log on and, with the right password, view your company as it will be 10 years from now. Pretend you could focus your webcam on a particular element of your organization's activity—large or small, people or product, finance or food, customers or community. What scenes would you want to see on the screen?

What Happens When You Don't Have a Vision?

Why bother with such futuristic esoterica when there's food to be sold and floors to be swept? Although the day-to-day, hour-to-hour, hands-on work we do is essential to the successful operation of our organizations (large or small), we can't do all of that work ourselves. Wherever we're going—unless we're working entirely on our own—we're going to be traveling with others. And our work with them is going to be a lot more effective if we agree on a vision of that future success.

Imagine I asked you to prepare for a long trip but wouldn't tell where we were going. It would be tough to get ready, wouldn't it? Or pretend you're trying to plot a course at sea without knowing what the ultimate destination is. Pretty much impossible, right? In either case, hard work, commitment, and all the best intentions in the world aren't going to be enough to attain success. Without a clear picture of where we're headed, about the only chance we have of being successful is just that . . . chance. It's true that things can sometimes work out well even when you don't agree on where you're headed. But setting aside that one-in-a-million chance, you're completely at the mercy of forces beyond your control. Not a good feeling? Well, that's how our staff members will feel if they don't have a clear vision of where our organization is going.

Vision vs. Mission?

As I said a few pages ago, a vision—at least as we define it at Zingerman's—is not the same as a mission statement. Both are important, but they aren't the same. A vision of greatness for our organization must, of course, support and be compatible with our mission statement. Unlike the mission statement, a vision is time-constrained. It should be something we can actually attain. While it's inspiring and exciting, it must also be specific enough that we'll be able to tell whether or not we've successfully arrived.

What's the Right Time Frame?

The bigger the organization for which you're writing the vision, the further out into the future you probably want to work; bigger ships take longer to turn. Since there are more people who are impacted by what you're doing, they need a better sense of where they're headed and probably more time to make organizational change a reality. By contrast, if it's just you and two other people and there's no major growth on the horizon, then you can probably work with a vision that's only a year or two out.

Certain industries have strategic constraints that may dictate the time frame for writing a vision. If you're working with wine and you want to do some serious cellaring, you need a vision that takes you 10, 15, or 20 years out. On the other hand, if you're working in e-commerce it makes little sense to try to figure out exactly what you'll do all day 10 years from now because even the experts barely know what technology we'll be working with in two or three years, let alone in 10.

Why Is a Good Vision So Critical?

Although there are always a hundred reasons why we don't have time to develop a vision of greatness on any given day, the reality is that there are few more effective uses of our time and creative energy. Why? Let me count the ways:

1. IT HAS A POSITIVE IMPACT ON OTHERS

You have probably heard the tale of the masons working on Milan's majestic cathedral. Asked what they were doing, the first worker said, "I'm laying stone." But the second looked up and said, "I'm building a cathedral." When we provide an effective vision of greatness our staff can see that their work is all about building a great cathedral, not, as they've been told in most other work experiences, just laying stone all day.

2. IT ATTRACTS GOOD PEOPLE

Face reality: These days we need our staff members far more than they need us. They get to choose where they want to work, where they're going to spend their time, how much of their emotional and intellectual energy they're going to spend on, and in, our organization. And where would you rather work? Somewhere where you just lay stone day after day after day? Or where you can help build a uniquely beautiful, world-renowned cathedral? If I were looking for a job I know where I'd hand in my application.

3. IT ALLOWS US TO CREATE REALITY INSTEAD OF JUST REACTING TO PROBLEMS

When we do effective visioning we're moving toward the future we want, not just reacting to the present-day reality we don't like. A good vision sends the message that we aren't satisfied with what's currently going on. It brings our fears, concerns, and needs out in the open. If we do our job well in this regard I believe that we keep our competitors reacting to what we're doing, instead of the other way around.

4. IT'S A STATEMENT OF OPTIMISM IN THE FUTURE

Laying out our vision says we believe that tomorrow will be better than today; that if we work together, we can make great things happen. That we don't have to be passive victims, but have the ability to create a future of our choosing. Instead of being victims whose fate is determined by others, we have a chance to become effective leaders and make a positive difference in the lives of those around us.

5. IT FORCES US TO ACT ON AND MODEL THE REALITY THAT THERE IS NO SAFE PATH

Risk and change are a way of life. When we put our vision of the future out in the open we're modeling this behavior for our staff. To not create a vision—or to create one but not tell anyone what it is—allows us to protect ourselves from disappointment by playing it safe. But, in truth, that path has its risks as well—trying to stand still in the rapidly moving stream of life is ultimately much more dangerous than swimming with the current toward a more promising future.

6. IT FORCES US TO HOLD OURSELVES ACCOUNTABLE

Putting the vision in writing and actively sharing it pushes us to be accountable for what we've chosen to go after. Once it's out there for everyone to see, it's a lot harder to turn a blind eye when we're not upholding our obligations or not honoring our commitments.

7. IT TELLS US WHAT WE AREN'T GOING TO DO

Because our vision for Zingerman's specifically says that we are committed to staying in the Ann Arbor area, it's clear that we aren't going to open in Chicago or California or the Carolinas. It's not that there isn't a solid strategic case to be made for opening a business in any of those areas. It's just that, for a number of reasons, we've decided we aren't going to. Similarly, if your vision is to put together an IPO within the next five years, it's pretty clear that remaining a small, family-oriented business isn't going to be part of your future.

8. IT TELLS EVERYONE WHAT'S IN IT FOR THEM

In order to get the staff excited about the vision we've laid out, it needs to show the opportunities available to those in the organization. It should make clear what possibilities there will be for them, how they stand to benefit, and how they can contribute.

9. IT CREATES POSITIVE MOVEMENT WITHIN THE ORGANIZATION

Once you've laid out your vision people can start moving toward it. Their energies can now be confidently directed toward an agreed-upon and highly desirable future.

10. It helps us keep good people

In their book, *First, Break All the Rules,* Marcus Buckingham and Curt Coffman cite research by the Gallup Organization showing that the single most important factor in retaining the best staff members for the long term is a clear set of expectations. Certainly an organizational vision isn't enough to get all the day-to-day expectations we may have of our staff out in the open, but it's a darned good start. And if it helps us hold onto a couple of good people each year that's a pretty worthwhile investment of our energies.

What Makes an Effective Vision of Greatness?

There are four major characteristics of an effective vision of greatness: it should be inspiring, but also strategically sound (i.e., attainable). It should be written down. And it needs to be communicated.

The first two of these characteristics are inherently at odds: the more exciting and unique the vision is, the harder it will be to make it happen. A vision that says that every one of us will be millionaires in the next two years and that our store will remain small, family-focused, and open only five days a week from 10 to 4 in order to enhance our outside lives sounds pretty great. But you and I both know it isn't going to happen. The idea is to get into the middle: to define a vision of greatness for the organization that's challenging enough to get people excited and energized, while still being attainable. An effective vision of greatness is:

1. Inspiring

In our experience, most people—especially the most talented people—want to be a part of something special: i.e., the cathedral you all are constructing together. Which is why an effective vision of greatness needs to be uplifting, even a bit spiritual. How will you know if it's inspiring enough? Ask your partners. Does it get them excited about the future? Share a draft with your staff. Does it tell them that they're a part of something special? Ask yourself—does it get *you* excited?

It's important that the vision of organizational greatness be something of a stretch. It's got to push us to the edge. If there's no chance of falling short, we're not stretching enough. Some people may be willing to settle for mediocrity, but second-rate certainly isn't very inspiring. We need to challenge ourselves, to create something that sets us on the path to creating something unique.

2. STRATEGICALLY SOUND

If we write a vision and it sounds great but we don't have even a slight chance of getting there, then what we've got isn't a vision of greatness but a great fantasy. Good for getting people excited; not so good for paying the bills. To be effective a vision also has to have some measurable components that we can use to assess our success.

A vision of greatness in the sports world might include winning an NBA championship. In science, it might be to bring home a Nobel Prize. But don't assume that "ultimate achievements" like those are the only worthwhile goals. If they were, almost all of us would be losers for life. Why? Although both are certainly inspiring, most of us have neither the athletic ability nor the intellectual acumen to get within hailing distance. In other words, given our abilities, those just aren't strategically sound visions. To be strategically sound, then, the vision must be true to who and what we are, building on our strengths, staying true to our personalities and our principles.

Even if you've quantified what being "the best" would mean, it would be only one aspect of an effective vision of greatness. It's just as important that the vision details what our relationships will be like, and what our daily life will be like. Look at such things as: What will make us unique in the marketplace? What will our customers' experience be like? What will it be like to be a staff member? How will our customers and our community view us? How will we treat each other? How will others in our industry view us? What will we be selling? Who will be selling it, and to whom? Approximately how much of it will we be selling (after all, there's a big difference between an organization with sales of $300,000 and one with sales of $300,000,000)?

3. DOCUMENTED

This one is huge. Putting your vision in writing gives it enormous power, by imbuing it with a degree of clarity and commitment that goes so, so much farther than the, "That's a good idea, maybe I'll try it" sort of stuff that we're all so used to. Documenting the vision (when combined with #4 below) makes the whole thing real. This is it—when we write down our vision and share it with the organization, it's where we're going.

I've learned that most folks will find a few hundred very good reasons not to get around to putting their vision into writing. I totally understand. Doing visioning work is scary: other people might criticize what we've committed to attaining; there are never any guarantees of success; we could fall short or even fail altogether.

But the problem is that when we don't put our vision in writing it's too easy to let a move that could have made a major difference become little more than the organization's "soup of the day." It's only when we really write it down that we can make sure all of us in the organization are on the same page (in this case literally as well as figuratively). Putting a long-term vision in writing insures that we're a lot more likely to stick to it when we run into the inevitable resistance. And it makes it magically and meaningfully a whole hell of a lot more likely that it's actually going to come true.

4. COMMUNICATED

I hate to even say it, but you know it's true. A great vision that no one but you knows about isn't going to be very effective. So once you've gone and decided on your organizational vision of greatness, you really ought to tell people what it is.

Let me take that one step further: just telling them about it isn't really enough. What we have to actually do is actively *sell* that vision to our organization. Just as the products on our shelves never sell themselves, neither will a vision sell itself to our staff—no matter how inspiring or strategically insightful it is. It has to actually and actively be *sold*.

How do you sell it? The same way you sell anything else. Talk about it. Teach classes on it. Make flyers for it. Put it in your staff newsletter. Get it on your intranet. Show your staff what's in it for them. Get excited about it. Make it something that people can remember. Display it. Promote it. Make people want it by telling them how their lives are going to be better when the vision is a reality.

With that in mind, our vision needs to be reasonably easy to explain. Everyone in our organization needs to know what we're doing so that they can support it (or, in some cases, so they can decide they can't and move on).

I'll add again for emphasis that for the vision to be effective, it really has to be put in writing. Oral history is wonderful. But there's something solid, something serious, an increased consistency that we get when we put something on paper (or on the corporate intranet). When it's in writing, the vision will be clearer, easier to pass on to new arrivals, harder to deviate from, and more likely to keep us on course.

Who Creates the Vision?

Initially, at least, the vision needs to come from the leader or leaders of the organization. It's rarely (though it can happen) something that is going to emerge spontaneously from a group of a hundred staff members at the company picnic. I don't mean that any one of them might not be more capable of creating an effective vision than I am; simply that the "out of the box" thinking that it takes to create an effective vision is unlikely to come from a large group.

Certainly, once you have a draft of a vision, it's important to get input from others. Talk to your staff members, peers, customers, community leaders, and industry experts. Each will have something to offer that will help you shape your vision into an ever-more effective document.

If you're in a leadership role and you don't have an inspiring vision with which to get the ball rolling, you can also ask others in the organization to create one. In this case the leader's role shifts to making sure that a vision gets done in an appropriate time frame and that, again, it's both inspiring and strategically sound.

If You Own the Business

We believe very strongly that one of the key components of an effective vision is a statement about what you, personally, are doing in the picture of success you're painting. There are no right or wrong answers. But how much you work, what you do at work, how much you get paid, how you feel about your work, and how others feel about you. . . . those are up to you. Because if you have a vision that doesn't even inspire you, what's the point? If you're not going to get into it, neither is anyone else around you.

With that in mind, we decided long ago that an important part of our role as owners and leaders of the organization was designing our work to be something we would want to do for a long time to come. Which means that the whole construct within which so many others seem to operate—the "I want to get out of this work so I can do what I *really* want to do" model—becomes irrelevant. If you want to work a lot, put that in the vision. If you want to weave tapestries instead, write that in. If you want to work from home, say so. If you want to be rich, say that, too. Again there really aren't any rights or wrongs. And we only get one life, so the one we want really ought to be prominently included in our vision.

With that in mind, it is then possible that what's right for us in our own vision isn't right for the organization. In that case we'll end up with two visions, one for us and one for the organization. The key is that they both have to be attainable: we have to adjust our organizational vision to accommodate the one we have for the (one and only) life we're living. If that means that the vision says we've retired rich, that's great. If it says we've sold the company, that can work, too. If it says (as mine and Paul's does) that we're still at work, a lot older but still contributing creatively and constructively to what the organization does, then that's cool too. The key is that if it's our show, it really better be a show we want to show up for.

How Do You Come Up With a Vision of Greatness When Your Name Isn't at the Top of the Organizational Chart?

This is a challenge. But it's our challenge. And the answer is actually pretty straightforward. You come up with the vision by working with your "boss" to develop one. It would probably help to gather input from your peers and your staff and your customers, too. Ultimately, if you and your boss can't come to agreement on a vision of greatness for your area, then, for the moment at least, we know that you're headed in different directions. In the end, it may be time to part ways. In hindsight, that's exactly why I chose to leave the restaurant group I'd worked with for four years before I gave notice and went on to open the Deli with Paul—I had a very different vision from them of what great food meant, and I had a different sense of what it meant to manage people respectfully and well. While getting people to leave their jobs isn't the desired outcome here, it's better for all involved to have any disparity of visions out in the open where everyone can deal with it than to continue on with hidden or unspoken expectations.

A Couple of Caveats

It's important to understand that if you do indeed map out a uniquely creative vision of greatness, you're going to catch some flak for it. Everyone who's ever set his or her sights on something truly remarkable knows that out of the ordinary ideas usually meet with resistance. The trick is to be able to distinguish between the resistance that's coming because your vision is so creative and that which comes because you're so far off course that your idea really won't work. Other than building a network of trusted advisors, or relying on trial and error, I don't have any great ways to help you tell the difference. But I will say that if no one's telling you you're crazy (or at least that you've pushed the envelope a little too far), then you probably haven't stretched far enough in creating your vision.

I will also tell you from experience that laying out a vision can create short-term conflict between various elements of the organization. As hard as this is to deal with, it's ultimately worthwhile because it's getting the real issues out in the open where we can deal with them. It forces us to confront the reality that we and our partners/managers/peers/staff don't always agree on what the future should look like. Working through this disagreement can be very, very difficult, even painful. But achieving mutual agreement on our future is the only way we're going to have a chance of getting there.

A Vision Is Not a Strategic Plan

I can't tell you how many times over the many years that I've been working with and teaching visioning that someone uses the word "vision" interchangeably with "strategic plan." It's become so common that when I start to teach now I usually say something like, "OK everyone. Write this down":

"Vision ≠ Strategic Plan"

While both are important they're two totally different things. The vision is where we're going; the strategic plan is how we're going to get there. And although big businesses and high-powered consulting firms seem not to let it bother them, I have no clue how you can effectively design a strategic plan if you don't know where you're trying to end up. It's like trying to get Mapquest to chart a route for you without first typing in your destination. So if we want to do this work, we always, always start with the vision. Only when we have agreement on that can we really begin to write the strategic plan we also need to get us there.

Which brings me to one of the most valuable things about having a well-written, documented, and well-communicated vision (that isn't a strategic plan!). A vision makes it much easier to handle the strategic opportunities that present themselves every day. See, most organizations and most people, in my experience, pick and choose from a palette of opportunities that come up all the time. The calls come in every day. And we then start to agonize over what to do on an opportunity-by-opportunity basis. But the beauty of having a vision is that the only opportunities worth even considering are those that are going to help us to attain the vision we've committed to.

This makes the conversations pretty simple, because, if you think it all the way through, not only does the vision state what we're going to do, it also makes pretty clear what we aren't going to do. That has enormous organizational benefits. It means that when opportunities crop up (and they will) that are out of the bounds of our vision, we can rule them out quickly and thus save extraordinary amounts of time and organizational energy. For instance, our vision for Zingerman's 2020 says that we're going to have 12 to 18 Zingerman's businesses, each with its own unique specialty, each with a managing partner onsite, and all located in the Ann Arbor area. So when we get a call about opening another Zingerman's Roadhouse in Rome or another Deli in Denver the conversation with the caller can be really short, very polite, and visionarily sweet. "We're honored that you're calling. But our vision says . . ."

Don't underestimate the value that visioning can bring to your work in this way. Life is short and time spent agonizing over opportunities that seem too good to pass up but aren't going to help us get where we really want to go is, in my opinion, time wasted and never to be reclaimed. I'd prefer to have my vision clear and then spend my time working toward the future I've chosen to create. Trust me—I've tried both ways, and using visioning as I've described here is about fifteen hundred times more rewarding.

What Do You Do with Your Vision Once You've Got One? *Do It!*

Once we have our vision in writing, it becomes the finish line toward which all of our organizational energies are directed. In a somewhat simplistic world, every major decision we make should include the question, "Is this going to help us move closer to our vision of the future?" I know that decisions generally come in 15 shades of gray. But still, our strategies, our plans, our behaviors, our actions, and our words should all be focused on moving us toward our vision.

Can You Change Your Vision?

Sure you can. But I don't recommend that you do it too often. Though it may be relatively easy for you or me to personally change direction, remember that every time we shift our focus, the rest of the organization has to keep up. If you've mapped out a five-year vision for your organization and then drastically alter it every 12 months, all you'll have done is confuse everyone.

On the other hand, to stick with something after it no longer makes sense isn't effective either. So the answer is: by all means, revisit your vision every year or so and make sure it's still valid. If you believed in it when you wrote it, if it came from the heart, and if you still believe it to be inspiring and strategically sound, then don't give up on it. If it was truly a vision of greatness it's probably going to take the fortitude to fight through all sorts of resistance to make it a reality. But remember that the Duomo (the cathedral) in Milan wasn't built in a day, and neither is any good organization.

making salads and sandwiches at the deli

Vision Back

Why Sharing Where You've Come from Isn't Just Important to History Majors

Granted, being a history major probably prejudices me toward taking the time needed to teach our organizational history to our new staff members. But, biases aside, I think it's a huge tool for us here at Zingerman's in terms of getting people bought into what we do. Sadly, I think we're more of the exception than the rule—few companies actually take the time to teach front liners where the organization has come from. Those that do so in a broad "corporate" context often forget to follow through at the departmental level—every part of an organization has its own story to tell and the more people know it, the more they can connect it with the work they do every day. Honestly I think that not sharing "Vision Back" is a huge missed opportunity. People really do want to know some of the interesting background of the business that they're a part of, whether it goes back two years or two hundred. If you doubt me, try this out once or twice on your own staff and see what happens. I'm betting you'll find that you have a lot of interested folks who are really happy to hear the stories and other seemingly "unimportant" bits of info that you and I might otherwise take for granted.

I'm certainly more inclined than the average American to advocate the sharing of stories about where we've come from. At first blush, someone could call this work "business history," but that's not really what I mean. While I'm interested in guilds, artisans, the first cheese factory in America (1851 in Rome, New York, in case you're wondering), and the early iterations of the Ford production line, I'm not really thinking about the trends and timelines of organizational development. What I'm talking about is how important it is that we, as founders and leaders of our organizations, take time to share our history with the people who work with us.

Why bother sharing history when it's already over? Actually, there's a whole host of very sound business reasons that make it worthwhile. I firmly believe that organizations that do so get better staff buy-in, make better decisions, and probably have more fun in the process.

People Want to Be Part of Something Greater than Themselves

After more than 28 years of co-owning and helping to lead our organization, I believe with ever-greater conviction that everyone wants to be a part of something that's meaningful, something significant, something lasting and positive. Everyone wants to know that when they sell a customer a loaf of bread, a piece of pie, or a bottle of olive oil, that it's not just about sticking a few more dollars in the cash register. Rather, we contribute positively to the quality of life of the customer who gets to eat great food; of the artisans who made that food; of the community we live in; of our own families; and of this very special organization.

"Vision Back" is enormously valuable for this purpose. Every organization is unique, with its own story to tell. That's not really news—it's actually kind of obvious when you think about it. The problem is that we forget to tell people so, and to explain how it came to be that way. And if we don't tell them, they lose out on the chance to be a part of what is almost always a really rich, interesting, and innovative past. After a business has been operating for even just a couple of years it's so easy to forget to talk about the early struggles, the first successes, the hard days, the laughter, and the tears that added up to make our organizations what they are today. And I would argue that the longer we're in business, and the greater our "success," the more important it is to share how special the past is that we're building on. The further those formative experiences fall away in the rearview mirror, the more important it becomes to revisit and renew them.

Sharing History Helps Keep the Story Straight

There is of course no perfect or objective history. As ZingTrain's Stas' Kazmierski taught me years ago, "Everyone's truth is their own." But the reality is that each person who comes to work with us will get some version of the truth—from their friends, from the media, and from customers and co-workers. While I think it's great for everyone to informally share their versions of history like this, I really want to be sure that anyone who works with us hears our account directly. I don't want them to get it second- or thirdhand, which would require that we invest extra effort in correcting their misimpressions.

I'm not talking about revisionist history here—merely about consciously choosing what we include in our storytelling. In her book, *The Jewish Community of Salonika,* author Bea Lewkowicz writes that, "Those memories that an individual shares with his contemporaries are part of the 'communicative memory.'" And that communicative memory contributes greatly to the culture of an organization and the decision-making of the people within it. In the "Welcome to Zingerman's" orientation class, which Paul and I still teach, we talk about the key highlights and challenges we've been through over the years. That means that new staffers are hearing the story of how we got started straight from the people who did the starting. It's history that informs our organizational decision-making and creates a context within which everyone can operate.

Take note that this isn't just about telling people what's worked over the years—it's not an organizational hit parade; it's also about sharing one's struggles. Communicating with vulnerability makes it all the more likely that the connection we build with our co-workers will be a solid one. Take note too that the stories we choose to share in the class are not random selections. To quote from folk historian Charles Joyner's *Shared Traditions*, "What remains after forgetting everything that is not truly memorable, is something primal, something very close to the basic poetic impulse of the human species. People neither remember nor forget without reason." Be mindful of which memories you share—each one carries with it a meaningful message.

Great People Want to Work with Great People

When someone chooses to take a job with us, it's in part because of the day-to-day work they're going to do, and even more so because of the opportunity to join an exceptional organization. But while people join the organization as an entity, the data suggest that the most meaningful factor in their decision to stay or leave is the person, or people, who directly manage them.

Frank Carollo, one of the partners at the Bakehouse, told me 20 years ago, "People want to work for . . . somebody!" What he meant was that they want to work for a man or woman they can connect with, someone with integrity, experience, insight, passion, and values; someone who's special and who, in turn, is likely to contribute something special to their life. One of the best ways we've found to build that connection is by sharing our history—breaking "emotional bread" together by sitting around the table and telling new staffers where we've come from. A rote bio on a company website may technically fulfill this need, but the only people it's likely to inspire are folks who write resumes for a living. So put some energy into it—share your passions and your past! Even if you didn't start the company, it's important to tell people where you came from, how and where you grew up, what got you into your current role, what you like about it (and what you don't), what you like to eat, and what you do outside of work.

The bond we create from this personal storytelling helps build more resilient relationships of the sort that make for healthier, longer term, more sustainable organizations. Think about things your grandparents told you that stuck with you, and why those things connected. Philosopher Rollo May wrote that, "There is an energy field between all humans. And when we reach out in passion, it is met with an answering passion and changes the relationship forever." Sharing "Vision Back" is a small investment that I think makes a BIG difference.

Getting to Know the Staff's Stories

To state what's almost, but not quite, obvious, this connection is made even stronger when the sharing is a two-way street. Getting to know the story of each staff member—who they are, where they've come from, why they're here—as well as knowing their vision of their own future, is pretty sure to solidify the connections we as leaders make with them. And it makes it more likely that each of those staff members will make a positive difference, in your organization and everywhere else they go.

Dates, Stories, Subtexts, and Pictures: The "Why" Behind What Happened

A lot of times when I bring up the importance of history, people's eyes glaze over and their minds start wandering—maybe even running—away. They think of history as dry, boring, and basically irrelevant: little more than a litany of names and dates. By contrast, for someone like me it's not so much the dates but *the story behind the dates* that makes the past come alive. For example, I don't just tell people when we opened—I tell them what it was like at the time, what the town and the country were going through (interest rates were at 18 percent!). I share a bit of how it felt to go through it all (working seven days a week, open to close). This sort of stuff is relevant info in any organization. What was going on in the world when you first unlocked your doors? What was driving everyone to get the business going in the first place? What was your industry like then, and how has it changed? How have *you* changed?

For anyone who's just starting work at Zingerman's today—at a time when the Deli is physically four times bigger than it was on day one, with nearly 200 employees doing more than $10,000,000 in annual sales—it's almost impossible to grasp what things were like when we started back in '82. Telling them that the original building—which is still the public's most common entry point into the Deli "campus"—was just me, Paul, and two employees running a place with five tables plus four vinyl-covered stools at the front counter, puts things in a little perspective. So too does sharing with them that for the first year or two we were open, there were people living upstairs in the apartment—a space that's been the Deli's office for as long as only a handful of us old-timers can remember. And then there's that story of how one of us used to drive an hour each way to Detroit every morning, through rain, snow, ice, or whatever, to pick up the bread from the bakery we'd selected—we liked their bread a lot but they wouldn't deliver to Ann Arbor. Sharing this story gives new employees a sense of how determined we were right from the beginning to do whatever we needed to, no matter how unglamorous, to make our food great. While we might have had big ideas, it was a pretty grassroots reality. And the message they take away, I hope, is that we've stayed true to what we were doing, thinking, and feeling back in 1982.

I often like to segue from these stories into our decision to open Zingerman's Bakehouse with Frank as the managing partner in 1992. While most business-people assume that we started the Bakehouse to make more money, the truth is that what was driving us was an ever-stronger desire to bake and sell more flavorful bread. Talking about the Bakehouse's beginnings also gives me an opportunity to share that when we opened it in '92, a lot of our customers were *not* happy with the move we were making—people don't like change and this shift was no exception. They thought the crusts were too hard, the changes unneeded, and they were fine with the way things had been for many years. This resistance is probably hard for newcomers to comprehend now that the Bakehouse is hugely successful and our bread and pastry are known nationally, and are generally acknowledged to set the standard for quality all over the area. But it helps get clear just how innovative the work was that Frank, Amy, and the other bakers were doing in our area back in the early '90s.

Tell It Yourself

While it's helpful for anyone in a leadership role to share their organization's story, the effort will be much more effective when the telling is done directly by the founder, or someone who's been through things firsthand and has a passion for what's been built. There's no way around it—there's just way more power when the message is personal and from the heart and head of the person(s) who lived the story firsthand.

Not long ago, I was out in Seattle and had the chance to sit in on a ZingTrain session that chef Tom Douglas had put together for the 50 or so managers of his restaurants, bakery, and catering facility. I think that Tom's is one of the best restaurant groups around: people care, they're bought in, they're exceptionally loyal, and the food is really good. They've achieved impressive longevity among their upper-level leaders and, really, throughout the organization—meaning that most of the people in the room were fairly well familiar with the story of how Tom and his wife, Jackie Cross, started the business back in 1989.

As part of the process of sharing his vision of the future, Tom started out with a look back. He shared the story of his success working for others as the chef of one of Seattle's best restaurants back in the early '80s, and about the craziness of the early years of opening his own place, the Dahlia Lounge, in 1989. He talked about the challenges of getting through times when money was tight, and of riding out the economic ups and downs of the last twenty-some years. Throughout the session he shared the sorts of laughs and laments that anyone who's been through a bootstrap opening like that can relate to.

I stood in the back of the room, completely caught up in the power of what he was saying. At first I thought maybe it was just me who was so engrossed—I wasn't intimately familiar with the history and figured maybe it was old hat for everyone else in the room. But later I heard people who've worked with Tom for years talking about how great it was to hear the story from him firsthand. I guarantee that the 10 minutes it took him to tell it increased the already high buy-in of the people in the room: you could sense the energy in their eyes and you could hear it in their voices. I'm sure that in small, both formal and informal ways, many of the stories probably still circulate throughout his organization of more than 400 staff members, enriching what was already a very positive and supportive culture.

Stories for Times of Struggle

While people who find history boring usually see it as little more than a static, frozen-forever-in-time photo shoot, the reality is that the way it's taught, interpreted, and shared varies over time. So it only makes sense to tailor which parts of it we share in order to make the learning opportunities as valuable as possible for those who are listening. Cultural memory, the historian Bea Lewkowitz explains, is not static. Rather, "It selects the themes which are important for the recent identity of a group." Different stories hit home for different people in different ways and resonate differently in different settings.

More often that not, it's the stories of struggle—and of successfully fighting through struggles—that stick in people's minds. While it would be easy to list all the kudos our organization has earned and act as if it were always thus, I'd rather review how success has only come by fighting through challenges, threats, and the nay-saying of experts who supposedly knew better. This gets the message across that going for greatness is not always about doing what everyone says you should do. People who want to do great things relate to that, and those are the kinds of people we want to work with.

When I asked Marie Mourou, who works at the Deli, about the value of learning our organizational history as part of her initial training, her eyes lit up and she said, "I think it's great that you started the business when people were telling you that it was nuts to try. Anything that has to do with people getting told they can't do something gets me going." It obviously worked—Marie has degrees in political science and anthropology from McGill and has done some very interesting work in restoration of ancient art, but she's at the Deli because she loves the food and the culture, cares about the past, and is committed to helping make our long-term vision a reality.

Right now we're all faced with a tough economy and a gloomy outlook, both nationally and especially here in Michigan, which currently has the highest unemployment rate in the country. Here again, history provides valuable context. I like to remind people that when we opened in 1982 the economy was also in horrible shape. Actually, the situation here hasn't been very good for most of the years we've been in business. While history can't guarantee that we'll weather the next storm, it does influence the state of mind of the people in the organization—if we've made it through this stuff many times before, then we can feel far calmer and a bit more confident (if still appropriately concerned) about what's coming.

To quote from Charles Joyner, writing in *Shared Traditions,* these sorts of stories "provide the present generation with a sense of continuity with generations gone before, a precious lifeline to courageous ancestors, a source of strength that still enables us to cope with the hail and upheaval of life." Knowing that your contemporaries, and those who came before you, beat back the pressures of their time to help get to where we are now often creates a big boost of energy—"If they did it, we can do it," and "If they made it, we don't want to let them down" are pretty common responses.

Share It Early and Often

When is the best time to share one's organizational history? Whenever you can. A new staff orientation class is one great place to start. When I debrief the attendees at the end of the Welcome to Zingerman's orientation session, the history section is pretty regularly one of the most highly rated parts of the class (others include the active role we play in the community and the specifics of what makes our food so special).

In truth, any time you've got people together is a good time to build in a bit of history. It can be personal stories or accounts of outstanding outcomes achieved in the face of overwhelming odds. At Zingerman's our big meetings, little meetings, and classes of all sorts are designed to help us use history as a tool. Every one of our managing partners teaches an orientation class for their own business, and shares their own stories of startup, struggle, and success. When we teach about finance, we share the history of how ours has developed over the years. When we work on service stuff we go over the timing of how much our service training has improved since our early days of just leading by example.

You can also use a number of alternative methods. An illustrated "Vision Back" is one great approach: it's different, and some people learn far more effectively that way. Cartoons, creative arts, fun movies are all OK . . . as long as your method is lively and engaging, you're pretty sure to connect with people who like to learn visually (and there are a lot of them!). Or you could share your history through skits, T-shirts, tattoos . . . pretty much any technique you can think of will probably connect with someone in your organization.

If you really get into the history, you could do what Clabber Girl has done down in Terre Haute, Indiana. I had the pleasure of visiting their corporate headquarters not long ago to teach our approach to leadership to their management team. While you may not immediately recognize the company by name, most everyone who has ever baked knows their product—the classic baking powder with the young girl on the label. This is a company that has been in business for over 150 years, and their entire headquarters is a testament to the organizational traditions they've built. They've turned their location, in the original brick building where the company was founded, into a living museum. Woven in with workspaces are displays of old packaging, hundred-year old recipe booklets, antique labels, fantastic photos, and beautifully restored old equipment, all labeled with information about the featured items. You really couldn't come away from even a quick visit to Clabber Girl offices without some sense of what the company is about and where it has come from.

Getting Them Involved—Writing a Living History

Writing a living history is a valuable team-building exercise that I learned from Stas' Kazmierski. It's not hard to do and it really does help create a common culture.

To get going, tape a long sheet of blank paper on the wall. (We use butcher paper because we have it on hand, but anything big will work fine.) You can set up a timeline that runs from a year or two before the business opened all the way up through to the present; or, if you have a long-term written vision, you can extend it out to the end date of your chosen future.

Then ask each person in the room to mark the date on which they started work with the organization on the timeline. The person who has worked for you the longest gets things going by telling stories of what it was like when he or she was hired. As this person speaks, someone else can record key bullet points or make pictures on the paper to illustrate each episode. When this person is done you go on to the next most senior staff member, and so on. By the time you've worked your way through the whole group, everyone in the room knows where you've come from. To really keep the history alive, Stas' suggests leaving the paper hanging for a long time—or even getting it transferred into a visual that can be reprinted and referred back to, so that the sharing of the "Vision Back" continues to happen on a regular basis.

Sharing the Past Gives a Better Shot at Future Success

When you play basketball for the Boston Celtics or sign on to sing with the Metropolitan Opera you know you're building on a great tradition. And you feel responsible for continuing that legacy of greatness. Put differently, I've come to see sharing history as "plowing people's mental field." When we tell staff the story of how we've gotten to where we are, they're significantly more receptive to hearing—and then supporting—our long-term vision for the future. When people feel like they're a part of something important, something that is grounded in history and has provided their predecessors with positive benefits, they're a lot more likely to see the possibilities of the future and actively work to help make them happen.

When I share our history in our orientation class, I talk to the new staff about how each of us who's currently here has a responsibility to learn from, and then build on, that past. That each of us has an obligation to take things to the next level, respectfully making things ever better in a way that pays homage to those who've done so much work to get us to where we are. It all adds up to make it just a bit more likely we're going to get where we're going in the way that we want to get there.

There's very little to lose by sharing "Vision Back," but a ton to gain. To quote Joyner's book, *Shared Traditions,* "People who know where they come from have a better sense of direction, a better sense of where they are going and how to get there." When I asked Mike Baptista, a manager at Zingerman's Creamery, about this, he perked up immediately. "Knowing our history builds excitement. It makes me feel plugged in. I know what's led up to me being here and how I fit into it. With everything in my life, I just feel more confident when I know the history."

illustrating the old fashioned way for zingerman's mail order catalog

An 8-Step Recipe for Writing a Vision of Greatness

*A Surefire Way to Get Clear
on the Future You Want*

Now that I've hopefully persuaded you of how effective and powerful a vision can be, for both your leadership and your life in general, I should probably share a recipe for how to actually write one. As with food recipes, there's no reason you have to follow the instructions as I've written them—if you're OK with writing a vision of greatness on your own, by all means, go for it. You don't need me, or any 8-step outline, to write out what your desired future is. If you're ready to go it alone, you have my full support.

That said, I've learned over the years (and re-learned more times than I'd like to admit) that most people work better when they have a good set of guidelines to help them get where they want to go. So with that in mind, here's our recipe for visioning.

Because visioning is a craft and not a science, feel free to adjust, adapt, and annotate as you see fit. Because there are a thousand applications of the idea of visioning, it's not like one recipe is going to be perfect for every situation. The real key for me is the idea of it—the recipe is merely a method that can help you to get out of the just "thinking about writing a vision" stage to actually getting one done.

Ingredients for Effective Visioning

1. Belief in the process

Seriously, and I mean this in the most productive and not at all passive-aggressive way, if you don't believe that visioning will work, it's not worth wasting time doing it. I can't explain that in a really rational or logical way but unless you're intent on proving you can waste time any way you want and don't have to listen to me (and I can certainly relate to that kind of anarchistic attitude!), I'd say just take my word for it and then find some new and more creative way to spend a few hours than working on a vision without believing that it's going to work.

2. Your gut

No, although we are in the food business, I don't mean your belly. I'm actually talking about that voice we have deep down inside us, the one that gets excited about what we really believe in, about whatever it is that gets us going before everyone tells us we're dreaming or irresponsible, or gives us 16 eminently logical reasons why it won't work. You know, that voice that really speaks for us, but that's gradually overridden by all those other accumulated voices we gather as we grow up and move into "proper," "mature," "safer," more often than not middle-of-the-road, adult behaviors. The sad state of the world is that that adult attitude so often buries our true feelings and passions, the ones that really are at our true core, our gut. You know . . . your loveable, creative, uncensored, often seriously silly, self. It's where we have all that stuff that—if we think about it too long, our logical brains (or our mothers, business partners, accountants, staff or the Wall Street Journal) will say you can't do. It's that little impish, creative spirit that, in *Ignore Everybody,* Hugh MacLeod calls "your wee voice."

How do you know when what you're getting at is really your gut? If you've fallen out of touch with it, that's no small challenge. It took me about 10 years of working really hard at it to get back to a point where I honored what my gut was saying and didn't let others back me off it without a fight. I think you're getting there when you share what you really truly are excited about doing, and your wee voice kind of laughs on the inside and says, "Duh! Of course that's what you want—you've known that for ages!"

3. SOME TIME

The process might take less time than you think. But there's no way around the reality that it will take some. More specific estimates are in the recipe.

4. WILLINGNESS TO MAKE YOURSELF VULNERABLE

If you're actually going to show your vision drafts to anyone other than your pet owl, there's definitely emotional risk involved—it's just the price one has to pay for trying to do something special. Don't let the opposition fool you. In my experience, the better your ideas, the more likely it is that a lot of people will quickly tell you why what you're envisioning won't work. If you're at all sensitive like me, that stuff can be very hard to hear. But, having been through the process a thousand or so times now, for me at least, listening to some people's opposition (and learning from it in the process) is a small price to pay for being able to successfully do something really special in the long run. And while most of the world may not be excited, you'll find some great people who are truly supportive of you and are able to offer great insight while still helping you nurture your newly formed little dream.

5. READINESS TO DO SOMETHING GREAT

After all, the last word in the title of the essay is "Greatness." While I suppose you could use the recipe in a risk-avoiding, CYA (in case you're not intimate with the corporate world, that stands for "cover-your-ass") sort of way in some bureaucratic-type setting . . . it seems such a waste to expend good creative energy writing a vision that doesn't really accomplish anything significant. If you're going to do something, why do it halfway? I hope to be able to look back and say, as early 20th-century anarchist Charles Plunkett did, "I never did anything by halves."

6. You gotta wanna

In *The Great Game of Business*, the book he co-authored with Bo Burlingham on the subject of Open Book Finance, Jack Stack, CEO of SRC Holdings Corp. (formerly Springfield ReManufacturing), lists one of his "higher laws of business" as "You gotta wanna!" Jack's right on (as he usually is) about the financial element of it, but it's totally true for visioning, too. If you don't really want this—either the act of visioning, or what's actually written in the vision itself—it's really just not gonna work. It may seem silly but it's really as simple as that. As Jack said, you really do gotta wanna. It won't guarantee success but it definitely increases the odds. And truthfully the more you wanna, the better the odds will be!

7. The willingness to stick with the process

I can't tell you how many people—many of them good friends of mine (you know who you are!)—have started to work on their vision but never seem to get it done. Starting to write a vision is nice, but honestly, if you're not going to get the thing finished it's probably not worth starting in the first place. To be clear, by "done" I mean really writing the darned thing down, getting agreement on it from all the key players, actively sharing it with everyone around you, and then going out and actually starting to live it. The good news is that when you do it, the vision thing really works!

Recipe Procedure

Step 1. Pick your topic

Because visioning can be used for just about any project you're involved in, it's important to start by being clear about what you're working on. Is it a vision for your organization overall? Or just for a particular piece ? For today's shift? Or your retirement? We do visions for all of the above and everything in between and around them.

Step 2. Pick your time frame

All of our vision work is pegged to a future point in time when we'll have succeeded at putting the particulars of our preferred future into place. How far out should you look? There's no right answer, but as a general principle visioning works best if you go far enough out to get beyond present-day problems, but not so far out that you have no sense at all of actually getting there. For our 500-person, 16-partner organization, we've done a long-term organizational vision that's set in the year 2020. We've been doing this sort of work for so long that 2020 seems right around the corner. But most organizational visions will probably be set somewhere between two and ten years out—five is a fairly typical place to start.

Remember: the vision is NOT the "strategic plan," so it doesn't need to say HOW you're going to get to there—just what success will look like when you arrive.

STEP 3. PUT TOGETHER A LIST OF "PROUDS"

Timing: 10 minutes at most. Don't overthink the list—it's always OK to add more things you feel good about as they come to you!

Think about the work you're embarking on and throw down a list of past, positive achievements that seem at least somewhat relevant. You might include specific contributions that you or your colleagues have made to past successes, or skills, techniques, and resources that could be assets in achieving your vision.

For instance, "I feel good about the last three projects we've successfully implemented: (1) the team really came together; (2) we've improved cheese quality a lot in the last two years; and (3) we've brought our staff turnover rate down 20 percent since 2007." Anything good that comes to mind is fine. And don't stress out about it—just do it. The idea is just to build a base of positive energy and high-quality experiences on which you can build for future success. The more people focus on the positives, not on the present-day problems, the more likely you are to attain the greatness you envision.

(If you're working in a bigger group, it may be helpful to go back through the list and identify the top three to five entries. But, again, don't fixate—just pick the ones that seem best. If you want six instead of five, go for it.)

STEP 4. WRITE THE FIRST DRAFT OF THE VISION

Timing: Give yourself somewhere between 15 and 30 minutes. Don't get too uptight about it. The vision police won't pop up on your screen if you do more or less than that—it's just a guideline that I've found works pretty well. For most people who haven't done this before, that time frame will feel like it's way too short. It isn't—I've written a lot of visions and I've worked with many others to help them do theirs, and it's amazing how much good stuff you can get out in half an hour!

This is it: the point of this piece, the Big Bang, the *raison d'être* of this entire exercise. While writing a vision is hugely important, don't let its perceived weightiness work against you. The results will be great regardless, but the amount of time you spend drafting it is, in my experience, generally NOT related to the quality of the vision. I'd actually posit that it's inversely related—the people who just dive in and get something down on paper almost always are the ones who emerge from this process with the most creative and inspiring visions. Those of us who get bogged down into worrying about the day-to-day details of how everything's going to actually be accomplished tend to lose the momentum, passion, and creativity that can come from just going with what's in our gut.

You can compose your vision in any style you like—in prose or in bullet points, by hand or on the computer. I've seen a few people draw it and then talk through what they've illustrated while someone else takes notes. Really, it's whatever's most comfortable for you.

I do want to emphasize the importance of putting the word "DRAFT" on your document. Unless you're writing a vision for, say, a shift that starts in a few minutes, what you're working on here is really just that—something that you'll revise on the basis of input from others you ask to help you. We've found that by simply writing the word "draft" at the top of the page, we get a lot more input, whereas without it people tend to assume the vision is final and there's no point providing any real feedback.

Before you start writing, let me review a few technical tips. I know I've referenced some of these earlier. But—for me, at least—working in the future as I've been recommending is so counter-intuitive that I need to remind myself of them regularly; it's not easy to break a lifetime's-worth of learned behavior that always had me starting out with reviewing present-day problems. On the assumption that I'm not alone in that, I stuck these in here to reinforce how important they are. Having used (and not used) them for years now, I can tell you flat out—if you follow these tips, the visioning work will be way better:

> **Go for something great:** The work here is about writing visions of *greatness*—if we don't put something special into the initial draft of the vision, it's not likely to get any more inspiring later! Remember, this is a first, rough writeup, so put something wild out there. I think about John Kennedy's call to go to the moon, Martin Luther King's "I have a dream" speech, winning the NBA championship ... Things that are big, but also specific; scary, but also exciting. Get past the 59

reasons that spring to mind for why it won't work. If the early draft isn't kind of scaring you a bit (or at least the practical-minded part of you), then you probably haven't pushed yourself hard enough or put down your true desires.

Write from the heart: To restate, effective vision writing happens from the inside out: go with your gut and put down what pours out, not just what you think other people want to see. I was recently reading an article about the state of the nation's economy that led with the headline, "Even the Experts Can't Predict What Will Happen." The good news here is that an effective vision of greatness is NOT an attempt to predict trends. Nor is it some business school case study where you have to recommend what someone else should do. If you're the one writing it, it's about what *you* believe in, what gets *you* excited. Often that means including what you've always wanted to do but have been told by others so many times that you couldn't, a mission that you've long since filed away under "impossible."

Remember, the vision draft at this stage is really just for you. So when you hear the voices of others cutting in to "kill" your ideas, just gently ask them to step aside for the moment. You can come back to their concerns later.

Get in the future: Having done visioning work a few thousand times, I can tell you that it works way better when you *write as if you're already actually sitting in the time you're envisioning*. Start by stating the future date of your vision. That could be tomorrow, two weeks, or 10 years, depending on what you determined in Step #2 above. If you're writing a vision of a wedding you'll be catering this Saturday, you might start out with, "It's a few minutes before midnight on Saturday night. The bride and groom just headed for home, the rest of the family members are lingering. Everyone is tired, but feeling really good about the event . . ." Again, this seems strange, but it really is critical: don't write it as if it's *going* to happen; write it as if it already *has* happened.

To help folks who have a hard time transporting themselves into the future we sometimes do seemingly goofy things like have ZingTrain seminar attendees wear special visioning hats. Now that

I'm thinking about it, maybe we should build a special transporter unit and have seminar participants pass through it before we let them start drafting their visions of future greatness.

Go quickly: I know it seems like a contradiction in terms to emphasize over and over again how important visioning is, and then tell you *not* to spend a huge amount of time worrying about it. But the truth is just that the visions I've been involved with come out much better when we don't drag out the process. So don't wait until the stars are perfectly aligned, the full moon is out, the stock market is at an all-time high, or the White Sox win the World Series (unless those things are incredibly meaningful to you personally). Just sit down in a reasonably comfortable spot at a reasonably comfortable time and get to writing.

Use the "Hot Pen" technique: Once you start writing, don't stop. Just keep writing for that 15 to 30 minutes, regardless of how smart or silly what you're saying may seem. Don't start self-editing—just keep writing. When you catch yourself starting to think a lot about what to say next, just keep the "pen" (or keys) moving. (Personally, when I start wondering what to say, I often just stick in lots of swear words—it's just the first draft and I take them out before anyone else sees it—to keep me going.) Believe me, this works—it's very interesting what appears on the paper. My own experience is that sometimes the most important/interesting/insightful elements of the vision are the ones that I started to edit out, but forced myself to put down anyway.

Get personal: One of the things we do in our visioning work is to blend the personal and professional so we arrive at a single, holistic vision, or at least two compatible and mutually supportive ones. If you're the one running the business it makes sense that you build your passions into what you write. If you want to teach, put that in the vision. If you want to work less, say it. If you've "retired" into an advisory-only role in the company, talk about how the person who took your position feels about his or her role, and how you relate to that person. In other words, don't write a vision that you aren't a part of (unless the vision is that you're no longer at all connected).

Now, with all these rules in mind, take the 30 minutes max that I've given you and put down a vision draft.

We usually start our writing with an introductory sentence along the lines of: "It's — (fill in the date you've chosen above). I'm about to head out for the evening. There are so many great things going on that make it clear that our long-term vision has come to be the reality that we planned and believed it would back when we wrote it." And then start listing what those things are and just keep going until your time is up!

Then put the draft aside. Go back to all the other stuff you do every day. Enjoy the rest of your day!

STEP 5. RE-VIEW AND RE-DRAFT

Timing: Again, I'd say give yourself at most a half an hour for this part of the vision writing. Go through what you have, make changes, and then run with it.

Depending on how long you have to get the vision done, I'd suggest setting your initial draft aside for a couple of days before you bring it back out to review and revise it. It's good to let a little time pass—when specifics we've stuck in the vision still sound good two or three days later my experience is that they're almost always things about which we feel very strongly in our gut. Stick with 'em!

When you're ready to revise, go ahead and take your draft out of the drawer (literally or figuratively). Read it through from start to finish. I like to do this out loud, which is a technique I learned by going to writing groups for many years—I can't really explain why, but it helps. Regardless, read it through. Don't erase what you wrote in the first draft. If you're on the computer, start the second round by copying your first file so you can edit what you wrote without losing the original version.

In terms of editing and making changes in this second-round review, my experience is that 80 to 90 percent of what I put down in that first scary rendition is actually pretty right on. But regardless, you'll have plenty of opportunity for editing both the content and the language. Still, I really recommend not taking out the parts that seem a bit too bold or feel slightly overly ambitious at this point—often those are the things that make the vision most inspiring and ultimately special.

As you read through, keep in the back of your mind: "Does this sound inspiring? Does it really say what I want it to say? Do I get more excited when I'm reading it?" Note that in this context, "excited" does not preclude anxiety about the challenges of implementation—for some of us practical types, the two almost always go together! Everyone is of course different. But my personal rule of thumb is that if I'm not feeling any stress around whether or not we can make the vision happen, then I probably haven't pushed things as far as they need to go. Similarly, if it strikes me that some element of the vision is in there pretty much just to placate other people (either folks who are actually in the room, or who are only imaginary voices in my mind), then I put mental question marks next to those passages. Designing a vision to please someone else means I'm not truly inspired to achieve it, and the only thing that's a recipe for is trouble!

How specific should you get? I recommend having more detail rather than less—it helps make the vision more real. If you're writing a business vision, stay away from vague statements like "we're busier than ever" and make them more specific by adding in sales numbers that actually mean something to others. Again, don't panic—it's not like you need "the perfect number." Just something that conveys a sense of the scale and size at which you want to be working. How big you CAN get is really not the issue. A business doing $1,000,000 in sales a year is radically different from one doing $10,000,000, which is radically different again from one doing $100,000,000. Same goes for whether you have only one store, a series of six all in one city, or 600 spread all over the southern United States. Mind you, all of these options are OK—there really aren't "right" visions or "wrong" visions. But the specificity is important because depending on which you choose you're going to end up with radically different organizations, sizes, scales, etc.

Along the same lines, a personal vision might say, "I spend a lot of time with my kids." That's great, but I think you'll get a lot further with something more specific, like "I'm spending two to three weeks a year traveling the country with my kids. It's amazing how much fun we're having." Or "One night a week I go out to dinner with just my entire family." Or "I go to three quarters of my kids' kickball games." Or, "I home-school them and we're together all but two weeks a year when they go to their grandparents to visit." While all of these are perfectly good visions, and all have you spending "a lot of time with your kids," clearly they're also very different.

I'd push for the same level of detail about organizational statements like "We're financially successful." Whether you're writing about personal or business finance, the use of the word "success" really only says we're "not failing." But without definition, we have no details on what success will actually look like. No offense to anyone who's said that (and most of us have at some point) but it's really not all that helpful. We need some specifics to see what we're really doing every day! "I want to be wealthy" is all well and good, but one person's view of what makes you "rich" is another's "only slightly-better-than-poor." So, I say, spell it out. What are the key financial numbers that define success for you? Sales levels? Salary? Savings? Status?

Same goes for service. If customers "love coming into your store," say why! Are they coming because they love the location? Because the food is so special? Because the prices are low or the fun factor is high? Again it doesn't really matter to me what you choose—the point is to add specificity to your vision so that those who will be working with you to get there have a good sense of (a) where you're all going, and, (b) how to get there.

STEPS 6-A, 6-B, AND 6-C. MORE RE-DRAFTS

Timing: Once again, I'd allow at most a half an hour for each go-round.

If you want, you can take this second draft and make additional adjustments to the language you've used. If you're really concerned, kind of compulsive, or don't have anything else to do besides work on your vision, you can repeat this early review and rewrite it as many times as you want. But at some point you'd better get your butt in gear and move on to Step 7.

For conversation's sake, I'm going to say that in the case of this recipe for writing a vision, there is no "6-D." If there were, the "D" would stand for "Done"—in other words, if you're working on your own, four re-drafts is the most I'll give you before you have to go out and let someone else look at it. More than that and I think you're headed down the long and unrewarding road of, "I've been working on a vision for the last few years but I still don't have it finished" thing. I've done it, and believe me, it really doesn't help you or anyone. At some point you really do need to move on to the next stage.

STEP 7. INPUT FROM ACES

This is the step where you let the vision cat out of the intellectual bag, and get input on the draft from people you trust and respect. Remember, it's just a draft, so the idea is to use their insight and assistance to improve what you've got. But remember, too, it's your vision so you're not obligated to change everything to fit what others want to see or think should be in there.

In our recipe for organizational change here at Zingerman's we call these people *ACES*, which stands for "Advisory Content Experts." ACES are folks who have experience, insight, and expertise relevant to your vision. They might be your business partners, colleagues, peers in your work community, or people from your neighborhood. They could be mentors, family members, close friends, or casual acquaintances. If you're opening an ice cream shop, they might have owned one themselves. If you're going to add a line of Moroccan foods they might have sold North African specialties for many years, or maybe grew up in the Maghreb.

Again, please don't obsess (I'm probably projecting). There are no perfect ACES. Just send people the draft and see what they think. You can always get more input later if you think of other people you'd like to hear from.

You can gather input in rounds if that works best. For instance, if the first draft of your vision is pretty reflective of what you really are passionate about, but it's a bit "out there" and you're (understandably) a little anxious about what kind of response people are going to give you, I'd suggest you start out by taking your draft to ACES who are very likely to be supportive. If you're sensitive to what others say, please don't start by sending the initial draft out to your most supremely cynical colleagues—when you've got your new little hatchling of a vision out there you don't want to put it out in front of a steel-toed-boot kind of corporate world captain to step on. As you gain a bit of confidence, then you can send it out to a round of more challenging experts for input.

At this early stage I rarely make my request too specific. I generally just ask folks to let me know what they think (and explain a bit about visioning, if they aren't familiar with the idea). That's all. Keeping it loose gives them more room to tell me which parts excite them, which others worry them, etc.

Inevitably, some of these ACES will shift away from talking about the vision into a discussion of all the action steps that will have to be in the plan. They're slipping away from working on where we're going into trying to figure out whether we can actually get there. Don't worry. Just listen carefully and take notes—some of those ideas might come in handy later when you actually start to write the action plan that will detail how you'll get to the vision!

I've learned that when people are offering input that doesn't fit with what I believe, it's helpful to seek more information. People's suggestions often tell you as much about them as they do about your vision draft. Which doesn't in the least invalidate their input. It just makes the process all the more interesting.

That said, I know that I definitely do not need to just do what everyone else says. Taking advice that goes against my gut and pushes me to put away the passions that I've included in my original vision draft is *never* helpful. So how do you know which input is worth adapting and which to respectfully set aside? I wish I had an easy answer. Practice helps. As does learning which ACES usually give supportive, helpful input, or have values and views aligned with your own. I like the advice I heard from John Williams, co-founder of Frog's Leap Winery in Rutherford, California, who said, "Don't let people beat the passion out of you!"

If You're Not the Only Decision-Maker— Getting Leadership Alignment

Some folks that write visions are sole operators who have enough authority to put a vision in place unilaterally. But most of us work with partners, family members, or key managers who are prominent—or equal— players in the picture, and we need to get in alignment with them around the vision of the future that we're working on. In fact, leaders pursuing different visions for the same project will almost always create enormous problems in an organization.

One alignment technique we use here is to begin the process with each of the partners in the group drafting their own vision. We're careful to be sure that everyone is clear on both the time frame and the topic we've chosen. Once each person has put together his or her vision, we compare drafts, listening carefully to what each has to say, capturing themes on a white board as we go. Usually you can condense the themes that you listed on the first go-round because there's almost always overlap in the various visions. We then give everyone a chance to weigh in on the strength of their feelings about each. If there are 10 topics up on the board, we might give each participant four votes, or something along those lines. The votes help the group get clear on the top priority items. Remembering that there aren't any "right" or "wrong" visions, we then work to identify common themes and come to agreement on a single vision that we can all work toward.

I don't want to make it seem like visioning work is always all bliss and harmony. We often wind up with themes that seem totally incompatible (though this happens less often than you might expect). We usually set those aside for a bit and come back to them later—often that move alone reduces tensions enough to allow the group to get to agreement.

Then again, sometimes it doesn't. While there are often ways to achieve compromise, other times there just aren't. All you can really do at that point is push back on the conflicting desires and work toward consensus. When we've got conflicting views, something has to give, or we have to come up with a different way to go forward.

On occasion, what we come to consensus on is the challenging realization that we actually have incompatible visions and that we might need to go our separate ways. While that's a difficult decision to make, if we have "preferred futures" that don't fit together, then the reality is that our vision needs to shift. It might become a positive picture of a future in which we're no longer working together, or at least not working together in the way we are now. It could mean splitting a company in two, living in different cities, etc. It's painful and difficult, but far more productive than having people passively go along toward a vision of the future that they don't really buy into. When that happens you get tension and trouble. Agreeing—openly and supportively—to pursue different but positive visions allows everyone to go in the direction they want to go. And ultimately that's a good thing.

Step 8. Let's Go—Start Sharing the Vision!

Once you're in alignment with your fellow decision-makers (or yourself) it's time to share the vision with everyone else who'll be involved in implementing it. (Naturally we have a recipe for this, too. It's called Bottom Line Change, and you can read more about it in Part Two of *Zingerman's Guide to Good Leading*.)

When you roll out your vision to the bigger group, it's pretty much inevitable that people will ask questions about how you intend to achieve the vision. Again, what they're asking you about is what we call the "how," as in "How are you going to get there . . . ?" The vision, however, is the "what"—a picture of what success looks like at the particular point in time in the future that you chose. It's totally appropriate—at least in our way of looking at things—that you don't know how you're going to get there (even though everyone will have been asking you). Later we'll figure out the "how"—that's what others might call their strategic plan, or, at least, the action steps that we believe will most effectively get us to where we're now clear that we're headed. (We're not down on strategic plans—it's just that we've found it to be way more effective to agree on the vision before we start to write out a long list of action steps that outline how we're going to get where we're going.)

I hope this recipe makes the potentially daunting or mysterious task of vision writing a bit more straightforward. Take it from a former skeptic: *writing a vision of greatness really is a lot easier than you might think.* As with any recipe, the more you work with this one, the better you'll get at it. And it's really, really worth the effort!

The Recipe for Writing a Vision of Greatness

INGREDIENTS

- Belief In The Process
- Your Gut
- Some Time
- Willingness To Make Yourself Vulnerable
- Readiness To Do Something Great
- You've Gotta Wanna
- The Willingness To Stick With The Process

PROCEDURE

Step 1—Pick Your Topic

Step 2—Pick Your Time Frame

Step 3—Put Together A List Of "Prouds"

Step 4—Write The First Draft Of The Vision
- Go For Something Great
- Write From The Heart
- Get In The Future
- Go Quickly
- Use The "Hot Pen" Technique
- Get Personal

Step 5—Re-View And Re-Draft

Optional: Step 6-A, 6-B and 6-C—More Re-drafts

Step 7—Get Input From ACES

Step 8—Let's Go—Start Sharing The Vision

Serves one entire organization liberally

How Long Should It All Take?

Writing an effective vision of greatness usually takes a lot less time than most people think. Ultimately I think the answer to the question "how long?" should be informed by your answers to two questions:

1. How long do you have?

    If you're working on a vision for a special salad that you're going to be serving in a few hours you don't really have a whole lot of time. Follow the visioning recipe quickly and get it out there where others can benefit from it.

2. How many people should be involved in writing it?

    The fewer people who need to be part of the draft the quicker it can get done—and the more likely that it will really be "out there" at the far end of the innovation and creativity scale. On the other hand, the more people you involve, the stronger their buy-in will probably be. And when the process is well managed, even large groups can come up with some pretty impressively out-of-the-box visions in fairly short periods of time!

Ultimately, there's not really a "right" time frame—you can move too slowly and you can move too quickly. Timing it all out is a craft, not a perfect, fancy PhD science.

A Long List of Questions to Address in Creating Your Vision

Let's say you're creating a vision for your business or organization. Look out three to five years (pick a date) into the future. Give your best shot at describing how things would look.

1. How big is your business? Physical size? Number of locations? Sales volume?

2. What are the most important factors by which you will measure your success (remember to get specific)?

    a. Your relative rank in the industry

    b. Financial success for the organization

    c. Personal financial success

    d. Contribution to the community

    e. Product or service quality

3. What standards of excellence are set by your organization?

4. What are the most important product lines or services you sell?

5. What types of products or services are sold in your industry that you won't offer?

6. How do you sell your products or services? Try to describe how the shopping experience at your business takes place. What makes that experience unique?

7. What special products or services are you offering to the market?

8. What sort of customers shop there?

9. Where do they come from?

10. If your customers were asked to list three noteworthy things about your business, what would they be?

11. How many staff members work in your business?

12. How would you describe your business's management style? (Participative? Top-down? Open book finances? Family style?)

13. What types of people are you hiring as managers? (Promoting from within? MBAs?)

14. How do people in the business relate to those around them? What sort of relationship do you have with your staff members? What do staff members say about their jobs?

15. What do you do? How much do you work? How much do you make?

16. How does your community view your business?

17. What do your suppliers say about you?

18. What do industry experts say about you?

This list is far from complete. It's meant to get you started in creating your vision, so feel free to add or subtract stuff as you see fit.

the bread crew laying farm loaves into willow baskets to rise

A Question of Systems

Or, "Yes, Anarchists Need Structure, Too"

Getting good at systems work is hardly what inspired me to get into business. But, as it turns out, systems play an important role in building any great business. I'm sure there are diagrammatic, schematic, academic sorts of articles and undoubtedly entire books on the subject that go into more detail than this essay. But since I'm not an engineer, an auto plant designer, an academic, or an MBA, what follows is . . . I guess it's a lapsed anarchist's angle on doing good systems work. While systems are usually perceived as the opposite of the art and spirit of a freewheeling anarchist approach to life, they're actually essential to the success of free-thinking people and the creative spirit in any kind of group setting. Mission statements, inspiring visions, high ethical standards, and big bottom-line results get most of the glamour, but without strong systems very little actually gets done well. As it turns out, designing and using them well actually calls for as much creativity as any painting, product development, or poetry writing you might do.

PART ONE: Struggling with Systems

One of the most important things I've learned over the years is that good leadership often depends a whole lot more on being able to ask the right questions than it does on immediately coming up with some seemingly brilliant answers. It's not that, eventually, we don't need answers as well. It's just that when the question we've posed isn't the proper one, it's really hard to move forward productively. Ask the wrong question and what almost always happens is that people end up expending way too much energy arguing over answers that aren't necessarily all that applicable anyway. And even when they do agree, it's more often than not only a matter of time before the question—improperly positioned as it is—is reopened again. I can say this is true with a high degree of certitude because I've spent way too much time screwing up all of it over the years.

So, speaking of questions, it might be smart to start with one now, maybe to get this piece going forward on the right foot, by asking the seemingly (but probably not so) obvious question . . . something along the lines of "What is a system, anyway?"

Being a book-oriented individual, I figured I'd get going by looking in the dictionary. Not shockingly there are a lot of answers. *Webster's* gives five.

Dictionary.com gives 16 (the last of which has nothing to do with what I'm talking about here, but which caught my attention anyway—it says that a system is, "in checkers, either of the two groups of 16 playing squares on four alternate columns"). Much more meaningfully for what I'm after here, I'll go with *Webster's* 3.a.—"An organized or established procedure."

Moving from the formal dictionary world to the Deli, as we define the term here at Zingerman's, "systems" are the way that we we've agreed to do what we do in our organization. Systems for us could be—and are—in place for payroll processing, recipes in the kitchen, procedures for packing orders at our Mail Order business, for double-checking carryout orders, for daily quality scoring, and for much, much more. Like every organization with more than 15 or so folks working in it, we have lots of systems at Zingerman's. Which is a good thing. The way I see it, systems are pretty much essential. Unless one wants to just run around in chaos (I'm an anarchist, but that doesn't mean I'm in favor of anarchy), systems are the structure around which the other parts of our work are framed. Sloppy, loose—or worse still, non-existent—systems can leave otherwise beautiful organizational fabric falling all over the place where it can get unpleasantly whipped by the wind, stepped on, or . . .

The Wrong Question: Take One

Coming back to questions then, in this case I think that an awful lot of time and energy have been expended over the years—both here in our own organization and I'm sure elsewhere as well—working with the wrong question. Depending on where you are, it might be some version of "What's more important? People or systems?"

I've certainly argued both sides of this debate at various times in my life. While one can build a logical case for either side, in hindsight I'd say it's a waste to spend the least bit of time debating the issue. The simple answer is really just "yes"—as in, "I'll take both!" Because:

(a) everything is going to be better for all involved if we have both really good people *and* really good systems. On top of which,

(b) why settle for one or the other when we can go after—and I think, get—both?

Which brings me to an insight that Paul Saginaw shared with me not all that long ago. After about a decade and a half of working with our Business

Perspective Chart (see page 79), Paul showed me a rather insightful addition to the way he teaches it.

Paul realized that the two parts of the chart that are usually pitted against each other when this "people or systems?" question is argued out—people (in this case represented by "Culture" on the left side of the chart) and systems (shown on the right)—aren't at all in opposition to each other, nor is one more important than the other. To the contrary, he pointed out, if you look at the chart you'll see that Culture and Systems actually look like the two weighing pans of a balance scale. And with that in mind, the organization actually works best when the two—people/culture and systems—are pretty much in balance.

Personally, I thought this idea of Paul's was pretty brilliant. The two do look like they're suspended from the three things above them on the chart—Mission, Vision, and Guiding Principles. Without the spiritual and strategic scaffolding that those three provide, the organization is likely to fall out of alignment all too easily—its "spine" will likely sway more than it should every time the economy swings up or down, the CEO gets some new strategic vision from Outer Space, or some big new opportunity is put into play without us doing due diligence. Any of those, or about a thousand other things, can throw the scales out of balance. But when the people and the systems are equally strong, I'm pretty confident that we're going to be operating at a really high level of effectiveness.

It's not that weird that the scale would be a bit out of balance on any given day. But if you get the two totally out of whack I think you're headed for trouble. Great people working with poorly designed systems usually leads to burnout, or worse still, a situation where the business fails to deliver, possibly so often that it will gradually go under. The opposite—great systems without good people— makes for a nice-looking structure, but creates a culture in which people follow the rules so religiously that they make what will seem like really silly mistakes (witness some of the more glaring *faux pas* of the current economic situation or the seemingly mindless questions cashiers ask you at so many chain stores).

I should clarify, by the way, for any hard-bitten bureaucrats or academics prone to shooting holes in other people's theories (I came from a family like that so I can pick on them) that while one could actually have the two (people and systems) in balance by having them both be equally ineffective that's clearly not the point here. It's obvious I guess but, what the heck, I'll just say it—if both systems and people suck, we're not going to be in business very long.

A Better Question:
"When It Comes to Systems, What's Your Vision of Success?"

Given my efforts to promote, teach, and practice the idea of visioning—which we've defined here as starting out with the end in mind and agreeing on a positive picture of what success looks like before we start mapping out how to move forward—it would make sense to provide a vision here, too. Because, as I've already pointed out a few hundred times in the many essays I've written on the subject, if we don't have a clear vision of what success is going to look like it's very unlikely that we're going to get there. Which makes it a seriously good question to ask: "What's your organizational vision when it comes to systems?" What follows is my own little draft—see what you think.

In our organization systems are embraced with the same passion as we do so many other things—traditional full-flavored food, amazing service to guests and co-workers, commitment to the community, open book finance, sustainability in all its elements (people, environment, soil, finance, personal energy), etc. We've got really well-designed systems, put together by a diverse team of smart, creative, collaborative, and curious people from all levels of our organization. People actively embrace those systems across the organization; they follow them because they believe that it's the right thing to do, and they understand the value that effective use of systems brings to our customers, the quality of our work, and the results that we get.

In every area of our organization—food, service, staffing, sanitation, administration, accounting, maintenance, etc.—our systems bring out the brainpower of the people involved, while providing effective structure and support in the interest of delivering ever-better results. Even where we have the most repetitive systems one might imagine, the people who use them understand why we use them, and when and how they were put in place ("the story behind the system").

To build an ever-stronger systems culture, we teach classes on systems design. Any number of folks who work here have learned how to do systems assessment, and also how to lead system repair in a relative hurry. Everyone here knows, too, that when the systems are in need of improvement—as they regularly will be—that each of us can and will take the lead on making that improvement. And they understand, and know how to use, our Bottom Line Change process when there's an improvement that they believe we should make. Their skill, insight, and willingness to take initiative to lead improvement means that they don't have to wait for a hundred weeks to figure out that a system isn't working. They know what good systems design means and have a . . . well . . . they have a working system for figuring out what's working well and what isn't.

In all of this systems stuff, we use technology—whether of our own design or of some already existing tools we take in from the outside—actively wherever it enhances the quality of the product we make, the quality of our customers' experience, or of our work environment.

As a result of all that we attract better, smarter, winning people who want to do great work, and their natural energy and desire is enhanced by having better systems. And to let them know how much we value their contribution, we have regular recognition—things like "new system of the month," "best systems improvement," etc.

Like I said, it's just a draft at this point. Thoughts, insights, and good questions are all welcome!

The Wrong Question, Take Two

Another sign that we're still asking the wrong question is arguing about whether or not, "The right system will always get rid of the possibility of human error." What's your take? Some say that the statement is supremely sagacious; others say it's somewhere south of superbly stupid. The truth, again, though, is that it's actually the wrong question. As in the case above—people vs. systems?—the answer here is actually, "Yes! Thank you very much, I'll take both!"

I love when some new learning comes into play that shows me the pointlessness of those sorts of arguments. It happened for me ages ago when I read Edgar Schein's essay, "Leadership and Organizational Culture," which made clear to me the silliness of the standard argument over what the "right" style of leadership is. Schein insightfully showed that there's no one style of leadership that's better or more generally successful than others. That, once more, is really the wrong question. The more meaningful query, he says, is, "What style of leadership is best for the particular stage of development that an organization is at?" That, for me, was a hugely helpful *aha!* It got me thinking of things in a new way, realizing that most all the styles good people espoused were potentially effective. But only if—and that's a big IF—they were applied at the stage of organizational development when the leader was supposed to be leading. Mismatches between stages and styles are common and almost always ineffective, and usually frustrating as hell for both the leader and the organization as a whole. So sticking a startup expert in to lead a mature company, or sending in a man who's great at managing maturity to run a startup, would both be recipes for high frustration and almost certain failure.

The same sort of late-in-life light bulb went off for me when I read an article in the *Harvard Business Review [HBR]* called "When Should a Process Be Art, Not Science?" Now, that, for a change, struck me as exactly the *right* question to ask. Written by Joseph M. Hall and M. Eric Johnson (speaking of questions, is it my imagination or do the folks who write for the *HBR* seem to have a much higher percentage of initials used in their names than the average American?), it did much the same thing for me on the issue of systems as Schein's essay did in regard to the argument over leadership styles.

Joseph M. and M. Eric have, I think, asked a much better question than all the people who argue one way or the other on this systems stuff. And the answer they have is basically the same as Schein's—*both* art and science are good, and the key is to match the type of system that one puts in place to the requirements of the situation. Sometimes, Hall and Johnson show, a straight-up system is right on. Sometimes it's not. To address the answer more effectively, they actually count four sorts of systems that one can, and should, embrace at appropriate times. I was struck right away by how well their model fit with what I'd known for years, but had been struggling to accept in light of other, more extreme, positions.

Training Problem? Management Problem? Systems Problem?

Before I get to the *HBR* framework, let me back up to another good question of a similar sort. This is one I learned from Maggie Bayless, managing partner of ZingTrain. She uses it when helping ZingTrain clients improve their training work, but I think you'll see it's of equal importance in relation to systems. Before you start trying to solve a problem, she points out, it's much more effective to actually first figure out whether you need to address a training issue, a management issue, or a systems issue. To that end, Maggie asks three good questions:

1. Is there already a system in place, agreed upon and documented, for performing the task—one that works if it is accurately followed?

   "If the answer to #1 is no," Maggie points out, "you're dealing with a *systems problem*. Training won't help you here until you've created a system that employees can actually be trained to use. What's needed is effective systems design."

2. Is there a system in place and the employees know how to use it, but it's not being followed?

   "If the answer to #2 is yes," she says, "you're dealing with a *management problem*. If employees already know how to use the system, they don't need more training. What's needed is effective leadership to ensure that systems are being used."

3. Is there a system in place, but employees don't really know what it is or how to use it?

   "If the answer to #3 is yes," Maggie concludes, "you have uncovered a *training problem*. What's needed is effective training. If you have no current training on this system the answer is obvious: create some. If you are currently offering training on this system, it isn't as effective as it needs to be, so you'll want to re-design it."

Since Maggie's focus when she wrote this was on training (I think she's pretty terrific at that work if you want to hire a consultant to come in and help you), she was primarily looking for folks who were answering "yes" to #3. In this case all three of her questions are good ones. Since I work in all three areas—systems design, management, and training—I use them to help me focus my energies in the right place. But for the purposes of this piece I'm going to address the problems that come up via Question #1.

PART TWO: Four Sorts of Systems

Type 1: Broken Processes

Type 2: Mass Processes

Type 3. Mass Customization

Type 4: Craft Systems

What Kind of Systems Are You Dealing With?

TYPE 1: BROKEN PROCESSES

If you speak the words aloud—"broken processes"—Hall and Johnson's first set of systems sounds a lot like "broken promises." Which isn't at all a casual comparison—that's really what broken processes are. When we have a system that isn't working, we're letting down our customers, our crew, our entire organization, and, actually, ourselves as well. While we as leaders can certainly continue to look the other way, broken processes aren't going to fix themselves. And the longer we wait, the worse the results we bring in, the smaller the pool of resources we have to dedicate to improvement, and generally the worse it's going to get for all involved. I've gone down that path and it ain't pretty. (I know the feeling, and all I'll say is that, if you even have a thought that you're on that path . . . you probably are—get off it as quickly as you can.)

To build on Maggie's question and answer about systems problems, it's important to be sure that the process really *is* broken before you start rebuilding it. Seriously, well over half the time I've discovered that a process wasn't broken—we just weren't using it as it was supposed to be used. (That begs another issue that I'll get to in a minute.) Again, my concern is to ask the right questions so that I'm effectively investing my limited resources.

Does the system effectively distribute the stress?

Well-designed systems usually don't require a manager to be the "bad guy" all the time—to the contrary, they minimize management's role in assuring that the system is effectively followed. Read through anything on the "Toyota Way" or work by Dr. W. Edwards Deming and you'll see what I mean. The more the system is designed to ensure that each stage can only proceed once the previous stage is done correctly, the more the pressure will come from within the team, not just from the "boss," and the more effective every person and process will be.

Are we as leaders doing our work?

To be clear, what follows is really a management problem—I just want to reiterate the importance of knowing when the burden is on us as leaders, and not on the system per se. If we as leaders regularly allow people not to follow the system as agreed, well . . . geez, that's on the proprietor, not the process. I'm embarrassed to say how many times I've come across this situation in our own organization. People keep saying there's something wrong with the system, but when I start looking for an explanation I find out that the problem is actually exceptionally straightforward—we're letting people avoid doing what we and they have agreed that they're supposed to do.

You've probably heard this one—the system says the manager (or someone) is supposed to check the work of the staff member, but they aren't doing it. What can I say? Changing the system isn't going to fix the problem—it will just expend time and energy remaking a process that probably wasn't broken in the first place. Meanwhile, most everything else is just as ineffective as it was before. In this context, getting different employees isn't going to help either— we, as managers, just have to do our work well, same as we're asking everyone else to do.

Do we have the right people in the right jobs?

All of this said, it is very possible that we have a really great system in place, that we as leaders are pretty much doing our part, that our training is actually darned good, but that things still aren't working as well as they really ought to be. In that case, part of our management work is to ask another question—like, "Have we put people in place who for whatever reason (physical skills, intellectual ability, interest, belief, or random acts of whatever) just aren't able to get the work done?" For instance, someone like me who has wholly illegible handwriting wouldn't be the person to put into a job that requires writing down anything important by hand. That's neither a systems problem nor a training problem. It's a management issue—it's our responsibility to make sure people are put into positions where they have a reasonably good shot at being successful. Mind you, if the right person is in the wrong job it probably isn't a reason to fire them. These folks are often a good fit for us organizationally, but our responsibility as leaders is to get them into a position where they (and the business overall) are more likely to be successful.

Then there's the other situation. The system simply doesn't work well. The process, as the boys from Harvard Yard said, is busted. To make sure this is the case you have to begin the repair work by actually using the existing system exactly the way it's been agreed upon. Follow it all the way through, diligently. If it works well, again, the system itself isn't the problem. It's one of the other options (management or training problem) listed a few pages back.

But when the agreed-upon process has been followed to a "T" and the odds of things going astray are still too high for your level of acceptance, *then it's time to redo the system*. I'm not going to get into systems mapping work here. I'm not the expert, and there's a wealth of good publications on the subject. On an informal basis, you know it's a systems problem when everyone is giving a hundred percent, you've got great people, everyone seems to spend hours talking about the need for better communication, and nevertheless failure rates are still higher than you think they should be.

How Broken Systems Can Be Fixed: The Story of the Greeting Game

It's not always that easy to sort out which type of problem one's dealing with. At times all three can overlap. The story that follows is about a situation in which we did some effective management work to encourage improvements, but then stalled after some initial headway. Ultimately there was also a "broken process" at the bottom of this thing. The management work helped, but it wasn't enough.

This is a tale about tables being greeted at the Roadhouse, our 175-seat restaurant that serves traditional, regional American food. We agreed years ago on a standard that said that every table should be greeted within five minutes of the time that a guest is seated. But as with many things we were falling short. To find out what was actually happening we started tracking our successes and failures. We fairly quickly discovered that we frequently had three or four "ungreeteds" a day, which obviously was not good—an ungreeted means that customers aren't very happy, we end up apologizing, and often comping items to make up for the problem. Costs go up, sales go down, and the situation adds unneeded stress to everyone's life.

So, to help get ourselves focused we set up what we called, "The Greeter Game." It offered a reward for the host team at the restaurant.

If we got to 50 days straight with no "ungreeteds" the hosts all got $50. There were smaller prizes at intermediate milestones. As games often do, this one helped get people to organize themselves effectively to make the system work. Within a month or so, things got *much* better. Awareness levels went way up. The hosts quickly found holes in the existing process and made changes to the way the system was set up. In less than a month they got it down to where any number of weeks actually had no "ungreeteds," and where a bad week was maybe two or three—a number we used to hit on a typical Tuesday alone.

As success became the norm after a year or so, the crew decided to raise their own bar. In the interest of making further improvements to service, they tightened the requirement for greeting a table from five minutes to three. Guests would get better service, sales and tips would likely increase, tables would turn faster . . . everyone would win. Wisely, they forecasted a higher number of "ungreeteds" for the first few weeks that we were running the new standard—it was likely that, in cutting two minutes off their goal, we'd fall short at least for a while.

With due diligence they worked their way down from about 40 ungreeteds in the first week to six or eight. From there the number went slightly up or down each week but made it down to zero only once, and that was it. People began to get frustrated—they certainly cared, but other than trying harder and talking over and over again about the need for better communication between servers and hosts, nothing really changed. Staff started to resign themselves to the "reality" that they wouldn't ever deliver a perfect week of greetings again.

To me these were signs that the process or system was broken—people were committed, training was solid, and the staff were following the system as we'd laid it out. But there were still too many misses. So what was wrong? Well, you'd have to map things out in detail to know for sure, but the story basically goes something like this:

- Hostess seats guests at a table.
- Notifies server, when possible (though of course it's not always possible), that s/he has done so.
- Server tries to get to table.
- If server is super busy or doesn't know that the table is in his or her section (this happens a lot when servers get sent

home and sections get switched at the end or early in the shift), the server doesn't get there in time.

- Hostesses *try* to check back to see if the table has been greeted. If not, they greet it or get a manager to help. When that happens it's a great save!
- It's also possible that a passing busser or manager might notice, but since it's not really their job they generally don't.

When I look at this "systems map," it quickly becomes clear that the process is broken. Why do I say that? Because nothing really radical or totally extraordinary has to happen for things to go wrong. I mean, if you told me that the only time a table didn't get greeted in a timely manner was when we had a hurricane hit or when a server slipped and broke his leg on the way to the table, I'd have a different response. Those truly are very rare occasions and we don't really need a system to prepare for those sorts of situations—the likelihood of either occurring is so small as to be irrelevant. But the truth, in this case, is that the way we set the system up meant that it wouldn't take a freak accident for us to fall short. All that was needed was a distracted host or a busy server—either of which is common in a successful restaurant. When we got the two happening in tandem, we'd almost always get an ungreeted guest.

So how should this system be set up? Well, proper process design work is the best way to figure it out. Working with the people who actually do the work, the ones who know what actually happens every day, we need to map the system one step at a time. Once we've done that we can look for the place where we'd like it to be much *more effectively self-managing*. I say that that's likely to be accomplished, in this scenario, by simply closing the loop on the system so that it's not dependent on any one server's ability to pay attention to all of his or her tables. Although I don't know for sure, I'm guessing that if we made the hosts fully responsible for checking that every single table has been greeted—instead of just having them do it when they have time or remember to check—the whole thing would work way better. In the process we'll be setting things up so that the host staff will actually self-manage: when the server hasn't been back to tell the host that the table has been greeted within two minutes, the hostess could then automatically go back to the table. Worst case? The guest has actually been greeted already, but we didn't know—no crisis there! A bad, but better, alternative possibility? The host finds that the guest hasn't been greeted but now will be, before they've sat for too long. While it's probably preferable that the server do the greeting, it's certainly better that the host does it than not having the guest be acknowledged at all!

To their credit this is pretty much what the Roadhouse host crew came up with—they divided the restaurant into "rooms," and each host is basically responsible for one of them. Plus they've put a system in place so that any time a server has more than two tables seated the host must ask the server before seating a third table in their area. It has already helped quite a bit!

(By the way, technology can often help. I think that if we're really getting going on fixing this, we might find some way to make our software at the host stand alert the hosts with a color code or "alarm ring" to get their attention. When they see or hear that, they act. The guest gets greeted in a timely manner and everyone wins!)

I don't think you need to be Six Sigma-certified to be able to make a pretty productive upgrade to a system. We've made tons of these sorts of improvements over the years. Our Mail Order crew has been particularly adept at it, but the same work has certainly been done most everywhere in the organization. It's not glamorous stuff, but truly it's way more effective than just telling everyone to "try harder!"

Type 2: Mass Processes

Let's shift from the broken to the bulletproof: these processes are truly made for careful, detailed, follow-it-every time, step-by-step scripting. It's the work that really is done best exactly the same way every time.

When you show this type of process to anarchistically oriented, independent-minded folks like myself, you often get a pretty negative response. The perception is that this is the sort of stuff that was at the heart of the whole early 20th-century industrial management approach, in which workers were treated like interchangeable machine parts. People were important only insofar as they performed a task that the system required. A manager didn't want to destroy his people anymore than he did his machines, but beyond that he didn't particularly care about their feelings or needs.

People who run factories probably haven't worried much about resistance to process—in their world, the idea that systems should be standardized is the norm. But since I work in the food world, not at Ford, I sometimes run into (understandable) resentment toward these sorts of strictly followed systems. I think it's just too easy for us to fall into a black-and-white way of thinking: "art is good; systems are bad." But this sort of oversimplification is not reflective of reality, and it's definitely not very helpful.

Paying proper attention to systems design and effective implementation—whether we're shipping $75-a-bottle olive oils or building big engine parts—does pay off. Our Mail Order crew has spent years studying and implementing the principles of the Toyota system, which is basically designed around the good work done by Dr. W. Edwards Deming in the second half of the 20th century. I've not done a thorough study of his work, but I've read a fair bit and seen a lot of it in action, and I will tell you that, in the right situation, it works really well. And contrary to those who see systems as restrictive, the approach actually appeals to the intelligence of the people who use it, and in the process usually makes their work more rewarding and effective.

Systems of this sort are perfect for products or jobs that are the same every single time—same stuff in, same stuff out. A process that takes into account the most likely problems and reliably keeps those issues from causing complications. Packing boxes, testing milk for sanitation before cheesemaking, quality testing products before they're sold or served—these are all good examples of instances where effectively standardized processes are totally appropriate and very helpful.

Anyway, I'm not the world's expert on totally industrial, effectively standardized processes. All I'm here to say is that as an anarchist and a decently creative person with a lot of innate authority issues I really do believe that great systems are critical to any organization's success. And that in the right settings—as outlined above—there's no reason that those systems can't be made fun, respectful of the people using them, and basically foolproof all at the same time. This is where consistency pays off big time because it reduces time spent on unproductive variations, and reduces waste so that resources can be applied in other parts of the business that can benefit from more creativity.

The Nick's Pizza's Sidework Story

I learned this approach from the folks at Nick's Pizza, who have a great business in suburban Chicago. I heard them present at the annual

Open Book Finance conference, known as the Gathering of Games, in St. Louis. They ran through a whole range of creative systems that they use in their restaurants, but this is one of the ideas I liked best.

It's a system that encourages staff to self-regulate their efforts in one of the most mundane, annoying, and oft-skipped bits of work in the restaurant world—what's known in the industry as "sidework." It's all that stuff like cleaning shelves, scrubbing stoves, stocking napkins, filling ketchups, etc. No one loves doing it; no manager loves checking on it. So morale goes down, problems proliferate, and people focus on getting away with not doing things instead of doing the right thing: thinking of the success of the group and going after greatness. All of which generally contributes to the negative energy that comes from that old command-and-control approach so common in the business world.

The pizza guys came up with what I thought was a brilliantly simple, easily-repeated system based on self-direction, trust, and individual responsibility. It's easy to monitor visually. And it retains an important teaching role for managers without forcing them to exercise their authority just to make the system work. We've put a version of it in place at our Mail Order business and it works well here, too. Basically it goes like this:

Each position's opening (or, later, closing) responsibilities are listed on a large laminated "Ops" card. They sit in slots on the wall in what looks like one of those old time-card racks. At the start of each shift—before the work has been done—the side of the card that's facing out is bright red on top. That allows everyone in the restaurant to see from a distance how much stuff still might not have been done. The cards list all the tasks that are supposed be done, including everything from filling salt and pepper shakers to oven cleaning. Which is great. No reason to make it a secret—information is shared equally. Having the list in writing and on-shift eliminates the oft-heard, "Oh, I forgot that we were supposed to do that" and the need for an all-knowing manager who walks around telling everyone what they have to do and looking for shortfalls.

When the team members are doing the work they take the card and use it as a guide. More experienced folks probably don't need the guidance and just use the cards to double-check themselves against the list. When the team members have finished all the tasks they put the card back in the rack, but this time turned over so that the bright green strip at the top is what's showing. There's no actual checkout: the system is based on the belief that all team members will take full responsibility for the quality of their work. To that end, they place great emphasis on using affirmative, proactive "I" statements on the cards. So, rather than the more traditional, "Stock side stand," the Ops card might say, "I have completely stocked the side stand." The language encourages a sense of ownership and responsibility.

If a task is left undone, the team member leaves the card with the red side out. In that case, the manager might ask this person how the shift went, and listen carefully to the answer. A manager can then go further, if necessary, by asking if there was any work that the team member wasn't able to do, was unclear about, or had a hard time with. As owner and founder Nick Sarillo made clear, the system is, "always a question of checking for understanding first, rather than telling them what you think they did or didn't do."

This, I think, is a pretty brilliant approach. By asking the "right" question the managers at Nick's give their team members the chance to be totally on top of things. Rather than having the manager presume that a team member is slacking, the team member has the chance to explain that, "I couldn't fill the ketchups on the side stand shelf because our order didn't come in today." In that case the manager can make sure someone else does the work the next morning. The team member might also reasonably say, "I wasn't able to change the light bulb in the ladies' room because the fixture is broken." Again, the team member, not the manager, is taking the lead on the tracking. Once that exchange is done, the team member heads out. As the shift gets close to its start or end time, anyone can see from 15 feet away that more and more of the cards in the rack are turned out to the green side. When they're all green, the crew is ready to go!

While the work is really self-regulated, the managers still have an important part to play. They have their own opening and closing Ops cards to use, and some of the items on their list may replicate those on the cards of their team members. Doubling up increases the odds that critical things will be done properly. Best case, the work is done as well as the team members said it was. Worst case, they said it was done well, but the managers don't agree and fix it to their satisfaction. Either way the manager has a meaningful way to communicate with the team member about work quality.

Nick says effectively putting together the Ops cards is one of the keys to making this system work—he and his colleagues are very mindful about the way they list the tasks (again, using affirmative, present-tense language) and including the right items. "Writing up and creating the cards," he shared, "can be pretty time-consuming initially. But once they're done they're good for years." The whole thing is based on trust, and Nick's has successfully built a culture where people operate at a high level of accountability. "They don't bring the card to the manager, they just turn it over to the green side and the manager trusts them," he says. And it works—Nick's has very low staff turnover, high sales, and operates with a high degree of effectiveness on all levels.

While it was helpful to me to hear the HBR *authors' thoughts on the first two sorts of systems, it was actually their ideas on the next two that really helped me move forward. Hall and Johnson made concrete what I already knew but wasn't really sure how to explain.*

Type 3. Mass Customization

This is the system that's really well suited to those sorts of situations I talked about at the beginning of this essay—the ones where people argue that you shouldn't even have a system—or, alternatively, that there must be something totally wrong with the system if the product or service doesn't come out exactly the same way every time. Again, those folks, I think, are asking the wrong questions. The right one would be something along the lines of, "Do you have a product that's made in significant quantities, and do you have a good system and/or time-tested recipe for making it, but, nevertheless, the product comes out slightly different every time?" If so, then I think you have a system that the *HBR* boys might call "Mass Customization."

The artisan breads we make at our Bakehouse fit this description perfectly, I think. We have great systems and well-tested recipes. And we do a good bit of training to help people learn to use them. But the reality is that, because of changes in humidity, temperature, etc., every day's bread will come out of the oven looking and tasting a little bit different than the previous day's loaves. We don't have to like that—it's just the way it is. To eliminate that modest variation, we would have to compromise on quality and make the bread a totally systems-friendly industrial product that would, Wonder of wonders (pun intended), look, smell, feel, and taste the same way every day. Instead, we choose to accept that small range of variability. In order to have the chance to hit the really high note—those few days a year where all the elements align and we produce a 10 out of 10, totally perfect, product—we have to accept that some days the humidity, the bacteria, and the temperature might mean that we only get a 7 or an 8.

So, again, my *HBR* heroes made clear what I kind of already knew: *mass customization is great as long as our customers are accepting of a modest level of variability in the product.* That isn't always the case—I don't think it would work well with car tires, computers, or pharmaceuticals. Consumers want and need total consistency in those types of products. But in the world of artisan food, consumers have come to expect that there's some natural, desirable swing in flavor and texture from one day's production to the next. In fact, they actually *like* the fact that that variation exists and understand that, to some degree, that's what they're paying for. In other words, if the folks who buy our bread like the fact that some days it's a bit crustier/darker/lighter/softer/whatever, then the process is working.

Mind you, mass customization doesn't mean anything-goes anarchy. It actually requires lots of training and very strict, well-designed, and well-managed systems that can be used to check quality and make sure that what we're putting out for sale is within an acceptable range of variation. Someone needs to taste and evaluate the bread—not just dismiss any aberration as OK because it's handmade. Here at Zingerman's we score products on a scale from 0 (terrible) to 10 (totally terrific). If anything scores below a six we definitely don't sell it. Actually, six is basically borderline. Seven is good, though not really great. Eight is better still—very good, if not exactly amazing. Nine is . . . pretty fantastic and special. Ten is super terrific. (Eleven on a ten-point scale is over the top. I call it "an Oprah" because "11" is what she scored our #97 sandwich from the Deli on her own scale of 1 to 5.)

Market the Difference That Mass Customization Makes

I'm not being disingenuous here: if the variation in product that comes from a system of mass customization isn't very interesting or meaningful then we're probably better off not bothering. On the other hand, if, for instance, all our tomatoes are grown the same way but they taste a tad bit sweeter some days, or if the color of the bread's crust varies a bit depending on the weather, we shouldn't hide that variation. To the contrary, I say: highlight it! If you have a spot that calls for a system of mass customization, then by all means make sure that your staff and your customers all know what that daily difference might be (no surprises!), and what they should look for to fully appreciate it.

Type 4. Craft Systems

This last of Johnson and Hall's four types really made me smile. The question they posed is, "When does a well-designed system need to be both systemically sound and still artistic?"

I've struggled with stuff like this for years. I tried reviewing and redoing any number of systems in a hundred different ways, but, no matter what I did, the "people" part of it was just too big. I couldn't for the life of me figure out how to guarantee that a counter person, server, or phone sales staffer was going to put the right amount of affect into their tone, actually make eye contact with the guest, or really bring the kind of energy to the interaction that we were looking for. We could train for it and test to see if they knew how to do it. But beyond that... there just wasn't any way to be sure that when they were actually working one-on-one with their customer, without a manager standing next to them, that they'd be able to manage the reality that customers come in in different moods every day and need to be handled very differently accordingly.

Seriously, I really wanted to figure out a way to make the work pretty much foolproof. But every way I looked at it, it just kept coming down to the fact that while we hire really well, train our staff to the ends of the earth, and set up the work involved very carefully, at the "end" of the process there is still this very human, variable, out-of-anyone's-control interaction. In these instances, good systems can certainly help, but they can't guarantee success. Like it or not, it's just not possible to take the element of chance out of a situation that involves two human beings communicating with each other.

Interestingly, in hindsight, I can see where I wasted way too much time arguing this issue and its systemic solution. Although the "people first" advocates don't worry about this sort of stuff in the first place, I'd spent years hearing from their counterparts—"the process people"—that we ought to be able to design systems so well that we'd never have problems. These conversations usually descended into the sorts of arguments I mentioned at the get-go: "There's too much emphasis on system"; "There's not enough emphasis on systems"; "People are paying attention to systems at the expense of the people"; "Good systems make it so that everyone will be successful all the time." You know the drill, I'm sure.

The *HBR* article got me to stop arguing and embrace the reality that what we have here isn't a failure to communicate, nor is it a broken process: while you can script service sequences and tell staff exactly what they're supposed to say in every setting, the problem is that service doesn't work that way. It's similar to the Wonder Bread example I mentioned in the last section: when you try to create a completely uniform system where everything is totally scripted, staff usually end up (a) sounding like robots, and (b) making silly statements and ineffective decisions because they're understandably afraid to depart from the script. Service just has way too many variables to be mass-customized.

So, back to the question at hand: When does a well-designed system need to be both systemically sound and still artistic? And the answer is:

When we have a sound system (no, not the kind you listen to your music on!), well-trained people, and so many variables that you can't guarantee consistency, then what we have here is what the *HBR*ers call an "artistic system." I've switched that up slightly to call it a "craft system," because "art," as I've learned the term, basically means you can do whatever you want as long as it's creative and inspired. For us it's not all art: there's actually a big need for good science and solid systems work.

The key with this fourth type of system, the *HBR* boys point out, is to design very specific processes that are rather rigidly used all the way up to the final "artistic" act. Their article includes a number of great examples: Steinway piano boards, Ritz Carlton service providers, etc. Let's take the example of the actual interaction with the guest. By making the system as tight and consistent as possible in the early stages of the work, we're able to minimize any unnecessary variability and bring us to the moment of systemic truth. While this systems funnel can't guarantee ultimate success, it definitely gives us a far greater chance of getting there than we would have otherwise.

Craft systems are, I think, exactly what we do in all our service work here at Zingerman's. We want very careful and thorough training. We want to standardize as many parts of the system leading up to the customer interaction as possible. And we want to prepare our staff members to handle all of the various sorts of service situations they may come up against. But once the staffers actually go out on stage, we have to rely on their ability to adapt, to use their insights, and to make great things happen all on their own. The fact that we actually free our staff to do this is a big part of what sets the service work we do apart from what happens at most other businesses. We've also learned that it's an important factor in why our best people enjoy working here so much. In all the service work we do, we expect our people to think and adapt in order to get the sort of results we're looking for—great service to customers and co-workers, great financials, and great product quality.

In this context, our 3 Steps to Great Service and 5 Steps to Handling Customer Complaints (see *Zingerman's Guide to Giving Great Service* for details) provide a broad framework, but they don't even attempt to script out entire conversations. Instead, they give effective, well thought-out and well-practiced guidelines: the kind of flexible structures (what we refer to as "organizational recipes") that prepare our staff members—i.e., the craftspeople at the end of the system—to use their expertise and insight to get to great results.

The Burger Challenge

Cooking on a restaurant line that uses scratch ingredients is almost always a "craft system." Take hamburgers. The challenge is that there's just no way I know of to ensure 100-percent perfectly cooked-to-order, hand-pattied burgers from the Roadhouse's oak fired grill. It's not like systematizing the proper packing of a box on our Mail Order production line. Here at Zingerman's, we choose the more difficult culinary course to navigate, which is to ask our customers how they'd like their burger cooked, and then attempt to deliver it. The reality is that our decision to pack the patties by hand, the temperature variation from the wood fire, and the number of other items on the grill, among any number of factors, all mean the cook has to be really skilled to get the burger properly cooked. In fact, the burger can easily be cooked properly on the left side but a bit under- or overcooked on the right.

The way they get around this problem in the corporate world is to simply avoid it—you get your burger cooked one way and that's it. Even when restaurants offer you a choice of "doneness," in most cases they're able to deliver it only because they purchase machine-pattied meat, ship it frozen, and then cook it on a more consistent (not wood-fired or open-flame) surface. The problem? Pre-formed burgers don't taste as good, freezing the meat affects its texture and taste, and you don't get that nice subtle smoky flavor we like from the wood. Consumers who go to the chains are apparently OK with that—no one orders their McDonald's

Quarter-Pounder rare, and I doubt that too many people ever send their Happy Meal back because it's "overcooked."

Both approaches—craft and industrial—can work in the burger world, but the final product will be pretty different in each case. We in leadership need to decide which problems we want to work with: in this case, that means choosing between a totally consistent mass-market process that yields a blander, well-done-only, burger, or a craft process that counts on the cook (and the sous chef, who does a final check on the food before it goes to the table) to use their skills and experience to manage the heat and the meat to come up with a great product almost all of the time.

(In fact, burger cooking might actually be a good candidate for mass customization. The problem is that customers seem to have much less tolerance for variation in their burger doneness than they do for that bit of inconsistency in our hearth-baked artisan breads. Which makes me wonder if we should shift the way we present the product? Food for systems thought, that's for sure.)

Why the Wrong Sort of System Can Create Suboptimal Results

A good friend of mine in the Midwest was having problems with some software she'd purchased. She called the company's customer service line to get the situation sorted out. Long story short, they failed to help her fix the problem despite her constructive efforts to get to a good outcome. Frustrated, as a final shot at getting things figured out, she explained to the service staff member that if he couldn't help her more effectively she was going to go out and look for another company to use.

Here at Zingerman's, where we have a craft system in place, the staff member would probably have apologized for failing to fix the problem, and then gotten a manager or someone else to provide her with more effective assistance. But instead, this fellow took her statement that she was ready to take her business elsewhere to mean that they'd arrived at some kind of resolution, and asked calmly if he could now mark her file as closed.

She was so stunned by this seemingly wacky response that she asked him if he'd heard what she said. He answered politely that he had, told her it sounded like things were now resolved (since they couldn't agree on a good way forward), and repeated his polite request to mark the file as finished. In the context of delivering great service, his question is completely absurd. But I'm sure he was following his company's system to a "T," since it more than likely said something like, "As soon as you've agreed with the customer on a resolution, mark the file as closed." He did his work according to spec, but in the process his subpar service cost his company a customer (maybe more than one, since my friend understandably told this story to hundreds of her friends and colleagues).

To add systems insult to service injury, my friend got an email moments after she hung up from the call, noting that her file was now closed and thanking her for being such a wonderful client. And, the auto-email added, if she needed further assistance in the future she should just give them a call. Yikes!

POST-PRODUCTION MEASUREMENT TO HELP MANAGE MASS CUSTOMIZATION AND CRAFT SYSTEMS

Whenever you have an element of "art" at work in the final stage of a system, tight post-delivery measurement can help keep things on track. For instance, we regularly survey customers about our service to see how well we've been doing. When it comes to burgers, the Roadhouse crew orders one secret burger per shift to see how well the grill cooks are handling their work. While this post-production measurement doesn't completely eliminate problems, it does allow us to reward staff when things are going well and correct course quickly when they aren't.

SYSTEMS AND SERVICE

From a service standpoint, systems need to be designed to exceed customers' expectations: to create a structure in which accuracy and attention to detail are stressed over and over again. Reviewing each element of your system and identifying all the ways that customer service can suffer or be improved can be a big step toward upgrading service quality. Having a great attitude while working with a poorly designed or inconsistently observed system is better than having a bad attitude with even a good system, but the optimal situation is when both attitude and systems are geared toward giving great service. No matter how good the people you hire, they're likely to work about 10 times better if you put them in a system that's customer friendly. For example, putting great people on the phone to back up a poorly constructed website is better than not having anyone respond to customer complaints, but clearly the whole system would be better if the website was working well!

Concluding Questions

So ... with all that said and (well?) done, I hope that I've at least given you a bit of new food for systems thought, and at best helped to frame what can be a very confusing jumble of organizational "stuff." When it comes to working on our businesses, the best single investment of time I can think of is attending to systems design, effective management of those systems, providing the training to support them, and identifying—and then asking—ever-better questions. While it's way easier in the moment to just complain about complexity, asking the right question and coming up with an effective systems answer can be the difference between long-term success and failure.

Let's leave you, then, with a few good questions to consider:

How does all this apply in your area?

When you list the systems in your organization, which ones are broken?

Which are Mass Processes?

Which qualify for Mass Customization or a Craft System?

How can those systems be improved to enhance the effectiveness of your already excellent staff?

Do you regularly review your organization's systems to be sure you've got the right types for the right settings?

And how can you use this stuff to make your work more fun, profitable, and positive?

I hope some or all of this thinking about systems will help you ask more effective questions in your own organization. And that doing so will allow you to more effectively allocate resources, get more done, and have more fun doing it.

anya pomykala pulling shots of espresso

Writing and Using Guiding Principles in Running Your Business

Putting Ethics into Action

It's hardly new news to advocate putting one's organizational principles down on paper. But, sadly, all too many places write them up and then fail to actually use them in any meaningful way. As with mission statements or visions, it may not seem urgent that you take the time to write your principles down and get agreement on them. It's certainly not the most glamorous work one can do. But if I had to choose between spending my time on a typical team-building exercise and reaching agreement on a set of values or principles, I'd take the latter 10 times out of 10. You actually get great team-building just by defining the ethics and values of your organization, and the document you end up with will help you make more effective decisions.

I want to preface this piece by stating up front that I know full well that we've never lived our own ethical standards perfectly; that we're always striving to improve, to more effectively close the inevitable gap between what we say and what we do. Getting guiding principles down on paper won't eliminate that gap. But, used well, the process can help us to more effectively become the organization of our choosing, rather than being constrained by the unpleasantness of present-day realities.

Whether you talk about "values," "ethics," or what we at Zingerman's call "guiding principles," the key is to be clear about what your values are and thoughtfully address the role they play in your work. At Zingerman's, our Guiding Principles define how we're going to behave and interact with those around us as we work toward our long-term vision and mission. In other words, the Guiding Principles are not *why* we're here or *what* we do; they're the framework for how we're going to relate to others around us while we work. Put simply, our commitment to these principles is a way of affirming that, for us, as for many others, the ends don't justify the means.

It's hard to remember exactly what triggered our decision to write down the Guiding Principles. I do know that it happened at a point in our organizational life when we had grown beyond just me and Paul and a couple of employees. As a startup business we'd done just fine without documented ethical standards. But 10 years on we found ourselves with nearly a hundred people on staff and half a dozen managers, all of whom were representing the organization to each other and our community at large. And it became increasingly clear to us that different people in the organization were driven in their work by different—at times, conflicting—values. As you might imagine this led to frustration for all involved, sapping energy that would have been better spent improving customer service and increasing sales.

We came up with eight guiding principles in the early '90s, and we still live by the same eight today. Although I believe strongly that ours are great for us, I would never argue that they're right for others. What's really essential is that everyone you work with be clear on what your principles are and agrees to live by them during their tenure in your organization.

Zingerman's Guiding Principles

1. *Great Food!*
   At Zingerman's, we are committed to making and selling high-quality food.

2. *Great Service!*
   If great food is the lock, great service is the key.

3. *A Great Place to Shop and Eat!*
   Coming to Zingerman's is a positive and enjoyable experience for our guests.

4. *Solid Profits!*
   Profits are the lifeblood of our business.

5. *A Great Place to Work!*
   Working at Zingerman's means taking an active part in running the business. Our work makes a difference.

6. *Strong Relationships!*
   Successful working relationships are an essential component of our health and success as a business.

7. *A Place to Learn!*
   Learning keeps us going, keeps us challenged, keeps us on track.

8. *An Active Part of Our Community!*
   We believe that a business has an obligation to give back to the community of which it is a part.

For the full Glossary of Zingerman's Guiding Principles see page 325.

What We've Gained from Having Guiding Principles in Writing

1. CLEAR EXPECTATIONS LEAD TO BETTER . . . EVERYTHING

At every level of organizational life we've found that clearer, more effectively defined expectations help a lot. Job satisfaction goes up. Less time is wasted arguing over things that were decided ages ago. Energy that used to go into mind reading can be diverted into more productive pursuits like reading good books or waiting on customers.

2. CLEAR EXPECTATIONS CREATE A MORE BALANCED LIFE

Living your organizational life in keeping with your values feels better and is less stressful and more rewarding. You're being true to yourself and your peers, family, customers, and friends. In *The Answer to How Is Yes,* Peter Block points out that the recent emphasis on balancing home life and work life is misplaced. I agree: *It's all one life.* Yours. While balance is all well and good as a goal, real life isn't broken down into completely clear chunks labeled "work" and "home." The reality of the world is that no one who's passionate about more than one thing is likely going to ever really have enough time to do it all. I think we're going to get farther by embracing the struggle than avoiding it.

What Block so insightfully argues is that the bigger issue of balance is the conflict between people's personal values and the values of the places where they go to work every day. Because suppressing your values while you're at work is a very difficult way to live. No matter how good the money may be, how scary it may be to consider changing jobs, how daunting it is to bring this issue up with co-workers, you can't deny the enormous stress caused by living this kind of double life.

Getting your organization's guiding principles on paper—assuming that they match your own values fairly closely—is the first step toward rectifying this situation. Even if you discover a gap between your personal values and those of the group, at least you're closer to understanding the situation, which is usually the first step toward fixing it. If it turns out there's no gap, more power to you. Either way, life is likely to be more balanced when you've written down the guiding principles and actively put them into practice.

3. YOU ATTRACT LIKE-MINDED PEOPLE

If we're up front about our principles we're more likely to attract people with a similar set of values. Think about it the other way, too: if we don't have clear values—or, worse still, don't live by the ones we have—then we may attract unprincipled (or differently principled) people to our business!

I should add that, while a solid set of well-implemented guiding principles makes a very big difference for us in recruiting like-minded staff members, we don't advertise the principles. We've always chosen to let the world judge us by our actions rather than our words. If others are aware of our principles, it's because we've actually lived up to our own standards, not because we're telling them what they should do.

4. YOU ACHIEVE ALIGNMENT AMONGST PRINCIPALS ON PRINCIPLES

It's unfortunately way too common for leaders of an organization to have significant but unstated conflicts over values. Failure to put our principles on paper allows us as leaders to avoid coming clean with each other: ethical differences will stay in the closet and we'll act out our conflicts on our staff or even our customers. Whereas I've found over and over again that if we agree on a long-term vision for the organization and a clear set of principles then we can get through almost any difficulty or challenge.

5. GUIDING PRINCIPLES LEAD TO BETTER DECISION-MAKING

Guiding principles form a framework within which we can more effectively make day-to-day decisions. Decisions in business are rarely black and white. A clear ethical framework makes our decision-making more consistent and effective in the midst of uncertainty and change—which in turn helps the organization develop in a positive and progressive way.

A Recipe for Writing Your Guiding Principles

1. DRAFT WHAT'S IN YOUR HEART

The first step is to draft a list. If you could have your way with the world—at least, your world—describe how you'd want your organization to work. What will day-to-day life be like: how will you talk to each other, work with each other, coordinate with the community or relate to the world around you? (By contrast, guiding principles are not bottom-line, strategically critical results. They aren't market differentiators. They aren't something to do just because you read about them in this book. They're values that you really hold dear. And hopefully they're values that most members of your organization share.)

Whatever comes to mind is worth writing down. But remember that this is about what you *truly believe* to be the core values of your organizational life. The principles you put your name to should be ones that you—as individuals and as an organization—are fully ready to live by.

Please don't just throw down what you think others want to hear—this has to really be from the heart. Remember, you're going to have to live with the results. In fact, I'd recommend that you hold true to your principles even if they become a strategic *dis*advantage. Why? Because if you're willing to forgo your guiding principles when they become inconvenient, then it's probably not worth your time to write them down in the first place.

When you're doing this work, don't be afraid to put down ideas that feel like they're common sense. What may seem obvious to you isn't necessarily so to anyone else. Take the issue of learning. Paul and I always shared the drive to learn more about what we were doing and seek out ever-better ways to do it. But through painful experience we learned (more often than I'd like to admit) that most folks don't share this drive; and that even those who are for it in theory frequently fail to actually follow through. Are they bad people? Not at all. It's just that, based on their behaviors, at least, they live a different set of values around learning than we do.

2. Take the "should" test

You know that internal monologue we have, where we critique the behavior of the people working around us? I call it the "shoulds": "people should be on time," "people should have more fun," "people should be more supportive of each other." That sort of stuff. If you have shoulds in your head about the way the people in your organization ought to be behaving, I'd suggest that you probably *should* include them on your list. Because if something's in your head that way, essentially it's an unspoken expectation. And in my experience unspoken expectations don't work.

Ironically, many folks with whom I've discussed this argue vociferously that they "shouldn't" have to bother writing down their principles because it's so "obvious" that this is the way adults/good staff/professionals ought to act. To which I just say, "No, you *should* have to." It's part of the work of building a great business. If we don't write it down, it's not going to happen. And we'll stay stuck in the "shoulds" instead of sharing the expectations we really hold in our hearts.

3. Test the draft with stories

For each item on your list of principles, find a few stories from your past that illustrate what you believe in. Share them with others. Talk about how they apply: how they helped you (perhaps unknowingly), or how you might have handled things differently. Real-life examples are important because they recognize the challenging and complex ways that life unfolds every day. As you do this it's likely that you'll discover that some of the items on your draft list don't work as well for you as you first thought. Nothing wrong with that—if everyone involved is in agreement, just take them off the list.

4. TEST STORIES AGAINST THE DRAFT

Now do the opposite. Think of some of the most difficult situations you've had to work through over the years. Is there a principle that would have helped? If so, make sure it's on the list.

5. WRITE A GLOSSARY

Having drafted, tested twice, and then re-drafted, it's time to sit down to develop what we call a "glossary," where you actually give written clarity to your broad, conceptual statements. In my experience this is the most difficult—but also most valuable—part of the work.

As you've seen above, one of our principles here is that, "At Zingerman's we are committed to making and selling high-quality food." Sounds good, right? Who could argue with that? Probably no one. And because many organizations stop with that sort of simple statement they never get to the more meaningful questions like, "What the heck do you mean by 'high-quality'?" The issue at this point is less commitment and more clarification: we need to have a definition of what the phrase "high quality" really means. Because, let's face it, quality is clearly defined very differently at Subway than it is at Zingerman's.

Since we've agreed on definitions, everyone here can quickly and succinctly tell customers who ask that "great food at Zingerman's" means:

> "Flavor in our food comes first. We choose our products first and foremost on the basis of flavor. We sell food that tastes great. We want our food to be full-flavored, delicious and enjoyable to eat."

And,

> "Traditionally made and great-tasting foods from around the world. We sell foods that have roots, a heritage, a history. We seek out traditionally made, frequently hand-crafted foods, which are primarily

of peasant origin. These are foods that people have been eating for centuries and will continue to eat for centuries to come."

Are those the only possible definitions of "quality"? Not at all. There are probably thousands, including many very good ones. But they just aren't ours. So when we're trying to make a decision on a new product we begin with those two simple but all-important statements: if a prospective product isn't really flavorful and if it isn't pretty traditional we're probably not going to sell it, no matter what everyone else is doing.

Is that a difficult decision to make? In a sense. Although I want things to be black and white, these sorts of principle-based decisions rarely are. But when we evaluate an opportunity in light of our guiding principles, we know in our hearts and heads what the right decision is—we'll pass up the short-term gain from a trendy product if it doesn't meet our ethical framework for quality.

I'll cite another example. Under the heading "Great Relationships" our principles state that, "Successful working relationships are an essential component of our health and success as a business." Again, that's nice, but it's still so general as to be almost meaningless. So in our glossary we spell out what a successful working relationship is:

> **"We are committed to each other's success.** Each of us is committed to the success of everyone else who works at Zingerman's. We go out of our way to support each other, to listen well, to facilitate and encourage each other's growth and advancement."

This has been a particularly important issue for us in our organizational development, but it's *not* an easy principle to uphold. Every one of us works with at least one other person who we believe could do better in his or her job. Unfortunately, standard social operating procedure is that the more we get frustrated with that person (we'll call him Bill), the more likely we are to tell everyone *but* Bill. But if we're truly going to honor our commitment to Bill's success, then we need to go directly to him. And if we, as leaders, allow someone who's frustrated with Bill to fail to share their concerns with him then we're sending a message that our principles aren't really all that important.

Take note that Bill's actual performance is a totally separate issue. If someone won't talk to him productively (even with our coaching and encouragement), then ultimately it's that person—not Bill—who is going to have to leave the organization, because that person is the one who is simply not upholding our principles.

Making Guiding Principles More than Just a Piece of Paper

Putting our Guiding Principles on paper was a significant achievement. But the far more important accomplishment has been successfully, if imperfectly, weaving them into our everyday work. Here are some of the ways we've made that happen:

1. MAKE THE PRINCIPLES PART OF THE HIRING PROCESS

Prospective team members need to know about our standards and understand that they'll be expected to live them and teach them. If there isn't alignment between our organizational values and the applicant's, then the working relationship isn't going to be successful, regardless of how impressive the person's resume may be.

2. TAKE TIME TO TALK ABOUT DECISIONS IN THE CONTEXT OF YOUR VALUES

Management decision-making, like cooking, is a craft, not a science. The only way to build understanding of what our values mean is to agree on how we'll apply them to real issues. This is no different than making time to taste food together: Without shared tasting experiences we're left with nothing more than platitudes about "high quality" and "full flavor." Only when we all taste the same dish at the same time and compare sensory notes can we really know what terms like "spicy" or "long finish" mean *to us.* Similarly, only by taking time to talk through ethical issues and how they impact our work can we really get straight with each other on what it means to "treat people with dignity" or "give service to the community."

3. TEACH THE PRINCIPLES REGULARLY

Without question the act of getting up in front of our peers, partners, and staff to teach the principles has made it far more likely that we're going to live them. If nothing else, it's embarrassing to talk about our values and then not live them. At Zingerman's I review our principles every two weeks or so when I teach the orientation for new staff. And we bring them up in every class we do, too, whether it's about cheese maturing, management, training, or trimming pastrami.

4. EXAMINE YOUR REWARD SYSTEMS AND SEE HOW THEY SUPPORT YOUR PRINCIPLES

It's essential that our reward and pay programs be in sync with, and actually support, our values. What message would we send if we were to say, "we work as a team" in our principles, but then have all our bonus programs based on individual performance? What if our values say that we "encourage people to stand up for what's right" but then someone gets the boot if they speak up about an ethical conflict? Conversely, it's imperative that we formally and informally recognize employees who exemplify our values in their work.

5. BEWARE THE "PRINCIPLE POLICE"

One thing that happens when you establish ethical standards is that a few folks will discover the pleasure of pointing out where they think others have failed to live up to them. At first these people may seem like well-meaning moralists. They will profess extreme loyalty to the organization's values. But don't be fooled. While they may be right about what others are or aren't doing, they'll spend a lot more time pointing fingers than they will working to turn the situation around. If you really look at their behavior closely you'll see that they're actually the ones who aren't living the values, because while they're quick to find fault with others, they're unlikely to appreciate what's working well. And while they're quick to criticize, they're typically very slow to actually raise their concerns directly with the individual involved.

6. MIND THE GAP

We need to schedule regular time to assess the gap between our stated values and our actual behaviors. Why? Because *we will fall short.* And when we find those shortfalls we need to quickly confront them: acknowledge that we've erred, apologize to those affected, figure out what to do to make the situation right. In most cases it's really more about quick and effective recovery from failure than it is about attaining perfection.

7. TELL STORIES

Talking about being a "principle-centered organization" is all well and good but it's about as meaningful as telling new staff that you're committed to "great service." I'm sure that Enron had a nice set of principles written down somewhere. The problem is that they weren't living them. And that problem is exacerbated greatly when principles are left as nebulous niceties. Telling stories is one of the best ways I know to imbue something that's otherwise vague or abstract with meaning. "Remember the time that Lou handled this situation . . . ?" Or, "one day this happened and it was really tough but this is how we handled it . . ."

Final Thoughts

Having a documented set of Guiding Principles isn't a panacea; it's not a cure-all for every issue your organization needs to confront. While it's easy to point fingers after the fact, big gaps in ethical integrity often happen gradually, even invisibly. In my experience the shortfalls that outsiders moralize about are almost always the result of a long series of small and seemingly innocuous decisions. As a result, it's easy for those involved—when they're working in isolation and not being pushed to assess their decisions in an ethical context—to rationalize each instance on its own. And then one day, the crisis comes and no one can figure out what went wrong.

Lest you think this stuff is all too earnest, let me share one of our Guiding Principles at Zingerman's: "Working at Zingerman's," we wrote, "means taking an active part in running the business. Our work makes a difference." And in our glossary one of the ways we define a great place to work is, "We like to have fun." As I mentioned at the very beginning of this book, we've learned that having fun isn't something that just happens. Instead, it's the result of conscious decisions that we make when we come to work every day (or go anywhere else we're going). It's really a perfect item to include in our principles, because when someone comes to work with us we want to make sure we expect them to have fun while they're with us. To make things all the clearer, we add in the glossary, "And we take our fun very seriously. So don't mess with it."

I guess the same goes for all our Guiding Principles. We take them seriously. So don't mess with them! They really have made a big difference in what we do and in the way our organization works.

working the counter at the retail shop at the bakehouse

5 Steps to Building an Organizational Culture

It's Your Company, You Can Cry if You Want to

"Organizational culture" has certainly become one of the hot topics in the business world. But more often than not the subject is framed either in terms of the culture that already "is," or of "not losing what we've created." The interesting thing to me is that, using that visioning stuff we talked about a few essays back, you can actually take an active role in making your organizational culture what you want it to be. It's very doable, if at times difficult. The "secret" is knowing what you want. Here's the recipe.

~~~

One of the most common questions people ask when they first come to visit us at Zingerman's is something along the lines of, "How did you build up this great group of people? How do you get people to care like they do? They all seem like they're having a good time." Basically what our visitors seem to want to know is the "secret" of our culture. And as you'll already have guessed there are a thousand things we do here that contribute, but no one of them alone (nor even a "top" two or three) makes the culture what it is.

Still, more often than not they're looking for simple answers in response to leading questions like: "It's all in the hiring isn't it?" Or, "Do you think it's because you're in a college town?" Or, "Is it the training?" Sometimes I look at them very seriously and tell them it's all in the Magic Brownies we make at the Bakehouse.

But setting my tongue-in-cheekiness aside, culture really is critically important. Here's a brief tour of what it means to us—and how we try to develop it here.

What Is a Culture?

Webster's defines culture as: "(a) the integrated pattern of human knowledge, belief, and behavior that depends upon the capacity for learning and transmitting knowledge to succeeding generations, (b) The customary beliefs, social forms, and material traits of a racial, religious, or social group; *also:* the characteristic features of everyday existence (as diversions or a way of life) shared by people in a place or time, (c) the set of shared attitudes, values, goals, and practices that characterizes an institution or organization, (d) the set of values, conventions, or social practices associated with a particular field, activity, or societal characteristic."

. As we view it here at Zingerman's, culture is the everyday reality of organizational life. Within that, all the *Webster's* stuff applies. The culture is not the mission statement, the vision, your bank balance, or the staff handbook (though, of course, all those contribute to it in various ways). It's what we really do and say, the way we really behave, the way we treat each other, our products, our customers, our community, and ourselves. In essence, it's the "personality" of the company; just as each of us have individual strengths and weaknesses in our personalities, so, too, does our organization.

Take note that while speeches, grand plans, and fancy training manuals certainly affect an organization's culture, they're actually just as likely to have a negative impact than a positive one. Why? Because if we as leaders make those big speeches and design those fancy plans but don't actually walk our talk and follow through on what we said we're going to do, then I can pretty safely say that the impact is much more likely to be negative than positive. Ultimately it's what we do—much more than what we say—that makes our culture what it is.

Creating a Culture

There are really only two ways I know to build an organizational culture: either with consideration and conscious intent, or by neglect.

I don't have kids, but it strikes me that developing a company's culture has to be a lot like raising children. Even if you work really hard to do the right thing there's never any guarantee that what you do is going to work. But there's also no question that doing the work in a mindful way will significantly increase the odds of your kids growing up to live the values that you wanted them to have. Of course both the kid and the organizational culture are still going to develop even if you pay no attention to them at all. And while it's not completely impossible that they'll turn out to be who and what you wanted them to be, the odds aren't great.

What follows is our recipe for consciously creating an organizational culture. If you use it well, you can radically increase the odds of successfully developing the kind of culture you really want.

1. Teach it

The more—and more effectively—we teach people in our organization what we want our culture to be, the more likely it is to become the reality of what we really do. Whatever orientation and training work you're doing—or will be doing after you read this—I highly recommend regularly talking about the kind of culture you want. Describe the way you'd like things to be working. Talk about the informal ways you envision the group working together, the way you want the customer experience to feel, etc.

I think it's perfectly OK to teach, too, about aspects of the existing culture that you're trying to change. There's nothing wrong with saying something like, "You may notice that there are still a lot of folks who arrive a bit late for their scheduled shifts. I apologize for having let that go on as long as I have. We're working on building a culture that's a lot timelier. In the meantime you'll probably notice that we're not there yet. But just to be clear, my expectation of you is that you're going to keep to the schedule regardless of what others may still do (or not do). And, in fact, I'm actually looking for you to help lead the way to making this cultural improvement."

As I've pointed out all through this book, one of the best ways to teach about an abstract concept like culture is to tell stories. There's something that resonates with folks when they hear tales of how a particularly difficult situation was handled, or how the organization has successfully gotten where it is. There's a substantive wisdom that comes from these stories, an experiential element of teaching that goes beyond the intellectual theories of what we're trying to do. And because culture is what's really happening, not just what we say should be going on, the stories resonate in ways that pure theory can't do on its own.

2. Define it

In order to teach about our culture, we need to get straight what kind of culture we actually want. Essentially this is where we're doing visioning—looking out to a particular point in time in the future and painting an inspiring but strategically sound picture of what our organizational culture will be like when we succeed. While this may seem easy, it rarely is. And if you have a number of leaders involved in running your organization you may find that you don't immediately achieve full agreement on what your vision for the culture really is. In that case, you've got some hard discussions ahead of you. So for clarity's sake, it's essential that you take the time to put your vision in writing.

Strengths and Weaknesses Wound Together; Success Means Getting Better Problems

Although most of the world hasn't yet realized this, I've learned that whatever we're really good at is almost always directly correlated to the problems we have. Since success is mostly about getting better problems, what I'm saying here is, when you're doing your visioning be sure to pick the problems you want to deal with and then prepare to deal with them.

Here at Zingerman's we've pretty successfully built an organization where people speak their minds when they disagree with something. We like that because we want to nurture free thinkers and avoid groupthink, bureaucracy, and all those other bugaboos that beset bigger organizations as they grow. But the "problem" that almost inevitably comes with this free thinking/mind speaking stuff is that sometimes we're going to get more dissonance and disagreement than we want. Since our vision is to build a cooperative culture, we've worked to counteract that problem by actively teaching techniques for more effective organizational change, good meeting facilitation, positive dialogue, and dispute resolution.

My point is that in visioning out the organizational culture you want it's important to understand and accept these sorts of tensions. Sure, I'd love to have a setting where people follow systems perfectly and have zero defects while simultaneously adapting quickly to strange service requests from customers. But in reality we will always need to accept, plan for, and manage the lifelong struggle to keep all that in balance.

3. Live it

This is, I think, the hardest part of the recipe: culture is very little about what we say, and very much about what we do. If we don't live it, it's never going to play out as we want. And unlike new products or new hires, organizational culture can only be built slowly over time, not through a quick decision or the writing of a big check to a consultant.

This is especially critical for those of us who are leaders in our organizations; realistically the people we work with see everything we do. To the best of my imperfect ability, I try to remind myself that every action I take and every word I speak is going to influence our cultural development. To pretend that my words, actions, and attitudes don't have a significant impact would be to live in big-time denial.

This is particularly true at a startup, where things are moving quickly and people are operating in close (mental if not physical) quarters, usually under high stress, and where our behaviors can have an impact way beyond what they would in more stable, longer-established settings. So although the pressure is very high in those settings I would urge you to be especially conscious of what you're saying and doing. We as leaders influence the culture of our organizations in many ways:

- by how well our words match our deeds
- by how we handle things when the two aren't in sync
- by our choice of which values we live and which we only pay lip service to
- by who we hire and who we fire
- by who we reward and who we don't
- by the systems/recipes/processes we put in place (and those we don't)
- by how we handle failure

Consider especially that last item on the list: the manner in which we handle difficult situations is one of the biggest contributors to the creation of organizational culture. It's relatively easy to build a culture when everything's going well. But strong cultures are more often built by what we do during hard times: How do we act when money's tight? How do we respond when a staff member is ill and we're shorthanded? When good customers can't pay their bills? When we're having a hard time in our personal lives?

As we try to make clear to anyone who speaks admiringly of what we're doing here at Zingerman's, we have all the same problems as every other organization. Over the last 28 years it's safe to say that I've probably fallen short on pretty much everything we've worked toward at one point or another. Fortunately I'm in (a) good company. What's different about our culture is how we handle things when we don't live up to what we said we're going to do. Because when we openly accept that we've erred, apologize, and then move forward to reaffirm our principles, everything works more effectively; by handling our problems in a constructive way, we're building the sort of culture we want.

Ultimately each of us has to take responsibility to personally live the culture that we want to create. None of us will get there perfectly as individuals. But that's where diversity is so great; if we can build a team that collectively embodies all of the characteristics that we're seeking and then manage that diversity with respect and inclusiveness, we're on our way to building the organizational culture we seek.

I want to add that, although that work has to start with those of us who are in leadership roles, ultimately it's incumbent on everyone in the organization to share the responsibility. It's understandable that front-line staff might want to wait for imperfect leaders to fix things before they (the staff) get in the game. But I don't think it works, any more than it works when the leaders go around getting mad at the staff for not knowing how to behave. The most effective organizations and most solid cultures are the ones where each of us comes reasonably close to living the culture we seek.

4. MEASURE IT

Once we've identified and written down the key elements of our desired culture in our vision, I'm pretty adamant that we can in fact measure our success in making these elements a (cultural) reality. Measuring something is often the first step toward improving it, and culture isn't any different. You're more likely to build a results-oriented organization if you measure the success of your efforts.

If you clearly define what it is you're measuring there's no reason why you can't assess almost anything, even something as abstract as "fun." Try it: have folks score (we use 0–10) how much fun they had at the end of every shift and tally the answers. If you track the scores from week to week, talk about what you can do to improve your "fun quotient," and then implement a good action plan, your organization will soon be laughing a lot more than it used to. And your culture will reflect it for a long time to come.

5. REWARD IT

Many organizations have a mismatch between what they say they want and what is actually rewarded. In some cases the mismatch is really just an absence of rewards. Companies say they want people to treat each other well but offer no recognition to those who do so. They say they want people to have fun but the only reward you get is . . . you're having fun. They say they want people to learn, but the only reward is that staff know a little more than they did before.

Sometimes the situation can be more extreme—all too many organizations actually reward the opposite behavior of the one they're seeking. They say they want people to be generous but they take for themselves first. Leaders say they want great guest experiences but they pay bonuses based on sales. Again, no company is going to ever perfectly align every reward with the behaviors it's seeking. But it's pretty darned important to at least recognize the key elements of your cultural vision and make sure you really do recognize and reward people for living up to them.

Take note that I'm not really talking about money per se. That's certainly one way to do it, but money alone will never be enough. You need to use multiple methods in various settings. It's not about a one-time bonus or a quick cash fix: positive cultures are built over time using a creative array of rewards and recognition.

Shining During the Blackout

One of the most meaningful measures of your organizational culture is what happens in those unique, crazy situations you could never plan for. One that sticks in my mind is the big blackout that took place in the East and Midwest back in 2002. No one—I mean, *no one*—at Zingerman's had ever prepared for an organization-wide, two-day power outage. But one sunny summer day in August of 2002 it happened.

We were actually scheduled to have our annual plan kickoff session that evening, so folks had been preparing their presentations all day. Suddenly, late in the afternoon, the power went out. Everywhere. It was less than a year after 9/11 so there were immediate rumors of some sort of terrorist attack. It turned out to have nothing to do with terrorism, but the entire power grid had gone down. Not sure what to do, I quickly made my way over to the Deli to help out. But when I got there, there really wasn't much of anything for me to do. The partners, managers, and staff were all so together that they simply kicked into action to make things work well in spite of the crisis. We may have been without power, but people definitely were *not* powerless.

One of the first things the crew did was pull the gelato out of the freezer case. Before the ice cream had time to melt they went out onto the street and started giving out tastes to drivers stuck in traffic. The Bakehouse—where we have a generator to run key parts of the operation during power outages—offered to take in perishables from the Deli coolers. Their wholesale sales staff set up their desks outside the office (no generator there) and worked off cell phones to find out which of their 100-plus accounts in the area would want products and which didn't. Folks from ZingTrain went out to the Bakehouse to brew coffee and bring it back downtown for Deli customers. The Deli staff set up tables outside the building and started selling foods that didn't need refrigeration (like bread and dry goods) using a calculator and a cash box.

As all this was happening, I kept feeling that, if I was a good leader I'd best find something significant to do to help. But it dawned on me that whatever work I'd had to do was actually done a long time before, because the entire organization—partners, managers and staff alike—had spent two decades training to deal with this, and clearly, from the way they handled it, they'd trained really well. They knew immediately how to think entrepreneurially, how to act cooperatively to help their peers, what to do to minimize loss and maximize gain both spiritually, for the community, and financially. They knew how to have fun in the face of adversity. And they darned well didn't need me to tell them how to do it. So I went back to the office, changed into my running shorts and shoes, and went out for an hour-long run. The power was out and so was the sun—it really was a beautiful day in the neighborhood.

Changing an Existing Culture

For better and for worse, there's really no quick way to achieve cultural change. Rules can be modified with a quick memo, but reshaping a culture takes a commitment to teach what we want, write a coherent vision to define it, model and live that vision as best we can, measure our progress, and then recognize and reward people when we succeed in making it happen. All of which requires tons of communication, years of stubborn persistence, relentless followup, and probably a little luck.

What I've learned over the years about cultural change is that you can never really get rid of the parts of the culture you don't like. The more realistic approach is to gradually build up your strengths until they overshadow the less-desirable elements, so that the problems become less of an impediment to getting where you want to go.

The analogy I like best for this process is someone with a foreign accent who has been living in the States for a long time. We have at least one such person here at Zingerman's—Jude Walton. Jude has been living in the States for more than 15 years now. By American standards she's still got an English accent, and she's still got some mannerisms that to American eyes would clearly mark her as British. But over the years those things have become less and less noticeable. And I know that when Jude goes back to Britain to visit friends and family they all lovingly accuse her of having lost her accent. That same sort of slow but steady transformation—often invisible to the people experiencing it—is the "secret" of cultural change.

How long does it take to change a culture?

I've always been taught that cultural change takes about a generation. In the food world one of the organizational challenges we've always faced—and probably always will face—is that there's a lot more turnover than we might like. Being based in a college town where it seems like everyone is perpetually thinking about leaving, going back to school, or traveling the world, tends to exacerbate this problem. Even though at Zingerman's we run at about 25 percent of the industry average for turnover, we've still got more than we'd ideally like. But the good news for the food business is that because we have higher turnover we can actually make cultural change happen more quickly than someplace like the auto industry, where the norm has until recently been for folks to be employed for life, sometimes across multiple generations.

My rule of thumb for meaningful cultural change here at Zingerman's is that it generally takes two to three years to get something new really well woven into what we do. I usually wish it would happen faster, and I'm often really impatient en route, but that's just the way it is. By accepting that reality rather than fighting it, I've found that I can do a much better job of managing myself and of leading and supporting the change process. I know that three or four weeks into most any change there are still going to be lots of problems and challenges; that in three or four months the glamour of the idea of change will have long since worn off. And that at that point we as leaders will probably need to get in there and help refocus folks on the long-term vision, providing the encouragement and energy needed to help get them through the seemingly inevitable zone of doubt and blame. And I know that if we stick stubbornly with our vision, if we really implement the action plans we agreed to early on (with of course some flexibility for midstream adjustments), we will ultimately get where we wanted to go.

The Culture Club at the Deli

Developing a Culture Club is an idea that I think we learned from Southwest Airlines (see *Nuts: Southwest Airline's Crazy Recipe for Business and Personal Success,* by Kevin and Joyce Freiburg). It's a work group that focuses on making an ever-better place for all of us to be a part of. While we haven't yet incorporated the approach across our entire organization, the Deli has done great things with it. But lest you think it was easy to do . . . let me say that getting the Culture Club going and woven into the culture of the Deli took—you guessed it—two or three years! Thanks to the leadership of Carole Woods, who runs the group, as well as the participation of a good number of Deli staff, managers, and managing partners, it's working really well.

Of course, because all this stuff is so iterative, the Culture Club is now itself a big part of the culture of the Deli. And that culture is, not surprisingly, probably the most positive it has ever been. Just by the very act of existing and working to do good things over a period of years, Carole and the group members have helped to create the culture they want—if you have a professional work group that shepherds your culture and supports positive culture-building by doing good deeds and good work, you will in turn create a more positive and more giving culture.

The group has basically lived the five elements of the recipe—teaching, defining, living, measuring, and rewarding—and in the process has helped make the culture of the Deli ever-more positive. Honestly, I don't know that the specifics of what the group has done are particularly innovative. What's so great is that they've taken things that we (and many other organizations) talk about all the time, and they've made them a *very* meaningful reality at the Deli.

It's no coincidence, I'm sure, that the Deli's bottom-line performance is better than it has been in years. And that the better the results the business delivers, the more positive the culture, the better the results . . . you get the idea.

Some of the programs that they've put in place include:

- Deli Sherpas: these are mentors who help new staff members "climb" the mountain of information and insight that they need to get through their initial training and seeming cultural confusion.

- Better environment: making the staff breakroom a nicer place to spend one's time before, during, or after a shift.

- Cultural Attachés: people who work to improve the effectiveness of the Deli's inter-departmental operations.

- The Deli Quarterbook: a "yearbook" of Deli staff, published every three months, that provides staff members with a simple but effective way to get to know each other, even if they don't see each other every day.

- Parties and celebrations: again, nothing particularly new here. But the key is that the Culture Club really makes the fun happen on a regular basis—and that a group primarily composed of front-line staff has taken responsibility for bringing celebration and positive energy into their workplace, rather than waiting for someone in authority to do it for them.

Ways to See What the Culture Really Is

Ultimately the culture—not the staff handbook, the CEO's position paper, or the company's marketing materials—is the best indicator of the quality of life in any organization. I try to pay attention to small sub-surface cultural signals like:

- What do people do when the boss isn't around?
- How do leaders treat others in the organization in casual settings?
- Are people laughing at work?
- What do people do when they're confronted with truly unique situations?
- How do people recover from failure?
- What do people say about the organization when they're with their friends or family?
- What gets discussed on the back dock?
- What do people joke about? Who's making the jokes? Are the people poking fun at themselves? Or at others?
- Every organization has its cynics. But how strong are they? Do they dominate? Or do people with more positive attitudes politely put the naysayers in their place?
- How do people in the organization talk about its products?
- Listen for the pronouns—do people talk about the organization in the third person ("they") or the first person ("we")?

Different Cultures in Different Parts of the Organization

If you have a business where people don't work together in the same space all the time—either because you have different locations, different areas of expertise (like production vs. sales), a big building, extended hours, or some combination of these factors—you're going to end up with different cultures in different parts of the organization. That's not a bad thing. It's normal. Look at it on a national level. There's clearly an American culture that anyone who arrives here from abroad is going to identify, no matter whether they land in New Mexico or New York City. In contrast to, say, Sweden, Sri Lanka, or southern Sudan, the U.S. is just going to seem somehow distinctly *American*. Of course if our new arrival pays attention and starts to travel around the U.S., he or she is going to start to see the nuances: within that broad American cultural context there are differences between the Land of Enchantment and Manhattan. And if they pay still closer attention they'll find that the culture can change quite a bit even from the Lower East Side to Soho to Midtown and on to the Upper West Side and Harlem.

The same is true here at Zingerman's. We certainly have one coherent culture across the organization. But you'll find a slightly different version of it at the Bakehouse than at the Roadhouse or the Deli. And within each of those businesses you'll find cultural variations between the various departments and shifts as well.

The key for us as leaders is not to fight against this diversity, but to focus on the positives. Look at the parts of the culture that are consistently working well and build out from there. Since we aren't going to have a Stepford Wives sort of uniformity, which elements of the culture are most important? Given the level of growth we've agreed on for the next five years, what actions do we need to take to build the culture we've visioned out?

Worrying About Losing What You Have/Building for the Future

This comes up regularly when we work with other organizations that have actually created the kind of culture that they wanted early on in their business development. While I think of this as a good problem, I revert back to my parenting metaphor. You can worry about what's going to happen to your kids if you let them out of the house. But at some point they're going to start going out. And you can't—nor should you—stop them. Worrying, as you likely have already learned, really won't help.

We can't stop our culture from evolving. It's going to change tomorrow, and the day after, and next year, and on and on. The key is to avoid slipping into working with a "negative vision"—one that focuses on what you *don't* want to happen. Instead, I'd ask something like, "Given the growth that we're going after and the way the world may change around us, what would the organizational culture of my dreams look like in five years?" I firmly believe—and have experienced—that, by writing down the vision of the culture you will create when you're successful, you really are very likely to get there. In fact, as I see it, why settle for what you've already done? Paint yourself a picture of a culture that's even better than what you've got now!

waiting tables at zingerman's roadhouse

Creating a Culture of Positive Appreciation

Being Kind Doesn't Have to Be a Coincidence

Here's something that I can safely say I never really gave more than two minutes of attention to back when we started the business. In hindsight it's clear to me that we sort of unconsciously created an appreciative culture anyway. Looking back, Paul was probably way better at it than I was. But there's no reason you need to count on happenstance, a good partner, and shared (though probably not very often spoken) intent, when you can mindfully make it happen—appreciation doesn't have to be an accident or an afterthought. Getting an already-positive organization to be a wee bit more appreciative is really not that hard. And, although it may not be the easiest thing in the world to turn a highly negative culture into an appreciative one, that can very definitely be done, too. In either case, actual costs are small. Kindness, as I told a group of about 50 grammar school kids a couple years ago, is free. Among the small and very easy-to-implement things you can do to make a big difference in an organization very quickly, appreciation is high on my list: the cost is next to nil, and the benefits are very big. It's incredible how far a bit of recognition and caring, heartfelt positive feedback will go.

I'm probably not all that different from a lot of high achievers—focused a great deal of the time on ways to improve our organization and the quality of our work. That's certainly not a bad thing—the drive to get better is a big piece of what creates any successful organization. But the very same drive that has helped me succeed by pushing for improvement all the time also makes it likely that I'm not always as appreciative of all the good things happening around me as I could be. At least that's my nature. The truth is that I'm sort of in recovery: I've spent the last 15 years trying to turn my overachieving nature inside out, by using my own drive to be as good at appreciation as I am at other things. I work on this in the belief that if I actually get good at it, I could help create an organizational culture where appreciation and positive energy are the norms, not the exception; in which people feel valued for their work and help those around them do the same. In fact, leading with appreciation for our own organization, I think I can—no, *I will*—say that people here have done an exceptionally good job of creating a positive culture.

It's very difficult for me to just come out and say these things without qualification. But working to be more appreciative has put me into a paradoxical box: in order to live the appreciative role that I'm committed to I need to recognize how much we've achieved in this area, even though it's hard for me to do so when I know that we still have a long way to go. Fortunately, I've heard so many compliments about Zingerman's from so many people—staff, suppliers, partners, neighbors, and of course our customers—that even I can't help but appreciate it. In the process I've learned to make peace with the reality that I can be both exceedingly appreciative of achievement and driven to make things better than they are. This paradox may seem natural to those for whom this appreciation stuff comes naturally, but it didn't to me, that's for sure. Which is why this is, and always will be, a work in progress.

In the interest of sharing this achievement with others, I got to wondering what it is that we've done to help create the kind of culture we have here. And it comes back to the basic recipe for building a culture, outlined in the previous chapter. So with that framework in mind, here's a quick look at what we do:

1. TEACH IT

Rather than just assume that being appreciative should be obvious, we actively teach techniques to demonstrate positive appreciation in a number of formal and informal venues:

- All of our training and teaching work is based on Zingerman's Training Compact, which includes our commitment to recognize and reward everyone in the organization who is meeting (or, all the better, exceeding) our expectations. And because we review the Training Compact in all of our classes, everyone hears about this appreciation regularly. While this may seem trivial, the feedback from our staff tells us it's critical. To quote Katie Frank from the Bakehouse, "When one's job expectations are made clear, it's easier to perform what is expected and one feels gratified by doing what is asked of them well, thus, appreciated. This may also transfer into a good performance review which may also turn into a raise, which is a sign to some that they are appreciated."
- "Welcome to Zingerman's": We touch on the importance of positive appreciation at least half a dozen times during the two-hour orientation class Paul or I do for new staff, citing specific ways that we show it. When I'm teaching it I try to model the desired behavior by appreciating specific things about what people in the class say or have done in their work to date, or in their lives before Zingerman's. I also try to appreciate the efforts

and achievements of others in the organization by mentioning departments or businesses that have had great successes, peers of the new staff who are doing a particularly good job, etc.

- We also mention the importance of an appreciative approach in training sessions on any number of other subjects, including classes on caring confrontations, how to do performance reviews, how to make meetings work, personal futuring, on-shift training skills, and the art of giving great service, just to name a few.

Through all this teaching, pretty much every staff member hears regularly from the organization's leaders that we value and model a positive and appreciative environment, and that we expect staff members to actively contribute to it, as well. Additionally, and interestingly, I've found from talking to staff that the number of classes we teach helps them to feel appreciated, so the positive culture-building comes out of education in a number of different ways.

2. DEFINE IT

There are many reasons managers so frequently fail to make time to appreciate their staff. There's the "People should know that we appreciate them—after all we keep paying them" angle. Others come at it with the "Why do we have to tell people this? They should take satisfaction in their work" mindset. There's also the "It's just the Golden Rule—treat others the way you want to be treated" approach, which sounds good until you find out that the manager was raised without much positive reinforcement. Having lived with, and through, all of the above, I've learned that it's far more effective to set clear, positive expectations up front and then share them through the aforementioned teaching. For example:

- Our mission talks about bringing a positive "Zingerman's Experience" to everyone we come into contact with. Regardless of title or seniority, we're all fully responsible for bringing that positive experience to every customer, supplier, peer, or neighbor we deal with. It's not enough to just make sandwiches, bake bread, do accounting, or whatever—our job is to make positive experiences happen. Right off the bat this puts us all into situations where we can both appreciate and be appreciated.

- One of our three Bottom Lines is "Great Service," and that service includes creating a positive workplace where everyone feels valued and knows that their work makes a difference.

- Our guiding principles outline a pretty appreciative environment.
  Specifically, I would note the statement that, **"We give great
  service to each other as well as to our guests.** We provide the
  same level of service in our work with our peers as we do with
  our guests. We go the extra mile for each other. We are polite,
  supportive, considerate, superb listeners, working on the basis of
  mutual respect and care."

- Visioning: By definition this emphasis on going after what we
  want—rather than fighting off what we *don't* want—creates a
  more positive and appreciative attitude throughout the organization. In short, visioning keeps us from getting bogged down
  in the present-day problems by focusing on creating a positive,
  appreciative future.

- The 4 to 1 Ratio: We all try to deliver a daily average of four
  parts praise to one part constructive criticism. Both aspects of
  this equation are important. The four parts praise is pretty significant—it really pushes people like me to make sure we take time
  to notice the myriad things that go right every day. And the one
  part constructive criticism is equally important, not least because
  it lends credibility to the four parts praise. Without helping others see how they can be even more effective, the praise can start
  to seem empty. Put together the two create a primarily positive
  environment, but one that's positively helpful, as well.

3. LIVE IT

Although most folks will agree with the suggestion that it's good to have an
appreciative culture, many organizations fall far short. But without actually living it, walking the talk, not a whole lot is going to happen. Here are some of the
areas where I've found that it's particularly worthwhile to invest my appreciative
energies:

- Appreciate Yourself: Like all meaningful organizational change, I
  believe that an appreciative environment absolutely has to come
  from within us as leaders. Which means that before I could
  even begin to be more appreciative of others I had to learn to
  treat myself with the same respectful approach that I wanted to
  deliver to those around me. While I can't prove this scientifically,
  my experience is that if I don't appreciate myself in a meaningful
  way, the praise I give to others won't connect, either.

Peter Koestenbaum, in *Talk Is Walk: Language and Courage in Action,* writes that, "You need a friend even if you are that friend." For me this meant learning to speak to myself respectfully, to appreciate myself for what I achieved (while still of course pushing myself to get better at the same time—don't worry, I'm not slacking).

• Appreciate Others: It's just too easy to lose track of the positives. They're always there—I just have to take time to notice them. In service of which, I've adopted an almost daily routine of making myself pay close attention to the many positive things, the great people and really wonderful food and service, that surround me. There are a few zillion examples every day. I also try to do a bit of journaling almost every day, a part of which is regularly making lists of people and things that I might have failed to appreciate of late.

• Train and Organize to Encourage Appreciation: Part of our job as leaders is to help the folks we work with to be successful. And in our world, one way we can do so is by being appreciative of those we work with and serve. While it's nice to think that appreciation is so much the "right thing to do" that it will spring up on its own, the reality is that one of the most effective things we can do organizationally is to set up systems and structures that make it easy—even require—people to be much more appreciative than they might normally be on their own.

• Start Doing "Appreciations": Speaking of systems, this is one of the best things we've ever done here. Thanks for it goes to my friend Lex Alexander who with his wife, Ann, founded Wellspring Grocery in North Carolina, and now runs the excellent 3CUPS coffee shop in Chapel Hill. The idea is simply that *each and every meeting* we hold always ends with a few minutes of "Appreciations." Appreciations can be of anything or anyone: someone in the room or not in the room; something work-related or not; accomplishments past, present, or future. No one is required to say anything, but people usually do. And this one small exercise has made a huge impact over the years. Think of it like ending a meal with a good cup of coffee: the people in the meeting almost always go back out into the organizational world with positive feelings. And because we do it at every meeting, it really disciplines us to devote time and mental energy to positive recognition. (Skip ahead to page 349 to read my appreciations for the work that went into this book.)

- Stay in Synch: We've also learned the hard way that some staff members are embarrassed by public praise. It's most effective to compliment people in the way that they most appreciate being appreciated. For some that's in public, others in private, some in writing, some with gifts, some with a pat on the back, some with eye contact and a head nod.

- Appreciations in the Staff Newsletter: We basically follow the same format in our monthly staff newsletter. Each issue contains three, four, or even five pages of appreciations and thank-yous sent in by various staff members.

- Code Greens: This is the name for the form we use to capture and communicate the compliments we hear from customers (the opposite, of course, is a Code Red). Could be big, could be small, but any positive comment we hear should be written up as a Code Green. These are shared with as many people as possible, sometimes by email, sometimes through bulletin board postings, sometimes by reading them aloud at meetings. The important thing is that the information is shared and that the people who work in the organization hear the positive feedback that their work has earned from customers.

- Performance Reviews: These certainly aren't unique to our organization, nor, I'm sure, are we the only organization that struggles to do them in a timely way. But they are a very good tool for keeping us focused on the positive achievements of those around us—every review here starts with a summary of the person's achievements.

- Specificity: In all of this positive recognition I've continued to learn that praise means more when it's specific. While general thanks and kudos never hurt, it's more helpful to be clear about what it is we really value, so that others know what they can do more of down the road to be even more effective in their work.

- Going the Extra Mile: Since we work to treat our staff here like customers, "going the extra mile"—the third of our 3 Steps to Great Service—applies to them, too. That means doing the unexpected (as in *good* things, not goofy stuff like dumping water on them) for co-workers, showing appreciation and creating the sort of positive feelings that we all want to experience. The effort doesn't have to be fancy, high-tech, or expensive. Something as simple as a Post-it note stuck to someone's computer screen, a handwritten card that actually comes in the mail, a quick unexpected email, a flower, a bouquet of fresh asparagus from the Farmer's Market, or a basket of just-picked cherries . . . these little things can make an enormous difference to people in the organization.

- The "3 and Out Rule": This is an internal mechanism that I've come to use regularly, and, in writing this piece, realized I should share more actively. When I'm having a really rough day (which of course happens) positive appreciation is the easiest way I know to turn things around. Appreciate, appreciate, appreciate... the old baseball saying "three and out" actually works pretty well and it's kind of catchy. So I think I'm going to officially adopt it right now: *When in doubt, three and out.*

The amazing thing is that by the time I've gone and appreciated at least three folks, it's literally almost impossible for me to still be in a bad mood. And in the process of turning my own day around, I've contributed something small but upbeat to those with whom I've interacted. They in turn are more likely to do the same for others. And in the end, everyone—the organization, the staff, the customers, and the community—will all be better off for it.

4. MEASURE IT

We probably don't do this as much as we should. But we do have ways to measure appreciation, both formally and informally.

- Staff Survey: We've based ours on the 12 questions advocated in the book *First, Break All the Rules* by Marcus Buckingham and Curt Coffman (which I highly recommend if you haven't read it). These include things like:
  - In the last seven days have I received praise for my work?
  - Does my supervisor or someone at work seem to care about me as a person?
  - Do my opinions seem to count?

The surveys are reviewed—imperfectly I'm sure, but nevertheless regularly—by each business and department, providing a basis for organizational "self-improvement" and a good sense of where we're successfully creating a positive, rewarding workplace.

- We also at various times track things like "extra miles" (going out of the way to do something extra for peers or customers), personal stress levels, Code Greens, etc.

- Turnover: This is a familiar way to measure how much people feel appreciated. Our rate has regularly stayed well below industry norms—and I appreciate everyone here who has helped to make it that way!

5. Reward it

- Thank-Yous: Here's an old-fashioned but surprisingly more effective than ever way to work on this stuff. Sometimes a simple note or an "appreciation" (as above) at a meeting can make a huge difference to those who are appreciated. Almost all of the verbal appreciations at our meetings get written up in the notes and then distributed. Believe it or not, others who weren't at the meetings regularly read them and notice whose names appear. Quick handwritten thank-yous make a huge difference. And I try to thank pretty much everyone on shift every time I leave work.

- Appreciate the Appreciators for Being Appreciative: In order to really seed the success of an appreciative culture I think it's important to make sure that those in the company who are already the most appreciative be recognized regularly for being that way. The more we acknowledge that their positive touch has helped take the organization to higher levels of appreciation the more likely they are to keep doing it! Which is, to state the obvious, exactly what we want—their appreciative nature is, in itself, of great organizational value.

- Service Awards: We have a series of awards that we give each month to the special service providers in our organization. I don't think it makes all that much difference what the rewards actually are, just that we have them. We also offer rewards to those who recognize the work of others—the individual who nominates the winner of our monthly Service Star award gets a cash bonus (as does the actual winner).

- Share the Success: This is the third in our 3 Steps to Great Finance, and it's where we get to pay bonuses, gainsharing, or give out assorted cool things in appreciation for attaining group achievement.

- Giving to the Community: I think that helping those in need around us demonstrates an appreciation of how fortunate we are to be able to do what we do. It inspires generosity of spirit and goodwill within the organization, as well as in the community at large. We contribute 10 percent of the previous year's profits to causes every year, which means a lot to the staff and to those in need in our area.

Why Bother?

I guess in my mind being appreciative is the right thing to do for all kinds of reasons. Above all else, most everyone wants to feel valued, to know that their efforts make a difference, to be part of something greater than themselves. And when they feel that their work is contributing positively toward those ends they're far more likely to reach way beyond the norm of what most people would otherwise do in their work. By maintaining an appreciative culture, we set a positive example for everyone who comes to work with us. I'm confident that when folks leave Zingerman's—either at the end of their shift, or to move to a new job elsewhere—they usually take at least some of this spirit with them. Which means that the world around them is slightly better off. And I think that's a great thing.

I've also realized that there's really no in-between when it comes to appreciation. The absence of it is not neutral—saying nothing leads most people to think that their work is not valued. And when they feel that way, the negative energy, the silo mentality, and the self-serving attitudes that mar so many organizations of all sizes, sorts, and specialties, starts to creep into people's work. The culture starts to go downhill. And I can't believe that anyone wants that.

Finally, life is short. I've learned by screwing up regularly over the years that no one can read my mind. If I think something someone's doing is great but I don't tell them, they have no way to know.

Does It Work?

I think so, but you knew that—I wouldn't have written this piece if I didn't. The best testimonials though really would come from the people who work here, or in any of the many other organizations that do this as well as (or better than) we do. Feel free to ask anyone who works at Zingerman's for his or her two cents on the subject. I don't know what they'll say, but I'll appreciate them in advance for openly owning and sharing their feelings, whatever they may be.

I will share one unsolicited note that came to me from a front-line staff member, and which captures this idea more effectively than I ever could. Tim Miller, who works in Mail Order, wrote to say, "Congratulations on the anniversary! Thank you for creating such a great company to work for—seriously. This continues to be the most interesting and fulfilling job I've ever had. I always wanted to work at a place where it feels like I make a difference in people's lives, and where I feel like I'm listened to, and that's what you've done. Keep on keeping on!"

Ultimately, I don't think you can isolate formal appreciation from everything else that's done in an organization to demonstrate its value. To quote Katie again, "All of the things listed above have one thing in common—none are vital or at all necessary to conducting business on a daily basis. I can only imagine their cost to the company, and it's hard to assign a Return on Investment to them. But, these signs of appreciation pay off in lower than average turnover, a special culture that makes the organization incredibly different and desirable as an employer, and all together a feeling of treating one another with respect and care. I also love being a part of a company that works so diligently in caring about its people so much and giving so much back to the community."

Thanks

In closing I want to say thanks to everyone who's helped me to learn what I've learned on this subject over the years, and to everyone who's been (and continues to be) willing to work with me as I learn how to do this more effectively. Their assistance, insight, and patient teaching have been a huge help to me and others who work in, around, or near our organization, and to the community—both the business world at large, and the community here in Ann Arbor, of which we're fortunate enough to be a part.

mixing classic cocktails at the roadhouse

Why I Want to Finish Third

Successfully Building Your
Business into a Third Place

I don't know how many people in the world have actually read through the whole 300-plus pages of Ray Oldenburg's The Great Good Place. *I really do recommend it—in honesty, of the thousand or so business-related books I've probably read over the years it's one of the ones whose ideas have stuck with me the longest. We use tools and techniques that are inspired by Oldenberg's excellent insights all the time, and with really great benefit to all involved. Like most everything else in this book, you'll see in this essay that the actual work of creating a third place costs next to nothing. Really what it requires is just the willingness to pay attention and connect people in your community in caring, engaging, and productive ways. When it's done well, everyone involved wins: the company, the community, the staff, and your co-workers all come out better when they get to be a part of a creative, special third place.*

Although I'm not a particularly competitive person, the truth is there aren't too many times that I'd tell you up front that I felt good about finishing third. But when it comes to a category that I'll call "places," third is actually where I want to be—becoming a third place is something that I think every community-oriented business would want to achieve.

Here's the basic concept: The first place, as Ray Oldenburg explains it, is the home. The second is work. Most every adult has experienced each of the two. But the bulk of the book is dedicated to a discussion of what he calls the "third place"—a public spot that's neither home nor work (other than for those who are actually employed there), where people gather and connect. In the old days the third place might have been the VFW Hall or the church; it could well have been the town square, the barbershop, or the tavern. They're places that people hang out, where they feel included, recognized, and accepted. Where people regularly go on their own or with their friends or family, where they know they're likely to encounter like-minded people. Often the folks you interact with in a third place setting are people that you don't see anywhere else. Spending time at a third place helps people maintain their social balance and provides joy, support, and stability to the community

One of Oldenburg's main points in the book was that, although the third place was once a common and critical piece of our social structure, the sub-urbanization of the country in the second half of the 20th century led to the disappearance of most of them. And with that loss, there was a reduction in the quality of life and the level of connection and community throughout most of the U.S.

That was the bad news. The good news as I read the book was that I immediately recognized that, without consciously intending to do so, we had in fact created a third place at the Deli. The more I read, the more it became clear that the characteristics Oldenburg ascribed to third places described our business almost to a "T." There were a series of regulars who were there . . . very regularly. Especially in the mornings. We know them. They know us. Even more important they know each other. Often they only know each other from having met at the Deli. And while a few may have gone on to see each other outside of our environment, I think that most don't; their interactions take place primarily at Zingerman's. While they're there, they connect over coffee; they stand around the tables, at the counter or cash register, and swap stories. While I wouldn't say that they're all there every day, many come in with impressive regularity. When they aren't there, their absence is almost always quickly noted—though more often than not another guest knows where the "missing" group member has gone, and you can hear folks sharing stories of their travels or having gone to see their kids at college, or wherever, when they come back.

(Those of you who've been to the Deli may chuckle at Oldenburg's description of a particular restaurant he classes as a third place: "The operation of it violates all the principles of efficient franchise management. One has to wait in a long and *very* slow-moving line, but here that curse of group life has been transformed into a pleasant experience. It's a 'talking line' within which people are 'pointed' in all directions as they shuffle and sip beer and bag their way toward the host." Other than the beer it could easily be us—or probably any number of other special spots around the country.)

Ownership Transfer

If you hang out for a while, you might begin to notice that many of our third place regulars act like they own the place. Mind you, I mean that in totally the best possible sense!

Some business owners I've talked to over the years don't actually like when this happens. They seem to resent the customers who tell them how to run their business, and they go to great lengths to discourage it. Sorry, but that approach has never worked for us. To the contrary, we expend a lot of energy actually trying to get the customers to tell us how to run our business: it's called feedback, and it's a heck of a lot easier to serve them well when they tell us how they want to be served!

Building this sense of ownership only makes sense. The business world talks a lot about how important it is to create a setting where employees feel ownership in the organization. And for good reason—it works. We all know that the more the folks who work with us feel that way, the more likely they are to go above and beyond. The same is really true of customers. The more we can do to create a business where our guests feel that sense of ownership, the more connected they will be to what we do, and the more likely they will be to stick with us over the long haul. They'll help us work through difficult times. They'll be a sounding board for us to deal with new challenges. They'll work like an early warning system on quality issues and clue us in to other customers who aren't happy with what we're doing. They'll promote us as they move through the community and the world.

When you really have this third place thing going well, you might find, as we do, that regular customers—folks who are basically "members" of the third place—actually end up informally "training" new customers for us. I'll hear someone in line at the Bakehouse telling a first-time visitor which breads and pastries not to miss, or how to get to the Deli or Roadhouse later, or how they can get a taste of anything they'd like just for the asking (thanks Harvey). At the Deli, "third place members" often act as unofficial guides for newer customers who may be confused by the layout, explaining where to order coffee or how to pay or where to find a table. For all of this—their loyalty, their support, their caring and concern, their willingness to share both positive experiences and suggestions for improvement—I deeply appreciate the folks who spend their time, money and energy with us so often.

Creating a Third Place

Having thought the whole concept of the third place through and watched it work for so many years, it's clear to me that creating a third place doesn't have to be accidental. There are things that we can do to actually help make it happen. I'm not suggesting some artificial construct—just that if our vision for the long-term development of our organization includes playing this sort of positive connectivity role for our community, then why not go out and actively help make it a reality? Here are a few steps that I think help increase the odds of finishing third:

1. PUT PERSONALITIES IN PLACE AND KEEP THEM THERE

Let's face it: interesting people are attracted to interesting people. While this isn't a huge revelation, creating a third place requires that we consciously find key "greeters" with big personalities and then keep them around long enough that the customers get to know them well (and vice-versa). The personality can, of course, be us as owners. But it can also be someone like the bartender on *Cheers* or the barista at an Italian café. These people become the masters of ceremonies, the hosts, the entertainment, the conversation partners . . . they're there regularly, welcoming the customers, holding court, remembering names, favorite foods, and drinks, noticing who's there and who's not, asking how things are going. They look out for their regulars and help welcome newcomers, all the while watching out for the interests of the business, too.

2. COLLECT—AND THEN CONNECT—THE DOTS

This is something I know we've done fairly well for years. But reading Danny Meyer's great book, *Setting the Table,* gave me a new way to express what I was already thinking unconsciously. Danny calls his concept "ABCD," which stands for "always be collecting dots." The idea is that giving great service of any sort is about gathering information—each bit of it is a dot. Dots could include details like knowing a customer's birthday, that a customer's child is starting kindergarten, that a customer has a new pet or just got a promotion. And the more we learn about our guests the more they feel at home and the better we're able to serve them. In the immediate sense that information is of great value to us as service providers in that we can better cater to, acknowledge, honor, and support our customers' needs. We prepare birthday cards for regulars, give them a bit of extra food to take on a plane trip, send them thank-you notes, etc.

But in the third place we want to take things further. We don't just collect dots to build our direct relationship to our guests. To take the concept a step further we built on Danny's brilliant idea and now teach what we call "ABCD III,"—"always be connecting dots." ("ABCD II" is "always be communicating dots.") That is, we use the information we gather to build connections that solidify our role as a third place. So, for instance, we might introduce two regular customers to each other, both of whom we know have seniors in high school. We may let a new customer with a dog know that the long-time regular sitting over in the corner is a big dog lover. We see one customer reading a book about Costa Rica and we let her know that Billy who's having coffee in the corner just came back from a week on the beach there. We see two people eating and enjoying the same sandwich and point it out to them so they can swap reviews. One customer is looking for a new house; another works in real estate. A first-time guest is a musician on tour; a long-time regular is a booking agent. The more we hook them up, the more connected they feel to the world, and, of course, to us.

Basically we want to connect the dots wherever we can—from customer to customer; from customer to staff; from customer to some other part of the community that we know well; and even to our suppliers. The more people in our business connect with new people the more likely it is that they will: (a) have a unique experience in our business, (b) feel a sense of ownership in our business, and (c) actively promote our business to others.

People who feel a part of a third place are almost always active promoters of that place. I don't mean overbearing salesmen. Sometimes regulars want to keep "their" place a secret. But despite themselves they'll still be promoters, saying good things about us when the subject comes up. They're an amazing resource to have.

3. MAKE THEM FEEL SPECIAL

From everything I've been saying it's probably pretty obvious that we really value our regular customers. But in keeping with our appreciative culture we don't ever want to forget to find ways to let them *know* that they're special and that we value them.

A few winters ago we had a big ice storm and a lot of folks who live in the area around the Roadhouse lost power. Fortunately ours stayed on so we were open for business as usual. We knew people lost power because they told us— good service dictates that we engage our guests to learn more about them; good relationships with regulars mean that they're telling us what's up in their lives. It wasn't any huge crisis, no Hurricane Katrina or Asian tsunami—most folks were "powerless" for less than a day, maybe a few for 48 hours. But in order to give great service and contribute positively to their lives we did any number of little things that helped let our regulars know we were looking out for them. Nothing fancy—just things like sending them home with a slice or two of coffee cake for breakfast the next morning.

One very nice couple had come in for dinner the evening after the storm. They looked fine when I saw them arrive. But when I passed by their table and asked them how they were doing, they shook their heads and very nicely (they aren't big complainers) told me it had been a rough day. They were without electricity themselves. And they were supposed to meet their friends here at the Roadhouse for dinner but the friends too had lost power and had left a message on their voice mail saying that they wouldn't be joining our regulars for dinner as planned. Add to that a rough day at work and suffice it to say they weren't in the best of spirits. They had a good meal and I'm sure felt better by the end of it. As they were getting ready to leave, though, we brought them over a small split of sparkling wine to take home with them. A nice touch to help them finish a bad day in a good way. To make it really good service—they had no power and hence no lights—we stuck in two "loaner" champagne glasses so they wouldn't have to rummage around in their dark cupboards to make a nice toast.

Mainly this was just about doing a nice thing for nice people. But of course it was good business too. While they were already regulars, I'm sure they're even more so now—in fact, I saw one of them back in with five friends two nights later. They feel valued and special (which they are). It's safe to say that they're going to tell that story many times over. And I guess, thinking it through even more, every time there's a power outage (which I'm sure we'll have more of) they're pretty likely to remember what happened and think positively about us. That's a pretty nice thing. We've built ourselves into their lives as a third place, a spot that they know is part of their community, one to which they return—physically or emotionally—even through hard times.

4. MAKE IT INTERACTIVE

One thing I've learned over the years is that the more active—and interactive—the guests are in helping to create the theater and action that goes on in a successful third place, the more effective it all is and the more they enjoy their experience. There are lots of easy ways to make this happen. One simple one is that when I take samples to a table or to a group of customers I bring at least one more sample piece than there are people in the group. Having an "extra" piece requires the guests to talk to each other, hopefully about how good the sample was and who gets to enjoy that last extra bite. Similarly I've asked customers to be "in charge" at their table by giving some samples to one member of the group and asking her to dole them out to the others. Sometimes to make it more fun I'll put a young kid in charge of a whole tableful of adults. All this stuff just gets people thinking and talking and creates the sort of entertaining action that's so important in a third place setting.

Similarly we create action by walking people to tables, taking them to their cars, introducing them to cashiers—the whole time we're walking, we're also talking and learning about them, stopping to connect the dots by introducing them to other customers, staff members, or products.

In truth I'm not sure I even thought about it at the time, but when we loaned out those champagne glasses the guests would have to bring them back; and that makes for one more way to connect dots, one more way to get the story told, a new connection for them with whoever works at the front door or serves them when they return the flutes.

5. GIVE THE GUESTS THE DOTS

One way to enhance all that dot connection and interactivity is to let customers be the bearers of good news, baked goods, or greetings on our behalf. Letting a customer carry a handwritten greeting card from me to their cousin who's moved to Colorado and hasn't been in Ann Arbor for a few years is more effective than simply mailing the card directly. While the latter is good, the former is at least three times that. I made up that stat to go with the third place, but sending the stuff with a well meaning, "connected" intermediary really is more meaningful. When they convey the card the guests feel valued; they've made a connection between two people they care about. Zingerman's comes up as a topic of positive conversation between two caring people.

The other night a customer of ours came in to get carryout for her husband and mentioned that her new grandson was in the hospital with pneumonia. I grabbed a bag of our brownies and asked her if she'd pass them along to the rest of the family, who were likely to be there that night, too. Again, she got to be the bearer of good news, and in this case, good food. And Zingerman's got to be a positive topic for conversation.

Another facet of this is the work we do to help our staff members. Their families are often also our customers, so we connect more dots by sending staff home with new foods or special greetings.

Again, in all seriousness I do these things happily just because it's nice stuff to do for good people. The spirit of generosity and caring that comes along with all this is hugely important. It's consistent with our Guiding Principles; it's good service; and it's just the right thing to do. But while we're likely to do these sorts of things anyway, we can simultaneously enhance our status as a third place by letting our customers carry the good word around with them. They feel valued, their friends are impressed, and everyone wins.

6. CREATE A "HAUNTED HOUSE"

In *Setting the Table* Danny Meyer makes the great point that we're more likely to become a third place when we can become a "haunt" for people from particular lines of work. If you run a third place you might already have done this. At Union Square Cafe Danny and crew did it by specializing in the literary world, but the choice of field doesn't really matter—the key is to become the third place for most everyone in whatever area of interest you'd like to appeal to. When you find two people who work in that field, you introduce them to each other; pretty soon they all feel connected, to each other and your business.

You can create a "haunted house" by doing things like:

- Staying up to speed on the industry you've got in your sights. Read its trade magazines, learn its lingo, know when there has been a big event or a major professional award has been given.
- Having supporting materials available. If you know that you want to be a hangout for fashionistas, have fashion magazines around, have the style page posted daily, etc.
- Educating the staff on a few key facts about the industry whose haunt you want to become.
- Making sure to promote the use of your space to outside groups that work in that field.

7. SHARE THE SUCCESS

We know that staff like praise, so why not customers as well? I'm always giving positive feedback to our third place regulars in front of their families, friends, and colleagues. If you like their jewelry, heard they got a promotion, or whatever else, let them know! The praise has to be genuine. As long as it is, the positive feelings it creates will reward them for visiting us so regularly.

8. CREATE COMMUNITY SPACES

Many of the best third places I've been to are far from glamorous. You only have to look at spots like airports or fancy office buildings to see that big budgets and long planning periods aren't what it takes to create a hospitable environment, let alone a special third place setting. Yet, much to my independent business-person's frustration, I've seen chain convenience stores on unappealing stretches of highway turn into third places without the slightest effort from anyone who cared much about the quality of life at a local level.

That said, it does help to actively create community activity in your third-place-in-the-making. Toward that end we make a point of offering to host meetings of local community groups of all sorts. I encourage families to gather at our spots for whatever occasion they have at hand. I like when customers linger and I don't try to chase them out. We put out picnic tables, offer free wireless, set up water bowls for dogs, and hook up air hoses for bikers. The more these folks come together in our business the more our space becomes "their" space, and the stronger the bond that keeps them coming back.

To help build that community energy we've also done things like host live music, create areas where kids can be comfortable, started an adjunct "off-night" farmer's market, and explored the idea of hosting a local radio show. There are thousands of things you could try. My point is just that the more diverse community-based activities (DCBAs?) are going on in our business, the more likely we are to successfully "come in third."

One key to me though is that to make this really work, things have to be done in a way that makes them—like us—feel authentic. There's nothing I've listed above that hasn't been done by some national franchise chain in one form or another. It's the uniqueness, the personal, the personality behind what we do that makes it special, as opposed to one more staged scene created at corporate world headquarters.

When it works, it's a fine thing to behold. "The casual environment," Oldenburg opined, "finally, is the natural habitat of the third place. Third place settings are really no more than a physical manifestation of people's desire to associate with those in an area once they get to know them."

Leaving the Community Better Than We Found It

There's no question in my mind that successfully building our business into a third place is good for us. But it's not all about us—*I truly believe that third places add enormously to the quality of life in the community.* As Ray Oldenburg describes it, "At the risk of sounding mystical, I will contend that nothing contributes as much to one's sense of belonging to a community as much as 'membership' in a third place. The third place also encourages people to hear others' stories; diversity grows because people are exposed to folks whose stories they might not hear otherwise." All of which, I think, enhances understanding, reduces the risk of stereotyping, creates positive community energy, and helps us as businesses enhance the quality of our community's existence. Which is why, in this one instance, I'm really happy if we can figure out how to finish third!

working the fields at cornman farms, our six-acre sustainable farm

Building a Sustainable Business

*Why Sticking Around Is Better
Than the Alternative*

I felt strongly about this subject when I wrote this essay a few years ago, and I feel significantly more so today. The act of creatively and constructively staying in business and, in the process, building positive benefits for all involved (the community, the people who work in the business, purveyors, investors, and, of course, customers) is probably more to the point of most "purpose-driven businesses" like ours than the more standard supposition of setting out just to make money. Although hardly anyone seems to teach it this way, the truth is that just staying in business is actually a pretty significant achievement. Seriously, it's way easier to go under than it is to keep going! To state the nearly obvious, staying in business does suppose that we will be profitable, but that alone isn't really what it means to me to be sustainable. In the old model of business, success looks like a hot poker player who hits it big, sweeps up all his chips, cashes out, and goes home while he's on top. In our case, by contrast, the point is to keep playing, and, in the process, to create wins for all the players at once while the pool gets ever-bigger and ever-more rewarding for all involved.

Over the last 10 or 15 years we've seen increasing support for the idea of sustainable agriculture. While we've got a long way to go before it's a widespread reality, many organizations are working in more consciously and ecologically sound ways than they ever have before. With that in mind I've spent a fair bit of time of late pondering the idea of sustainability, not just in the critical environmental context, but in a broader business sense.

Leaving Our World Better Off Than We Found It

While there have been many formal and legal definitions of sustainable agriculture in recent years, the one that's stuck in my head came from something I heard about 20 years ago at one of the hundreds of food-focused conferences I've been to. I can't really remember anymore who said it, so I apologize for not being able to give proper credit. It was early in the move toward organics. Someone on one of the panels was a grower and he was responding to challenges from folks in the audience who were asking about the higher price of organic produce. What he said was that when we, as consumers, purchased industrially-produced foods we were really paying only a portion of the full price—there were significant costs still to be paid, for things like restoring the soil and cleaning up the environment. In essence our initial purchase was like a down payment, with the full bill to come due later on, and with a huge interest rate, too.

By contrast, he went on, when we purchased sustainably raised food, the price we paid was all-inclusive. Rather than depleting natural resources and leaving less for those who would come later, the soil in which these sustainably produced products had been grown was left at least as good—and often better— than it had been when the farmer started working it.

The idea of business sustainability is, to me, about taking this concept and applying it to all elements of our organization. The results should be similar to what that farmer described: we should leave the world around us a better place than how we found it.

We've actually built this notion into our long-term vision for Zingerman's. I admit to having a bit of hesitation to actually state this out loud—inevitably we'll fall short in any number of ways in our efforts to make this happen. But if we don't commit to making it a reality, it's safe to say that we're not even going to get close. To put things in context, I should say too that this isn't really a very radical departure from what we did in our first 25 years. But as with so much organizational evolution, it's about taking something we've long worked at and stating it as an overt commitment, with clear guidelines for ourselves of what it really means in day-to-day life, not an ad hoc thing that sort of just happens.

The idea of seeing business in a sustainable context like this is still sort of new to me, so I'm sure I'll adjust my thinking as we go, and as I gather input from others who do similar work. But here are some of the basic components of what I mean. Sustainability isn't just about soil or air; it's also about staying in business, staying alive, staying engaged, and doing good things for a long period of time, all in a way that's rooted in the values and views that we hold dear.

Staying in Business

Good intentions alone aren't enough to build a sustainable business—you have to be financially viable, too. Which I guess points to an essential aspect of what it means to be a sustainable business: you have to actually stay in business for a long period of time. While the glamour usually goes to the new idea and the new startup—and more power to 'em—I think it's far more challenging to actually stay in business and do so in a way that's rewarding for all involved.

That idea stands in pretty sharp contrast to the prevailing reality of the business world. One thing I've come to realize over the years is that most businesses are not flourishing. A handful thrive, others survive, and the vast majority are actually in some stage of going out of business.

Paying the Full Price Up Front

I think that this idea of staying in business bleeds into a topic that hardly anyone ever really wants to talk about—charging enough for our products for our business to actually be financially viable over the long term. The funny thing about this is that even in the world of sustainable food production there are still a whole lot of folks pushing for ever lower prices. Which is certainly their prerogative. It's not like I'm an advocate of raising prices on principle. Nor have I ever thought that life is all about maximizing your financial return. And I definitely don't think higher prices should be used to cover up inefficiencies.

But the reality is that higher prices that allow healthy, sustainably minded businesses to do all the things we're talking about and still stay in business are, I think, a good and necessary thing. By contrast, driving prices down at all costs is the exact model that we all say that we want to get away from in the food world. And we know what happened there. Personally, I think back to what Michael Pollan wrote in an piece for the *New York Times Sunday Magazine* entitled "Unhappy Meals." Among his principles of healthy eating, number five is "pay more, eat less." He goes on to explain that:

> "The American food system has for a century devoted its energies and policies to increasing quantity and reducing price, not to improving quality. There's no escaping the fact that better food—measured by taste or nutritional quality (which often correspond)—costs more, because it has been grown or raised less intensively and with more care. Not everyone can afford to eat well in America, which is shameful, but most of us can: Americans spend, on average, less than 10 percent of their income on food, down from 24 percent in 1947, and less than the citizens of any other nation. And those of us who can afford to eat well should. Paying more for food well grown in good soils—whether certified organic or not—will contribute not only to your health (by reducing exposure to pesticides) but also to the health of others who might not themselves be able to afford that sort of food: the people who grow it and the people who live downstream, and downwind, of the farms where it is grown."

Having worked in the food world for nearly 30 years now I'm still shocked and awed to hear, over and over again, stories of restaurants and retailers that were generally considered to be big successes who, it later turns out, never made any money. Although some of them charged high prices, they ran cost of goods numbers that simply weren't viable, yet struggled along for years anyway. Some survived on infusions of cash from corporate parents, wealthy-from-other-work owners, or public stock offerings. Others stayed in business, in part, by not paying themselves a salary, either because they didn't need the income or because there wasn't any cash to pay it.

To the consumer, of course, these businesses look perfectly healthy. And the prices they charge set a standard that others see as the norm. But the problem is that using these failing businesses as a benchmark is akin to setting your weight target by looking at fashion magazines. In either case, the model (sorry, pun intended) is not very likely to be sustainable. It survives, maybe even looks glamorous for a bit, but eventually starves and collapses. And, in the process, it leaves the world around it—staff, suppliers, customers, and community—worse off than when it first arrived on the scene.

What that means to me on the upside is that we have to have the courage to charge what we need to charge to stay in business in a healthy way. That we have to back that up by delivering great experiences to those we interact with— staff, suppliers, community, shareholders, and of course customers. We have to share what we take in with all of those groups, so that everyone gets something positive out of the work that we do in order to create the kind of abundance we're committed to delivering. We have to back that all up even more by using good business practices, careful costing, and effective purchasing, so that we're not wasting cash that customers contribute to our cause.

To me, that's the crux of what sustainable business is all about. Staying in business in order to sustain the lives and livelihoods of the people and the producers of our community.

Community

This is where I started to realize that the panelist-farmer's model was relevant to a much broader field than just the organic agriculture he was addressing. His explanation and expectation applies perfectly—we want Ann Arbor to be at least as good and hopefully better because of our work than it was when we got here.

This is all part of what's commonly called "giving back to the community." On a very tangible level it could mean contributing money, time, or information to help those around us. Here at Zingerman's we focus on assisting people in need, specifically working to fight to reduce hunger in our community. We actively support the arts and education. But we also help the community in the traditional business sense—keeping jobs in the community and buying from other local businesses helps us keep our town economically viable and a place that other like-minded organizations opt to be a part of.

Leaving the community a better place than we found it is also about the less explicitly stated, but maybe even more important, contributions. I truly believe that by giving great service, by sharing constructive business practices with staff and others, by just being nice to our neighbors, we really do make a difference. Just by staying in business for a long period of time an organization helps build solidity and continuity for the community in which its located.

Staying Put

In *Kinds of Power*, James Hillman writes that, "The best way, maybe the only way, to change a situation is to imagine, even to declare that you will stay where you are, in your locale, the rest of your life." I can't say that's the only way to be sustainable, but it certainly makes sense.

A few years ago, Ann Arborites unwrapped their afternoon newspapers to find out that the corporate headquarters of one of the largest employers in town had decided to close its local office. The decision came at the cost to the community of over 2000 jobs, a lot of good people, a fair bit of cash, and all the other things that go with these sorts of closings. I'm not sure exactly what the implications will be for the community—other urban areas have experienced far worse catastrophes, and I'm confident that the creative and resilient folks who live here will turn this into a positive growth opportunity.

Although I'm saddened by the company's decision, this is not an evil organization. They gave to the community very actively for years, and were in many ways outstanding corporate citizens. But the reality was that they were a branch of a multinational corporation, headquartered elsewhere. Inevitably, their decisions gave less weight to community impact than a local business's would have. Mind you, I'm not saying that a company that finds itself in economic straits should keep a facility open just for the sake of staying open. These are very difficult situations.

But the closing reminded me of the importance of sustainability in a community context. This was a company that was wooed here with tax breaks and a whole lot of city support. In many ways this seems akin to organizations—in business, sports, or whatever—where huge amounts of money are spent to bring big names in from the outside while those who've been contributing all along (and who would likely have stayed rooted for the long haul) are basically ignored.

I'm not criticizing the effort to attract good businesses. But it does make me wonder what might have happened if those incentives had been directed to local businesses or to organizations that had a commitment to commerce and community that extended beyond immediate economic opportunism. In the environmental context an analogy might be forsaking strip mining for the restoration of wetlands or native prairies. By staying in business, we keep jobs in the community, we keep cash flowing through to other local businesses, we keep delivering quality experiences every day—to state the obvious, if we fail, all of that will be lost.

The Environment

This is certainly the most common application of the sustainability concept, and for good reason: it's critical for keeping our world intact for future generations. In the years to come, we've committed ourselves to do much more with ecologically sound work in food, fuels, carryout containers, and other facets of our everyday operations.

Food

It won't be any shock that we apply the idea of "sustainable business" to the food that is our daily business. The more we can demonstrate to people that they really *can* taste the difference between great foods and the so-so stuff, the more we can prove that most consumers care about quality and are willing to pay what it takes to get it, the more we encourage like-minded businesses to go out and do good things in their communities, and the better off we all are.

There are dozens of sources that enumerate the benefits of local agriculture, traditional farming techniques, sustainable seafood sources, and humanely raised and more flavorful meat. The point is that by supporting suppliers who share these values we can build a solid foundation for positive work in the food community. That support can come in the context of cultivating relationships, sharing techniques, paying the higher price that supports the production of sustainable and more flavorful food, sticking with new suppliers when they're struggling to get going, providing advice, and being patient so that we can get to win-win solutions over the long haul.

The People We Work With

The concept of sustainability can also be applied to the lives of the people who work in our organization, which we hope will be better when they leave us than when they arrived. I hope this is true whether their experience of working at Zingerman's was just a three-week stint at the holidays or 20-plus years of partnership. In small but meaningful ways we want to offer them a richer, more rewarding experience than they might have had elsewhere. So, if they stay with us for a long time, fantastic. And if they leave to go elsewhere (in or out of the food world), I feel confident that they'll be able to use the concepts they learned from us to benefit everyone around them in their new home.

How might we make that happen? Well, in part it's simply by giving our staff the chance to participate in, and contribute to, a sustainable business. By living (imperfectly though we do) our guiding principles, treating others with care and consideration, and being actively committed to the success of all those around us. By demonstrating every day that, though it can be hard to do good work and draining when you're in the middle of doing it, it's a *good* kind of hard! By helping people see that contrary to common wisdom work can actually be something you look forward to, not something you try to get out of.

I also think we impact people's lives through the use of the "organizational recipes" I've shared with you—systemic approaches that help each of us be more successful in our work. Having employed them for many years now, there's no doubt in my mind that by simply teaching and modeling ways to run constructive meetings, effectively manage money, resolve conflicts, give great service, appreciate the wonderful nuances of food and life, we make work and life better for everyone here. Whether they use this stuff at home, in managing their personal finance, at a non-profit they volunteer for, or in their next job, all these techniques can be of benefit.

We also want to provide benefits in the more conventional sense of the term, and at a level that helps people lead productive lives: health care, staff discounts, employee assistance programs, flex time, creative non-financial benefits, child care, scholarships, and so on. None of these are terribly original to us, but they really do make a difference in helping people manage their lives. In the end, I think people feel better about, and more at peace with, themselves. And that in turn makes for a more peaceful world for all of us to live in.

Balancing the Near Term with Long Term

Much of life in the big business and political worlds seems to be about responding to immediate pressures, about delivering short-term results at a negative cost that comes due much later. But I think we can achieve short-term sustainability—i.e., we can stay in business—while also creating long-term benefits for all involved. The two will always be in conflict to some degree, but the point of business sustainability is to embrace the struggle and find ways to achieve both!

We as businesspeople need to use our power and authority wisely and judiciously, in much the same way that sustainable producers limit their inputs. We need to stay true to our values, not just react to market pressures. And we need to be respectful of what nature has given us while still shaping a path of our own choosing. Despite the "wisdom" of agribusiness experts, farmers who do a good job of raising sustainable crops are very much able to succeed financially while maintaining their values and supporting their communities. We can do the same.

Getting Good with Gray

While I believe strongly in everything I've said in this book, I don't for a second suppose that there's some set of simplistic, black and white answers that will magically make a business sustainable and successful. Rather, I've learned enough in life to know that pretty much all this stuff comes at us every day, every hour, only in shades of gray.

We are, of course, constantly faced with difficult business decisions to make—is it better to get so-so, local mass-market milk or to ship better-tasting, sustainably produced dairy from 500 miles away? Is it more responsible to forego foods that don't grow locally in the winter, or to support indigenous growers in warmer climates? Is it more desirable to stay local, as we've decided to do at Zingerman's, or to spread the positive energy and word more aggressively by opening branches all over the country as others have?

Honestly I have no easy answers to offer to these or any of the other ten thousand questions everyone leading an organization struggles with every day. I guess what this is really all about is framing; anyone who's working toward this sort of sustainability in business is going to arrive at their own answers. While each of us may take issue with the decisions of those around us, I think that organizations that are honestly trying to do the right thing are going to make a positive difference no matter what choices they make.

In her novel *Eva Luna,* Isabel Allende writes, "I just do what I can. Reality is a jumble we can't always measure or decipher, because everything is happening at the same time . . . I try to open a path through the maze, to put a little order in the chaos, to make life more bearable." That's a nice summation of the world we have to live—and thrive—in. At the least, let's make a positive difference!

Much of this, of course, runs counter to conventional business thinking. But our vision here is to fight that tide; to stay in business in a constructive way; to still be here, contributing to, improving, and enriching the world around us for many years to come. While that may not sound all that exhilarating if you describe it in a business school case study, my experience is that pulling it off is a pretty big achievement.

I hope this whole piece doesn't come across as presumptuous, because it's not intended to be. It's extremely humbling, really: just stating our commitment hardly guarantees that we'll be able to meet it. But if we can make sustainability work—and I think we can—the world around us will win in most every way imaginable.

Last Minute Add On: Sustainable Business

Pete Garner, who's diligently led the work to put the pieces of this book project together, is probably gonna kill me. It's less than a week before we send this thing to the printer and here I am trying to sneak in a 1200-word postscript on sustainability in business. But what follows has been on my mind a lot of late, and it's not the concept's fault that it didn't come to me until a few months after the rest of the copy went in for final editing. I'm sure I'll write more on the subject down the road, but I don't want to let this piece go to print without at least sharing the thought.

So . . . here's the deal. I've increasingly come to consider what we do here at Zingerman's to be akin to a successful, sustainable (read, "organic" if that makes the point more clearly), small farm. The ZCoB is far from perfect and blemishes abound, but in its own weird, sustainable way it's been working pretty well for nearly three decades now. By contrast, the old mainstream business model, I think, is more akin to industrial farming. I know I'm generalizing, but you'll get the idea. The work in that conventional setting is all about output maximization, crop consistency, and cost control. The farmers' job at that scale (and lord knows the work is still very hard) is to take nature by the horns and wrestle it to the ground as best they can. People spray for pests and fertilize heavily with artificial inputs in order to elicit short-term high returns. Crops are grown in straight, orderly rows. Seed varieties are selected for consistent appearance and high yields, not for flavor. The weeds, the native pests, the slightly strange looking heirloom vegetables, and the high flavor but low yield seed varieties—all the stuff that seems suboptimal or underperforming—have long since been scrapped.

It's not like this industrial approach can't be made to work, and it's not like some folks, or at least large agribusinesses, don't still make good money doing it. Like all moderately dysfunctional systems (I've contributed to many myself) it works well enough that it's hard to make a big break and shift to a more long term, sustainable approach. Most folks involved, I'm sure, mean well, and while it may not be ideal, living mostly in the moment, it's hardly infernal. Still, innocence aside, we all know what the system has done to the food, to the environment, to the quality of life for farm families and rural communities across the country. Way too many small, old-school farmers survive economically only by borrowing more money from the bank each year, then hoping and praying for weather that will allow them to pay their loans back properly so they can then borrow again. Farm subsidies seem to keep it all kind of afloat, but the monotony of monoculture seems to wear ever thinner. A few win, a lot more lose. Bigger companies may come out OK, but communities—as reflected in nutrition, quality of work, environment, etc.—often don't.

The problem in the standard business world today is . . . not surprisingly, very similar. Both systems were driven by the desire to make the world succumb to the standardization of modern science. Both brought some short-term, systemwide benefits to the people at the top of the pyramid, but over time, big problems to those at its base. While profits may stay somewhat steady, quality and service have tended to fall ever lower. Resources are sapped, not replenished or renewed, and the less than totally tangible spirit and energy in the workplace slip ever lower. Stock prices, not sustainability, drive planning and production. In the corporate world as in the fields, instead of being encouraged, personality and diversity get pushed out of the picture. The focus instead is on fault-free, long-lasting, often all too bland (for my taste at least) middle of the market movement, making as much money as possible without all that much concern for the others impacted. The interesting "imperfections" that come from involving creative, smart people at every level, the diversity, inclusiveness, ingenuity, and innovation that occur naturally when nurtured, have been stripped out in the interest of conformity, cost cutting, and compliance. Despite the constant emphasis on scientific efficiency, yields gradually go down and the quality of the "soil" in which people work every day steadily erodes.

By contrast, what we have here in our little anarcho-capitalist Community of Businesses probably appears kind of chaotic. We don't really fit into any of the standard models. We have 10 separate businesses acting as one organization even though the latter really doesn't even, formally, yet exist as a legal entity. Command and control is kaput; 16 partners sit down to make organization-wide decisions using a consensus model, in open meetings often attended by front-line staff and out of town visitors. There are lots of people who definitely don't fit the "dress for success" profile flourishing in leadership roles, while refugees from bigger business backgrounds step willingly into supporting spots. Finances are posted on smudged-up white boards hanging on the walls, and most everybody actually reads them. Bosses are here to serve busboys, not the other way around. Bakers in jeans ask questions of bankers in suits. If you walk around it's not all that easy to tell exactly who's in charge and who's just helping out. Most all the food is made by hand, using highly labor-intensive methods and ingredients that cost way more than any industry expert would say they should.

But somehow, knock on a lot of well-worn wood, our odd-looking sustainable garden of an organization is working. While what we produce tastes great, it's probably way too quirky to conform in the standard commercial setting. We have "weeds" all over our organizational "rows," and, although our results are consistently strong, things don't look exactly like they're supposed to in the storybooks. Sustainable business may not make for org chart optimization, but just as the organic farmer works with nature to grow food in a sustainably sound way that builds effectively on, and bonds with, his or her environment, if you go back and read the essay on the Natural Laws of Business, we actually live—and live with—all 12 of them fairly consistently well.

As is the case with sustainable agriculture, it's hard to scientifically suss out exactly what contributes what to what in our world. In a sustainable farm setting it's tough to prove just how much those little beetles in the back contribute to making the melons so marvelous, and it's hard to say with certainty what it is about the compost that's contributing to some weird looking, but great tasting, heirloom tomatoes. Honestly, I can't really say which single "secret" of our work sets the pace here—who knows whether it's visioning, the culture of positive appreciation, the belief that people here have in doing something special, the 3 Steps to Great Service, open book finance, the quality of the product, working in a principle driven business, a shared sense of history, a clear understanding of the mission, or some other *mishegas* (meaning, as my grandmother often used it, "nonsense," in Yiddish). But at the end of the day, the food tastes better, the people working on it feel better about what they're doing, the bills get paid on time, the bank likes to loan to us, investors get paid back, the community wins, energy is high, and it all seems to come together in its own, organic, mindful, kind of anarchistic, but, ultimately, oddly effective way.

What does it all mean? That's for everyone who's interested to decide on his or her own. Let's just say that, while this may not be what they're teaching in most business school settings, at the least, it's full flavored food for organizational thought for anyone looking for a bit of a different, broadly minded, sustainably sound way forward.

the cheese counter at the delicatessen

28 Years of Buying Local...

All Over the World

One of the things that I believe makes organizations like ours (and there, of course, are others out there) so much more effective than most is that we get clear with each other around the words we're using. Most businesses, it seems, are comfortable sticking with buzzwords (quality and service are prime culprits), or bending with the winds as trends come and go. Here we've worked hard to get clarity around meaningful shared definitions that carry us past the clichés in which so many companies get bogged down. In the years since I wrote this piece, the subject of "local" has become even bigger than ever. Clearly it's a critical issue for any caring organization to work on. Even in the last few years there has been tremendous headway made in getting more flavorful, locally made foods onto Americans' tables in place of the mass-produced, not very tasty stuff that was previously shipped in from some faraway spot. That said, to me the issue is far less clear-cut than most people make it out to be. Here's our take on it, offered up in the spirit of trying to make sustainable business a reality by serving and selling the full-flavored and traditional foods to which we've been committed since we opened in 1982.

There's something about marking our anniversary each year at Zingerman's that makes me want to take a look at where we are and where we want to go. More than anything else it pushes me to appreciate how much great food and how many great people we have around us. As I've said many times before and will say many times again (because it's totally true) I feel incredibly appreciative of the opportunity to be associated with all these great customers, great artisan producers, partners, staff members, and suppliers.

On a different note, I've spent a lot of time in recent years thinking about the question of buying local. I have to admit that I've always struggled some with this one. Folks out in California talk a lot about it I know, and I've always agreed with it on a broad intellectual level—the issues of fossil fuels, supporting local economies, getting to know the people who produce what we use . . . these are clearly all good things, ideas that I believe in and very much want to support.

So what's my problem? (That's a question many people who work with me probably ask regularly.) Well, in honesty, there were three things that kept catching me about it:

- We live in Michigan, not Marseilles or Marin County. So while I'm all for eating locally, around here that would mean about six months of potatoes, cabbage, onions, turnips, and dried beans. And while I like all of those things a lot (just had some great braised turnips for dinner last night), I'm not sure that I'm ready to go back to that sort of a diet. In fact, let me state that more strongly: I'm not willing to go back to that sort of 17th-century diet any more than I am to living without running water or electricity.

- When I really started to think through the "buy local" thing in my very literalist way (in one of those belated glimpses of the obvious), it struck me that not only would we not be eating raspberries air-shipped from Chile, but we also couldn't be consuming coffee, tea, chocolate, or spices, all of which we get from sources that are so distant they might as well be on the moon.

- All I have to do is look around the Deli and see that while buying local is a great idea, we don't. I mean, we do it where we can, probably way more than most food businesses have over the years. We get ever-greater amounts of ever-more flavorful produce from local farms each summer. The milk we use to make our cheese at the Creamery comes from only an hour away. We roast our own coffee, make cheese and gelato, bake bread and pastries all right here in town. Our pork is coming from one of the new Niman Ranch network pork farmers here in Michigan, and, of late, even from our own spot, Cornman Farms in nearby Dexter. But it's hard to create an all-out "buy local" agenda around a menu of olive oil from Spain, pasta from Italy, and cheese from all over Europe. Even though we bake those really great Buenos Aires brownies at the Bakehouse on Plaza Drive by the Ann Arbor Airport, the Dulce de Leche that contributes that amazingly creamy, caramelly center comes to us all the way from a farm in Argentina.

So, all that said, this is merely my personal struggle. Others may or may not worry about it in the least, in which case I guess I should apologize for taking up all this space talking about it. But one of the things that probably sets us apart is that we actively acknowledge and then openly work on the values issues and conflicts that come up every day in our organization. For me, this is one of those issues. And one thing about me is that once I engage in a struggle I stay in it for as long as I need to in order to get to clarity. While it takes a while, after enough conversations and enough reading and enough journaling the clarity usually comes.

In this instance it came to me when I led a panel at the Terra Madre conference in Turin. Part of Slow Food's bi-annual Salone del Gusto festival, it was an amazing conclave of traditional food producers, food sellers, and food writers (I got to be in all three groups) from all over the world. There were 5000 attendees from dozens of countries. The panelists on the list I'd been given were literally from all over the world—some from Europe, two each from South America and Africa, a couple more from North America. Trying to prepare myself for the subject, I really started to struggle with all the issues I've already put down in this essay. Buying local sounded like a great idea but . . . there were all these issues that I hadn't been able to sort out on the subject. To say the least, I was anxious—I felt like I was going to be some sort of a fraud, getting up in front of this huge group of prestigious Slow Food members to speak about the importance of buying local when I knew full well that so much of what we buy isn't.

In fact, a lot of what we purchase comes from producers that were also attending the conference so I guess the burden was on them, as well as on me. But at the time I was mostly just trying to figure out how to balance the reality of what we do at Zingerman's and how much work we put into bringing non-local foods from faraway places with being the seeming spokesperson for the buy-local campaign at this prestigious conference. What turned the tide for me was the brilliant commentary of one the panelists.

It's funny how these things work out because Paul Muller wasn't even on the original list of panelists. Fortunately for me (and the audience), he showed up about three minutes before we were due to start and introduced himself as a speaker. I told him he wasn't on my list but invited him to stay anyway. Glad I did. Paul is a partner in Full Belly Farm, an organic producer near Sacramento. I don't know that what they're doing there is all that different from what goes on at the small farms we buy produce from around Ann Arbor.

What was different, though, was Paul's intellectual construct. To him, "buying local" means "having a relationship with the end user." This is not what I expected to hear from an organic farmer from California, where it's easier to buy local produce for a lot more of the year than will ever be possible in Michigan. As soon as he said it, the concept stuck in my head. Because what Paul described is what we do here at Zingerman's. And it removed, in an appropriate, intellectually, and principally sound way, all three of the obstacles I'd been mentally tripping over for so long.

In that context, I've long thought that one of the most important things we do at Zingerman's is to build connections among people who share our values.

- We connect people in Ann Arbor with food made by caring craftspeople around the world.
- We connect people who grew up with a local cheese or dish that they haven't had for years, and through the chance to eat it again give them a chance to enjoy all the memories they associate with it.
- We help people we sell to connect with other good people—we know that eating good food offers an opportunity to commune with others we care about.
- We connect communities through food. I love that we have settings in which people are experiencing full-flavored chopped liver and traditional Carolina pork barbecue at the same table. That people from all walks of life come in to our places to share with friends what they love to eat.

There are a million examples I could share to illustrate the emotional and culinary connections that happen through the food community we've been privileged to help create. One that comes quickly to mind is that of a customer who stopped me just before Christmas to tell me his story. He grew up here in the States in a family that had recently come over from France. He said that a few years ago he used our Mail Order to send his elderly grandfather a loaf of Farm Bread at Christmas. It was his grandfather's last Christmas, so the customer remembered it particularly well. His grandfather ate the bread and said, "I didn't think Americans could make anything so good!" The son felt pride in being able to get his grandfather something to remind him of his past, and his grandfather got to reconnect with a long-lost taste from his childhood. Really good bread from the Bakehouse and a team of Mail Order shippers made it all happen.

This has happened a lot at the Roadhouse too, often for people who grew up with North Carolina pulled pork. There was a musician who played here not long ago, a North Carolina native who'd been out on the road for a long time. He was so excited to get the kind of vinegar-based Eastern North Carolina barbecue and good greens that he'd grown up with. He just kept talking about it over and over. Same happens with pimento cheese—while Northerners are happy to taste it (it's really good!), Southerners living here in the Great Lakes region go wild when they get to partake of this little piece of their past. The memories are that strong.

We also connect people with their dreams. John Loomis and Allen Leibowitz are passionate, respectively, about making artisan cheese and roasting great coffee. Through Zingerman's Creamery and Zingerman's Coffee Company they now get to live their passions every day. And we and others in our community get to enjoy the fruits of their labor. I was at the Roadhouse one night in December and a guy who lives here in Ann Arbor stopped to tell me how much he'd enjoyed his dinner. I noticed that he'd had a press pot of coffee and asked him how it was. He loved it. Which coffee was it? The Coban from Guatemala. Turns out he'd spent two years working in the Coban region of Guatemala and loved the coffee there and was totally jazzed that we were roasting it here in town so he could drink it and in the process connect with his memories of great times down in Guatemala. Another guy who was at the Roadhouse the night before had traveled a lot in Uganda and loved the coffee there and was thrilled to find that he could now get some of it here in town. Small stuff but it makes a difference.

In thinking about this idea of connection, I realized that I'd actually like to take Paul Muller's definition of buying local one step further. For us here at Zingerman's, buying local means three things: having a relationship with the people who make the food, a relationship with the people we work with here in town, and, as Paul said, a relationship with the end user. Which leads me to the story of Ben Ripple, Five Foods, Bali, and the Sea Islands.

I write an electronic newsletter for our staff every few weeks that I call "Five Foods." It's really just my take on five foods that are on my mind that week— whatever I've tasted that seems particularly great and interesting and that I like. In addition to our crew, I'll sometimes "cc" friends, food writers, or producers that I think might be interested. Last fall I was writing about the arrival of Balinese long pepper. It's an amazing spice, one that the Romans raved about and used extensively a few thousand years ago, but that has fallen almost completely out of use in most of the world, certainly in the West. We'd been getting this really great sea salt from Bali, which comes to us courtesy of Ben and Blair Ripple, an American couple who settled in Bali and have worked for years to help the people there build a sustainable economy based on local produce. The Ripples had recently added this delicious long pepper to their line.

This is an example of one of the places where the idea of "buying local" always stumped me. Because if I want to help people in Bali find sustainable ways to live, then buying sea salt and long pepper from them is one way to help make that happen. Anyway, I wrote about this long pepper (a delicious, slightly more exotic relative of black pepper that I highly recommend) and cc'd Ben on the email to let him know what I was saying. Funny thing is that one of my other five foods that week was the sweet potato fries that we'd been doing at the Roadhouse. I learned about sweet potato fries in the process of studying the foods of the Sea Islands off the coast of South Carolina and Georgia. (One of the fun things about the Roadhouse has been the chance to introduce people to the obscure but delicious corners of American cooking.) So, I sent out the Five Foods featuring both the Sea Island sweet potato fries and the Balinese long pepper. And within about an hour Ben writes back to tell me that in fact he grew up on the Sea Islands and remembered eating sweet potato fries. Small world. Connections. All the way from Bali, but nevertheless, extremely local. We know the people that are producing the long pepper even though it's half a world away; we know the people here that are buying it; and the people we're buying it from grew up eating the foods we're introducing at the Roadhouse.

Realistically we really do know most of the suppliers we buy from. We've been to visit a whole lot of them. We know our customers. Even those who buy mail order, we talk to on the phone or via email and meet them when they come to town. We visit with customers over the counter at the Bakehouse. They can come into the Creamery and see where John makes our (very local in every aspect) cheese. They can sit at the chef's counter at the Roadhouse and visit and taste with us while the kitchen crew works. On top of this, there's the whole thing of our vision. Which is to stay local, to have 12 to 18 Zingerman's businesses here in the area by the year 2020, each with its own specialty and each with a managing partner or partners who devote their long-term passion and day-to-day attention to detail to helping that business succeed. In essence it's a pretty local vision. Because although we've obviously gotten a lot larger we're still here in town, still talking to staff and guests every day, still tasting the food all the time. It's never finished, this tasting and talking, this effort to improve in all we do all the time. At least I hope not.

Again, my thanks go out to everyone we work with, to everyone at every level who's helped to make this strangely global yet still ultimately local network of culinary and cultural connections that we're a part of; thanks for everything you do to make this a reality. I feel incredibly lucky to be a part of it.

Buying Local in Britain

One manifestation of all this has been our relationship with Neal's Yard Dairy in London. I first came into contact with Neal's Yard back in 1989. I was on vacation in Ireland, and, as I'm wont to do, had arranged to meet Irish cheesemakers, chefs, salmon smokers, etc., while I was there. About halfway through the three-week holiday I made my way down to see Tom and Giana Ferguson, who make Gubbeen cheese down near the town of Schull (it's about as far to the southwest as you can get in Ireland and not be in the ocean). When I arrived it turned out that Jane Scotter, then a partner at Neal's Yard, was also visiting. We struck up the usual food person's—or in this case, cheese person's—conversation. Turns out that I'd been to visit the Neal's Yard shop near Covent Garden a few years earlier. Turns out, too, that we were interested in the same sorts of traditional cheeses. That we were already buying from many of the same farms. That although Neal's Yard was selecting and maturing British farmhouse cheeses, they hadn't done any exporting. All intriguing, all exciting. All about connections. Very local. Jane invited me to come to London to visit. And sometime (I can't remember exactly when) in the next 12 months, I went.

In London I met Randolph Hodgson, Jane's partner and the man who'd started Neal's Yard back in 1979. Turns out we had a lot in common—views on food, cheese, people, business, life. We became friends, and, after much discussion, agreed that it was time for Neal's Yard Dairy to experiment with export. We agreed, too, that Zingerman's would be the ideal place with which to do the experimenting. And we did. Fifteen years later, we're still buying, a lot. And, through this story, I realize that we again are living Paul Muller's local thing. Funny (non)coincidence—Randolph was one of the speakers, along with Paul Muller, on that Terra Madre panel.

P.S. Long Ago Local—An Anarchist Ahead of His Time?

A great many of the important issues we're talking about here were addressed by one of the best-known anarchists of all time, the Russian-born Prince Peter Kropotkin, in his 1912 work, *Fields, Factories and Workshops; or Industry Combined with Agriculture and Brain Work with Manual Work*. His book includes lines like:

> "Home-grown fruit is always preferable to the half-ripe produce which is imported from abroad . . ."
>
> "For thousands of years in succession to grow one's food was the burden, almost the curse, of mankind. But it need be so no more. If you make yourselves the soil, and partly the temperature and the moisture which each crop requires, you will see that to grow the yearly food of a family, under rational condition of culture, requires so little labour that if might almost be done as a mere change from other pursuits. . . . You will admire the amount of sound knowledge which your children will acquire by your side, the rapid growth of their intelligence, and the facility with which they will grasp the law of Nature, animate and inanimate."

He also wrote extensively on the subject in *The Conquest of Bread*, published in 1906, from which the came the following quote:

> "It is to the advantage of every nation to grow their own wheat, their own vegetables, and to manufacture at home most of the produce they consume. This diversity is the surest pledge of the complete development of production by mutual co-operation and the moving cause of progress, while specialization is now a hindrance to progress."

zingerman's delicatessen, at the corner of detroit and kingsley

A Recipe
for Making
Something
Special

or, as Jim Hightower says,
"There's nothing in the middle of the road
but yellow stripes and dead armadillos."

Here at Zingerman's we've always worked to create unique and out of the ordinary things. Honestly we've spent nearly 30 years steering clear of the same sort of stuff that everyone else is doing, working to build businesses, develop products and services, marketing, merchandising, and work experiences that consistently stand out from the crowd. More often than not this stuff starts out running completely counter to the current trends, or to what everyone tells you is the "way you're supposed to do it." Having done a fair few (if never as many as I'd like) special things over the years, I can tell you with confidence that when you start going after almost anything that doesn't fit nicely into the boxes everyone else is used to operating with, you can pretty much count on catching a lot of flak over what you're proposing to do. Of course 10 years later, when you've made it to "great success" (whoever it is that bestows the blue ribbon of "success" on you), everyone will likely tell you how "brilliant" you were for doing it.

I decided to stick this essay near the end of the book because, in a way, I think it synopsizes all of the ideas in the previous essays. While it's probably easier in the short run to go with the mainstream flow, to me (and I think most everyone at Zingerman's) it's a lot less rewarding in the long term. If you're going to do something, make it memorable. Life is short—go for greatness. Do something special. And have fun doing it!

I have a natural attraction to the strange and different, the trendsetters, the people and organizations that have the emotional and intellectual wherewithal to do something special. In a world of increasing sameness, what I'm almost always drawn to are the places where there's that special energy, a sense of aliveness, of something cool, creative, and compelling. As someone who travels a fair bit, I'm pretty confident that I can track down two or three of those spots in any town I go to. In a big city there might be a whole bunch of them, but even in small towns there are usually a couple of places that catch my eye; a small café, an antique shop, a restaurant. Wherever you find 'em, they're the businesses that are the total opposite of those standardized settings in strip malls and chain stores.

In putting together the "secrets" in this book, I've spent a fair bit of time thinking about what it is that makes those places so unique, and, more important, what drives the people who run them to do all the work needed to make their places so special. It's been on my mind and in my makeup for as long as I can remember: making special things happen—whether it's a special organization, a special product or service, or just a special experience with each staff member or customer we run into—is a BIG piece of what we do here at Zingerman's.

Which is one reason it was nice to be honored as such by being included in Bo Burlingham's book, *Small Giants: Companies That Choose to Be Great Instead of Big*, where we're associated with creative businesspeople like Fritz Maytag from Anchor Steam Brewery; Danny Meyer and the crew at Union Square Hospitality Group (that's Union Square Café, Tabla, Grammercy Tavern, etc.) in NYC; and singer and musician Ani DiFranco and her record label, Righteous Babe—to name a few. All are companies that have shown a long-term dedication to creativity, community, and positive experiences for the people who work in their organizations. Each has chosen a unique way forward, a path that's true to their own vision and values.

What pushes these people to pass up conventional growth models to do something special? I'm not sure that what follows are the "right" answers, but they're the ones that I've come up with after many conversations with folks I respect, both inside and outside of the ZCoB.

1. A VISION OF UNIQUENESS

Most everyone in Bo's book, and most every business I know of that builds something special, seems to start with a unique vision of the future. Rather than just responding to problems and opportunities as they come up, these folks dream of bigger things, and unique ways to do what they do. That uniqueness energizes those in the business to go after greatness and attracts a clientele interested in making life a bit more interesting, special, and more substantive.

2. A WILLINGNESS TO BUCK THE TRENDS

It's very, very rare for people who really do something special to start out with a ton of support. To the contrary, most of them have to put up with considerable flak from the folks around them: the "that'll never work," or "we've done that before and it failed," or "what are you, crazy?" Only in hindsight does the public see how smart you were for going after whatever it was that you were working to build.

3. HIGH AWARENESS AND A GOOD SENSE OF PERSPECTIVE

To believe that you can create something great, you have to have a sense of what "great" is. If you've never tasted incredible cheese, then you have no sense of how it's different from the stuff that's just OK. Which is why one of the most important things I can do for our staff in this regard is to help bring them into contact with peers who really do amazing work: to let them visit other great retailers, to dine in exceptional restaurants, to read about other businesses that have created something truly special.

With those experiences comes the ability to notice a difference. Achieving this kind of heightened awareness is often painful. It means worrying about things that most folks are blissfully unaware of. Is there slightly too much salt in the soup? Are we answering our phones with enough enthusiasm? Is the finish on the espresso long enough today? Is the spelling on our specials list correct?

4. A Belief in a Better Tomorrow

Most everyone I've talked to about this has said that they started their business with a conviction that things would eventually be better than they were at the time they got going. And they believed they could personally contribute to that improvement. Without that sense of a better tomorrow, there's really little point in pushing yourself to create a unique and out of the box business. Whether you see the future in terms of the community at large, or of a single customer or staff member, or a supplier you want to help to succeed, it makes it worth doing those little extra things, staying just a little bit longer, or trying a little harder to make something special happen.

5. The Importance of Giving

Another consistent theme is the value that these people place on contributing positively to the lives of others. Margaret Wheatley, in her book, *Turning to One Another,* said that, "when we serve others we gain more hope. We gain energy." What keeps me going through the ups and downs of daily life in the food world is the realization that we made a positive difference in someone's life. The former staff member who's still using what she learned here 10 years ago even though she's gone on to great success elsewhere. The customer whose French-born father let go of decades of frustration about bad American bread after the Bakehouse opened in 1992. Knowing that through our community giving work we've helped feed a lot of people in Ann Arbor who were very much in need.

6. A Willingness to Go the Extra Mile

As I've mentioned, Paul taught me early on that difference-making organizations regularly do the things that everyone else knows they should do, but don't.

We allow longer rise times for our breads, drive 25 miles to deliver something to a customer after an item was left out of their bag, work with small local growers when it might be easier to order from the big guys, ladle fresh goat curd by hand (rather than draining it in bulk) to protect the quality of the cheese. Almost every supplier we buy great food from adheres to this same principle. In the end, the willingness to do the little things day in and day out is how you turn a great idea or inspiring vision into something real—and really special.

7. THE RELATIONSHIPS

People who create special businesses are usually motivated by the relationships they build in the process. Through their work they're contributing to the lives of the people around them, developing win-win relationships with staff members, suppliers, even competitors. These relationships pay a dividend for many decades, in the form of support, insight, and emotional sustenance to fight through the inevitable challenges faced by anyone who's trying to do something out of the ordinary.

8. FUN

Building a special business is definitely a lot more work than building an average one. But when I speak to people who are actually doing it, nearly all of them seem to be having more fun than their peers who have stayed with more standard models. The old image of work as a burden, as the opposite of enjoyment, just doesn't fit. These folks have fun at work and, in truth, in the rest of their lives, as well. Visiting many of them in my travels I've realized that there's just a whole lot more laughter and joy, the sort of simple pleasure that keeps people motivated to do all the work they need to do.

9. APPRECIATION

The special businesses and organizations that I've been around almost all have a really strong sense of appreciation for what they've achieved. Maybe it goes with the idea of service. But those who work this way say that they've come to really appreciate how it's much more about enjoying the journey than it is about any arrival at a final destination (as if there was such a thing . . .). In this sense, I guess they're not at war with the world around them; they avoid slipping into the victim role, instead finding the positive pieces in even the most difficult situations they encounter.

10. Sticking with Things (for a LONG time!)

The often-frustrating reality of life in business is that we're very rarely on a linear path. Instead, it's usually a crooked, winding, two-steps-forward-and-one—and-a-half-steps-back kind of experience. For us at Zingerman's, that means · tasting the bread, the coffee, the cheese, the sandwiches over and over and over again. It means constantly working to improve our service, to raise the quality of the workplace we provide, to contribute more to the community.

Whatever glamour there was to this work has long since worn off. But I still love what I do and value the chance to do it. I'm pretty darned thankful to have had the chance to deal with our everyday challenges, and I look forward to dealing with more of them—as well as new and exciting ones—in the years to come.

Special Conclusions

What's the point of this particular "recipe"? Just to give those of you who are starting out a bit of encouragement to push ahead with doing something different, even when it seems difficult and everyone around you is saying that you're never going to make your project work. Over the years I've learned so much from so many people who have been incredibly generous with their time, ideas, experiences, and insights. Thanks to their inspiration, I mark every anniversary at Zingerman's with an ever-greater commitment to help make something special happen in the year to come.

A Special Spot in Paris

There are innumerable food businesses that have committed themselves to being special. Some are well known around the country, or even the world. But rather than rattle off a list of famous folks I thought I'd share the story of one small place in Paris—while there are many shops and restaurants there that get lots of press, I'm kind of pulled in the other direction . . . I like the little spots, the ones that you could easily walk right by if you didn't know they were there, and the ones that keep on keeping on regardless of trends or who gets written up in the popular press.

Finkelsztajn's is a name that a few food folks will be familiar with, but one that hardly hits the tourist headlines. A little (maybe 700 square feet) bakery and prepared-food shop that has been operating in the Marais

District for 60-something years. It's not all that glamorous. It isn't perfect. It's just special. I love it. The shop is small, maybe 12 seats and a couple little food-covered counters. It's not fancy, and it's painted a really cute canary yellow that you just don't see in many food stores. The food is different, too—it's focused on old Eastern European Jewish dishes, prepared with a French flair that I'm guessing has slowly blended in over all those decades. The counters feature treats like *vatrouchka* (a not-very-sweet Russian/Polish cheesecake), an amazing poppyseed cake, a flaky *borek* pastry stuffed with fresh cheese and herbs, a delicious fig-filled coffee cake, beautiful braided loaves of challah, gefilte fish, and chopped herring salad.

On my last visit I went in to grab a quick bite to eat and some tea (served, much to my delight, in a glass, the way my great-grandparents would have taken it back in Russia). When I was done eating I walked back to the cash register, where this high school-age girl was working. She had this very big smile and eyes with the sort of sparkle that I often see in people who are part of something special. I paid my bill and asked her for directions to the Jewish Museum, which I knew was somewhere in the neighborhood. As I walked away I noticed a colorized old photo on the wall. It obviously dated from the early 20th century, so I assumed it was the original Mr. and Mrs. Finkelsztajn. It took me a minute or two longer to recognize the resemblance between the people in the picture and the young woman working the register. I asked her when the people in the photo had opened the business. "1946," she said. Then I asked her if she was part of the family. She smiled. "It's my grand-grandfather and great-grandmother," she said in very good but very French-accented English.

Finkelsztajn's fits my bill of something special. They're certainly not the richest, the biggest, or the most famous food sellers in Paris. But every day Finkelsztajn's serves special food to special people. They seem to feel good about what they do, and they're generally smiling while they're doing it. And for that, they've earned a spot at the top of my list of people who are making something special happen: people I look up to, people I can learn from.

John Loomis, managing partner of zingerman's creamery, hand salting his cheeses

Finally, Some Food!

Taking "Quality" Beyond the Cliché

I actually got awfully close to finishing this thing before it hit me that I couldn't in good conscience put out a Zingerman's business book without saying anything about food. It's so easy to miss the obvious, but you don't need to be a business genius to know that without great food, Zingerman's wouldn't be what it is today. For context, please know that full-flavored traditional food wasn't something we decided to do solely in the interest of building a great business. Food is our foundation. It's where we started—our roots were in restaurants, and, at least for me, the food is one thing that I can always come back to for comfort, and I can always count on to inspire and inform. The food is—spiritually, intellectually, physically, and financially—our sustenance. Whether it's corned beef, candy bars, or croissants, the cooking is what keeps folks coming back, which in turn makes it possible to pay people and bills, contribute to the community, and come back to do it again the next day.

—⁄—

I don't really want to go on at length here about the importance of quality, but . . . well, it's not as simple as just running an ad to say that you're all about high quality. What sets us apart, I think, is that (a) we actually define what we mean by "quality"; (b) we've set a very high bar for ourselves; (c) we actually clear that bar pretty consistently; and, (d) we've been able to make a living doing it. There just aren't all that many businesses that actually fulfill all four of these day in and day out for any meaningful period of time.

Doing all four at the same time is the key. Strange as it may sound, it's not all that unusual to have a good product but still fail to make a profit. Or, conversely, to get rich by selling mediocre stuff. In fact, my experience in the food world is that there's probably more money to be made selling slightly better-than-average stuff to the middle of the marketplace than there is by working at the very high end of the quality scale. Fortunately, this doesn't really bother me any more. Seriously—I say it without even the slightest tinge of bitterness—I've worked through my issues and come out, smilingly, on the other side. Honestly, I don't worry much about how much anyone else is making; only about creating a positive, caring, and financially sustainable business. I'm OK with the problem of not being the most profitable business around. To quote the country music classic, "Satisfied Mind," written by Red Hayes and Jack Rhodes, "The wealthiest person is a pauper at times, compared to the man with a satisfied mind."

Here's the thing—even if making really, really good, totally traditional food isn't the most super-lucrative corner of the market, it is most definitely the best place to be in terms of passion, vocation, and positive energy. I've got to believe that that's probably just as true in basketball, big business, and donation-driven non-profits as it is in baking bread. After all, who wants to go to work and make mediocre stuff every day? High quality begets high levels of caring, which, in turn, beget ever-greater attention to quality and better results all the way around. All of which fits in well with our anarcho-capitalist approach of appealing to everyone's intelligence and creativity, and requiring people to actively participate in putting out a great product every day!

So, after that little preface, here are a few quick comments on quality. I've used the term "food" because that's what we do, but you can, of course, plug in your own product as you like—I think these ideas are valid whether your business is corned beef, cars, or day care.

1. Make Something Special!

If you want to have a really special business, well . . . I know it's obvious, but I'll state it anyway: the product has to be really special, too. I'm *not* saying it has to be expensive. Just special. Exceptional. Engaging. Interesting. Better still, unique. (Or at least unique to your part of the world—pimento cheese is found in just about every kitchen in the South, but in Ann Arbor you won't find it anywhere but Zingerman's . . . at least not yet!) Put something out there that people will get excited about, take note of, talk about, and want to actively get behind, through good times and bad. I'm sure there are exceptions to this rule, but almost any great company that comes to mind was built around a special product or service.

Keep in mind that even products that now seem unremarkable were once unique. Offering drive-in restaurant service was something special back when the McDonald brothers got going, and the burgers probably weren't all that bad, either. Parking outside the Golden Arches back in the day was a cool thing to do—not just something you did for convenience or to keep your kids quiet. Sears was once a huge innovator in catalog sales and service, not just a department store struggling to survive in the 21st century mall. (They were social innovators, too: check out the Rosenwald schools, started by part owner and president, Julius Rosenwald, back in the early years of the 20th century.)

2. Make Something People Want

I almost skipped this because it's so "obvious," but . . . yeah, making something really fantastic that no one is going to like or be interested in paying for . . . isn't going to get you very far. To wit, I once tasted some very special handcrafted confections from Japan. The family's history in the business goes back a staggering 17 generations. The sweets are beautiful and handmade and in Japan people hold them in the highest regard. And for good reason; the family's standards in service and quality are exceptional. I have great admiration for what they do. But even at Zingerman's we work within the confines of the marketplace—while the sweets are highly esteemed in their homeland, their flavor just isn't (I think) in synch with the palates of even the most discerning Americans, especially not at the (understandably, given all that goes into them) very high price tag.

How do you know what people are going to want? Well you can certainly survey them—nothing wrong with that. The thing is, though, that surveys mostly just suss out what people are already into. Which, while it's not unhelpful to know, isn't very likely to get you into a part of the market where you can do something new and compelling. In fact, it totally misses the stuff that we at Zingerman's are after—the foods that people don't know about yet, but are going to love once they get to taste them. Seriously, I can safely say that no one in Ann Arbor was clamoring for a handmade, high-end, artisan candy bar, but this past January we sold over 4000 of them at the Deli, Roadhouse, and Bakehouse. The same rule applies for almost everything else we do: estate olive oils, super-aged vinegars, or handmade cream cheese. The key in each case was going beyond the pale of popular consciousness to find something that fairly quickly became compelling to our customers.

What's a good substitute for surveys? Well, one option is learning to go with your gut. I don't want to get overly mystical on you, but there's a lot to be said for intuition, even though it won't ever nudge the needle in any kind of significant consumer study. It's about finding those foods that feel right even though anyone in their "right" mind would tell you will never sell. One local cheese distributor in the early '80s told me he had "as much interest in carrying the specialty imports I was looking for as the man in the moon." Fifteen years later he called to solicit our business. Having done that dance dozens—actually hundreds probably—of times over the years I'm pretty well familiar with it. Seriously, I think it's safe to say that nearly every significant product we have here was either unknown in Ann Arbor, was something most everyone said would never sell, or in many cases, the two in tandem.

One of the ways we do that here is by homing in on foods that hardly anyone in our part of the world has ever eaten but that are traditional and pretty darned popular in their place of origin. That might mean pimento cheese, harissa from Tunisia, vinegar-based barbecue from Eastern Carolina, the Bakehouse's Paesano bread in the style of Puglia, fried cheese curds from Wisconsin .... To me there's not much research needed for this stuff: people from the American South, Tunis, North Carolina, Southern Italy, or almost anywhere in the Badger state will tell you, respectively, exactly how good these foods are. So it's not a huge leap for me to forecast that as yet unsuspecting Ann Arborites are going to like them, too.

We've followed a similar path to success by taking foods that most people already *are* familiar with—corned beef, fried chicken, macaroni and cheese, brownies, baguettes, ginger cookies, cream cheese, corn dogs, candy bars, etc.— and making them with such fantastic ingredients and solid techniques that they taste radically better than the mediocre commercial versions that most people are used to and already kind of liked. We know the demand for this stuff is out there. All we have to do is make it much better than everyone else does—even if it costs more, caring customers consistently have shown themselves happy to pay for high quality.

To quote Paul Hawken from *Growing a Business:* "Take a prosaic, everyday, kick-around sort of product and make it real again. Hamburgers, for example. There are so many bad burgers in this world I venture to say that anyone with a hot grill who makes an honest one with generous portions and fresh fried onions will never lack for customers. In other words, take a product and reduce it to its essence." No shock then that one of our biggest sellers at the Roadhouse is our ground-daily from fresh whole chuck, from humanely managed, Niman Ranch beef, hamburgers, hand-pattied and grilled to order over oak. They aren't cheap, but they sure are good.

3. You've Gotta Believe!

I've come to realize over the years that what we sell has to be special, not just so that it stands out in the marketplace, but because the people in the business absolutely 100 percent have to believe in what they're doing. And that's hard to make happen if what we're selling is only so-so. I don't know if they teach much about it in business school, but belief is a big thing. Without it ... food is at best technically correct, but almost always lacks the soul that makes it special. Seriously, it's hard to envision anyone getting—and staying—super excited about selling mediocre goods. By contrast, it's actually pretty easy to get pumped up to promote something special. Employees feel comfortable selling it, press people like to report on it, and customers like buying it. There's nothing to hide, so you can just come at it from the heart—the more customers learn about the product, the more they're going to like it. From whence we generate the solidity, trust, calm confidence, appreciation, and abundance mentality that are found in any mutually rewarding relationship.

4. Substance Sells

I want to build off that last one a bit: when your product is really good, believing in it is not a shell game. Glitz or hard sell will only get you so far; to achieve long-term business sustainability, your product actually has to be really good—not just have really good marketing. In order to get the emotional buy-in and passion we're looking for, those who work in the business—and those who buy from it—have to really understand the stuff: how it works, why it's unique, why it costs what it costs, how it will make their lives better. Which means, in turn, that we need to do a lot of educational work; this is all about being a learning organization, doing a ton of teaching, helping everyone involved understand what it is that we all do and why it's really worth spending more money and going out of one's way to get it. (See Natural Law #6 on page 52 for more on this subject.)

5. Definitely Sweat the Details

Ideas are wonderful and all, but when it comes down to the food, what we serve does actually have to taste good *every day,* not just in the test kitchen. In order to make this happen we really, really, *really* have to watch the details. All the time. And I don't mean supervisors monitoring hidden cameras from back rooms. In the food world, maintaining outstanding quality is a lot of work—as soon as we stop tasting all the time, it's pretty safe to say we'll be headed for trouble. Since everything is done to order and by hand, it can actually all come apart at a moment's notice. Just because we made one good meal doesn't mean the next one will be good, too. All it takes is someone forgetting to add the salt, or serving tepid soup from a steam table, and (literally) before we know it a guest is having a way-less-than-stellar experience.

For all our enormously good intentions, it's shocking how easy it is to screw it all up. While smart, well-trained, caring, and careful staff members certainly count for a lot, the truth is that we still have to systemically taste and double-check everything, all the time, for quality. And to make it happen we have to effectively share responsibility for quality with everyone in the organization: we need all eyes, noses, hands, heads, and palates on deck! We know all too well that well-written visions and great guiding principles are pretty much worthless once we overcook your walleye. And, I'm sorry to say, we don't get any big breaks because we've been at it as long as we have; a bad sandwich doesn't taste any better just because the business you bought it from has been around for a long time.

6. Keep Getting Better

While we may have made great things happen up to now, there's just no way we can serve you the same sandwich tomorrow that we sold you yesterday. Anyone who's really committed to greatness knows there's no resting on laurels (see Natural Law #8 on page 54): if your food isn't getting better then you're sinking inexorably, if slowly, into the morass of the middle of the market. I don't need to dwell on this point. Everyone knows it. The hard part isn't awareness, it's actually doing it—having the internal drive and focus to keep getting better year after year after year is no small thing.

Speaking of which . . . the best thing that happened to me last week was Frank Carollo, 18 years the managing partner at the Bakehouse, leaving me a voice mail on a miserably cold Monday night in February, talking about how he was starting to rework some of the fine details of the production of our Farm Bread. For context, I should tell you that the Farm loaf has probably been our biggest selling bread for years, one on which (knock on wood) I can't even remember the last time I got a complaint. And yet, to Frank's (and everyone at the Bakehouse's) credit, there he was, pushing the quality envelope—living that old Sly and the Family Stone song, "I Want to Take You Higher!"

This drive for improvement wasn't part of any problem solving; it wasn't in preparation for a Presidential visit; and it wasn't because business was bad (to the contrary, sales have been strong). Frank's push came just because he knows in his heart that the bread can be better, and that our work is to keep making it better all the time, preferably, as in this case, by getting on the case long before any customers start commenting.

7. If the Food's Not Really Good, People Aren't Coming Back

Well . . . I don't know, maybe that's not always true. There are a lot of businesses that manage to survive—sometimes even thrive financially—by selling mediocre food. So I guess I need to qualify this statement by starting with what "quality" really means to us. At Zingerman's it centers around two things: full-flavored food and traditional recipes. The key in this context isn't how we define the term, but, rather, the fact that we've actually arrived at organizational clarity and consistency—everyone here understands what we mean by "quality." Once we've defined it, we have a far better shot at delivering the consistent product that customers care so much about.

Of course you could clearly define quality and still make something that's mostly memorable for being mediocre. Most big chains do exactly that. Here, clearly, that's not the case. From the day we opened back in 1982 we've believed that the burden was on us to produce something—food, service, or, better still, both—that would make customers want to travel a long way to buy from us. And it's still totally true today. When we score quality—we do it here on a 0 to 10 scale—we're driving for the hard-to-hit 9s and 10s at the top of the chart. While 7s and 8s aren't likely to cause customer complaints—that's the range where people are usually perfectly satisfied—we want to sell stuff that leaves people talking and shaking their heads in a good way. We want to make the kind of food you want to tell your favorite cousin about, stuff you start calling, twittering, and facebooking about—and within hours of eating it.

While we never get it all right, and we know everything we do can be improved upon, it's those 9s and 10s that have taken us to where we're at today. And make customers start thinking about coming back not long after they finished their lunch. As Jim Van Bochove, longtime director of the Henry Ford Museum (half an hour east of here, in Dearborn, it's an amazing place in its own right), once said with his trademark enthusiasm, "Zingerman's is the only place where you wait 15 minutes to order, you pay $15 for your sandwich, you wait 15 more minutes to get it, and when you're done you go, 'Damn, when can I do that again?!'"

4 Steps to Great Food

The basic premise of all our business building really has been that anyone who's even moderately interested really *can* taste the difference between what we're doing here and more mainstream (and very often less costly) alternatives. In order to support that heartfelt supposition, we take staff through our simple, but effective, little "recipe" for great food at Zingerman's. As with all the other organizational recipes, this one really can be used for any product we work with, from pastrami to pastry and pretty much everything in between. Since so much of what we make here is artisan food, of the sort that I touched on on page 172 in the context of "Mass Customization," we need to be aware of pretty much every little detail, and this recipe really can help both novices and veterans alike.

1. Know It

This sounds simple, but given the complexities of handcrafted artisan food, this is no small challenge. Nevertheless, if we don't know our products, we know that we're in trouble. Which is why we ask everyone here to learn as much as he or she can: what's the flavor of each product supposed to be like? Where does it come from? How is it used in its home territory? How long is its shelf life? How was it prepared? What should it look like? What should it smell like? Why is it special? How is it different from all the other comparable offerings on the market? The list is long but you're getting the idea I'm sure.

2. Look at It

When we're eating two or three times a day, every day of the week, it's all too easy not to notice the visual variations of our food. But as professionals we need to break out of that routine, to slow down some and take in all the nuances of the food. The color, the shape, the size, the smoothness or roughness of the surface—every detail tells a bit of a story.

3. Smell It

Aroma isn't everything, but, since our sense of smell can account for roughly ninety percent of what we taste, it's about as close as you can get to flavor without actually eating. Taking time to take in the aroma is absolutely essential to proper evaluation and appreciation of any good food.

4. Taste It

This is, of course, the point of this whole process. To notice the flavors and intricacies that make for great flavor. Here at Zingerman's we define great flavor to mean, "complexity, balance, and finish." When a well-made, traditional food (or drink) has all three in profusion, then it's pretty likely we're onto one of those 9s or 10s I was talking about earlier in this essay.

zingtrain seminar attendees learning about open book finance

Afterthoughts on Lapsed Anarchism, Motivation, and Eternal Optimism

While I've probably written a couple million words for books, articles, essays, and the like, I'm pretty sure that I've never done one of these. So here you go—my first ever epilogue. It's included at the suggestion of Jim Reische, skateboard park champion, history major, the man behind bacon fat mayonnaise (see *Zingerman's Guide to Better Bacon* for more on that one), and seriously good editor—he's usually pretty right on about this sort of stuff, so I figured if he said the book could use an epilogue, I ought to get to work and put one together.

Of course, to do that, I had to find out what the word actually meant. *Encartus* says it's:

1. a short chapter or section at the end of a literary work, sometimes detailing the fate of its characters

2. a short speech, usually in verse, that an actor addresses directly to the audience at the end of a play

3. the actor who addresses a short speech, usually in verse, directly to the audience at the end of a play

I'm going with #2. Now that I've written this book, edited it, rewritten it, and gone a few dozen more rounds like that (I'll spare you the details) it makes sense that I take a time-out, give a little post-game report, and share a few stats to put all this in perspective.

As we go into the final months of work on layout and the like, the business world around us continues to struggle with all the upheaval of the last few years.

273

Yet in the midst of a still rather tepid economy the ZCoB has just finished one of its best Christmas seasons ever. In the last six months, we've started a Candy Manufactory; planted the seeds for a few possible new businesses (stay tuned to see how they play out); paid out gainsharing in most (though not all) parts of the organization; and are hard at work on improving any number of already successful, longstanding, big-selling products while adding new ones to the mix, as well.

Honestly, I'd say that the energy within the organization right now is probably as high as it's ever been. But, still, there's no sense that this is a time for laurel-resting or lily-gilding—collectively I think we're more driven to get better at everything today than ever, and more intently focused on having fun in the process. That's not just my opinion—we recently received incredibly high scores (placing us in the top few percent of the over 5000 companies involved) after our staff participated in the national Dennison Culture Survey, so some of this stuff must be working fairly well.

Getting into the meat of my epilogue . . . I've spent a fair bit of time thinking about the book you just finished reading (or have skipped straight to the end of). Someone told me a while back that if you want to really write a business book that sells well it shouldn't be more than a hundred pages long, and it oughta be at about a fourth-grade reading level. I'm pretty sure I've failed miserably on both counts. While I don't actually doubt that there's evidence to back up that theory, having reread this entire book a couple more times in order to 'logue epically here at the end, I'm going to stick with what I've got. It's real, it's from the heart, it's what we do, it's working pretty well, and I really do believe in it. In fact, though many of the essays were written years ago, each actually left me more inspired than I was before I pulled up the files on the computer and reread them. And, seriously, I'm not just saying that because I wrote the darned things!

Since this is the first book in our new series on leadership, it makes sense, I guess, to look ahead just a bit. While we've focused here on building a great business, the next entry, *A Lapsed Anarchist's Approach to Being a Better Leader*, will look inward instead of outward, exploring methods for effectively managing oneself and those whom we're privileged to lead. It will share our approaches to Servant Leadership (the belief that the leader's primary role is to serve the organization, not the other way around), Stewardship (a way to work together as peers, regardless of a person's formal role or authority in the organization), our Entrepreneurial Approach to Management (or why the free market works as well for management as it does for selling food), thoughts on effective energy management (the kind we each generate from within, not the sort that we use to run power plants), and our recipe for effective organizational change (and what it has in common with Tex Winter's Triangle Offense). And it will include my top-secret secret, the story behind "Managing by Pouring Water."

Part 3 in the series will be about our approach to Open Book Finance, which I pretty passionately believe is an amazing and exceptionally effective—if still seriously little known—approach to building a great business. It's all about getting everyone involved in creating, measuring, managing, and sharing financial success, rather than setting up the bosses to be the only ones who know the rules by which the "game" of business is being "played," let alone see the score to tell how the organization is faring. Part 4 will look at additional insights on service, adding to the basics that were laid out in *Zingerman's Guide to Giving Great Service*. And Part 5 will focus on our approach to merchandising, marketing, and selling lots of good stuff that hardly anyone ever knew they wanted until we told them about it and gave them a taste. Damn—that's a lot! I'd best hurry up and get to work.

But first, back to the issue of self-reflection for a moment . . . Sometimes I think of my life as being bookmarked: not so much in the usual sense of marking pages with pieces of paper, but in the sense that so many of my ideas are bracketed by the somewhat random reading selections that happen to coincide with what's going on with (and around) me at the time I crack open the covers. Books often pop up for me at fortuitous moments. To wit, I got to thinking about the idea of anarcho-capitalism only because I happened to be reading Paul Avrich's *Anarchist Voices* at the same time that I started working on putting this business-building book together. And the compatibility of old anarchist ideology and cutting-edge corporate thought came clear really only because I'd recently read Dean Tucker's excellent, if still little known, tome, *Unleashing the Power of Purpose*.

So, with that idea of bookmarking in my mind, just as I was thinking epilogue-ically it happened that my friend Anese Cavanaugh (see her website at leadingwithbootson.com) gave me a copy of Daniel Pink's book *Drive*. Anese does really innovative work around leadership, and she'd already steered me toward a slew of other good reads (including Hugh MacLeod's terrific *Ignore Everybody*), so I was pretty keen to dive into *Drive*.

That eager anticipation fairly quickly turned into antipathy. Nearly the first third of the book was devoted to proving that people aren't really motivated much by money. Which . . . let's just say that in this day and age I could barely believe that such an incredibly obvious (to me at least) statement was worth 84 pages of a serious 21st century study of business, let alone interesting enough to make the book a bestseller. In frustration I started skimming paragraphs, then skipping pages altogether. "Old news in a new book" was sort of what was going through my mind . . . and, honestly, I couldn't believe Anese had sent me something so . . . well . . . you know, if I were letting out my inner fourth-grader I'd say, "stupid." I knew there had to be more to it than this to have earned praise from someone as innovative in her leadership work as she is.

The funny thing is that I actually agreed with Pink's premise that people aren't particularly motivated by money. But the first conclusion that he drew from this observation—that bonus plans are generally a bad thing—had my frustration level going up steadily with each passing page. It just didn't jive with my experience, and it seemed like a rather superficial slam on a subject worthy of much more complex thinking than what I was reading.

Not surprisingly, part of the problem was actually mine. When I talked to Anese about this later, she reminded me that she'd suggested I should actually skip the first part of the book. For whatever reasons of fate, I failed to hear her. In fact, though, my faux pas was fortuitous, for it got me thinking about all this stuff in a new, and, I think, kind of interesting, way. Following Paul's long-standing advice, "when furious, get curious," I journaled a bit to try to figure out what was getting me so wired up. I went back through the first part of the Pink book, journaled some more, and . . . a couple of days later I finally realized what it was that was getting me going.

See . . . although the book makes a big deal of the fact that people aren't motivated by profit (I agree), I actually *like* bonus plans a lot—we use profit sharing, group "games," and bonus programs at Zingerman's all the time. But there's a difference: unlike the old-line management approach that Pink was putting down—where people are basically beaten into submission by stacking bonus plans in front of them, my reflection helped me realized that I don't actually regard "variable compensation" as a carrot to motivate an otherwise uninspired employee.

As I view things, bonuses, games, and profit-sharing plans are really just one element in a multifaceted approach to creating a positive and rewarding place to work. They're hardly a driving force, but they do have value. For me, bonuses, games, and profit-sharing plans are:

1. A way to share success or stress on any given project, or for a specific period of time. It's just always made sense to me that a business should align its employees' compensation with the entrepreneurial activity of the organization. When the team does well, everyone on it should do well. And when the team takes it on the chin. . . . well, everyone should feel a bit of the pain, as well. Performance-based bonus plans shift the focus away from effort onto what we're actually after, which is, I think, real, ethically attained, results in a setting in which everyone in the organization has an opportunity to gain by group success.

2. A very good way to get groups focused on a shared goal. Getting everyone working toward the same vision of success reduces distractions and gets everyone pulling together. You can read a lot more about this in *The Great Game of Business* (a fortuitous read for me back in 1995), and you'll get at more of my take on the subject when we get to Part 3 of this series, *A Lapsed Anarchist's Approach to Finance.*

3. A way to support autonomy and freedom of choice. I think they're actually an excellent example of lapsed anarchism in action. Including a work-specific individual bonus as part of a pay plan gives the staff member a choice: if they don't feel like pursuing the same goals I do, they don't have to. They aren't judged badly for it; they just don't get the bonus. At the same time it pushes me to get clear on my end about what I really believe is of value to the organization, and then to put my money where my priorities are. Better still, if the staffer doesn't like the bonus plan I've presented he or she can propose an alternative plan—and many do. Money may or may not be an incentive, but it's an up-front, adult-to-adult, free-market statement that certain levels of work are worth more than others.

So chalk up two points for self-reflection—exploring my anger actually got me to realize some interesting new things about the way I think! For me, I can now say that this bonus stuff actually starts with an anarcho-capitalist approach, one that admits that each of us is motivated by different things. That working hard is great, but that, like it or not, good results are usually worth more than bad ones. That whether everyone in the organization agrees on any given day, some results simply have a higher value than others. And that, in the spirit of anarcho-capitalism, each of us in the organization should get to choose what we want to do with our time and energy en route to wherever it is we're headed; a staff member coming forward to propose a bonus plan of her own design is pretty sure to make my day, even if I don't at first agree with all its content.

But I kind of have the reflective horse ahead of the chronological cart here; none of this actually came clear until well after I'd finished reading the book. As I went further I saw clearly why Anese had given it to me—without a doubt it backs up a lot of what we do here at Zingerman's (and what she works on with her coaching clients). It starts out with the author's hypothesis that "intrinsic motivation"—not money—is what gets people going. In other words, employees do their best work when their *drive* comes from within, not when they're being pushed or pulled from without: i.e., people feel better when they have freedom to go after the stuff that gets them going, when they're having fun and feeling good about themselves, acting on free will, and enjoying the process of learning and achieving en route. When you get all that stuff aligned, work feels good, not like something you want to flee from. "TGIF" turns into, "Wow, I can't wait to get back to work." What was once "just a job" becomes fun, often a passion, sometimes even a vocation. It's productive and it's very powerful.

A business, Pink points out, is most effective when not just the organization but each individual within it is pursuing greatness, or as he calls it, "mastery." "Autonomous people," he posits, "working toward mastery, perform at very high levels." I couldn't agree more. I'm one of those people. So, too, I think, are most of the folks who choose to work at Zingerman's. And while *Drive* isn't a case of dressing Emma Goldman, the "Queen of the Anarchist's," up in pink (sorry, couldn't resist even though I can't really imagine her wearing pink very often), it's not really that far off, either: the "intrinsic motivation" Pink identifies is basically the same as Goldman's passion for free choice—the drive to make a positive difference and the commitment to do great things as part of a creative group one chooses freely to engage with is central to what both had to say. Pink's point about intrinsic motivation is, pretty clearly, the core of the positive end of anarchism. You can hear echoes of the same idea in Emma's words a century ago: the workplace of the future would be built by people, she wrote, "to whom the making of a table, the building of a house, or the tilling of the soil, is what the painting is to the artist and the discovery to the scientist—the result of inspiration, of intense longing, and deep interest in work as a creative force."

So what started out as a stressful read ended up being, as Anese knew it would be, more support for the way we look at business. (I noticed, by the way, that Pink's book is well over 100 pages in length, and, I'm pretty sure, far above a fourth-grade reading level. I haven't looked up any stats on how many copies have been sold, but supposedly it's a lot. So maybe there's hope for higher end business books!) Without question, Pink provides a lot of good data to back up our anarcho-capitalist (or whatever you want to call it) approach. To sum up, I think it's safe to say that Emma Goldman, Mr. Pink, and I are all about free choice; about being motivated from within; about doing what we do because we want to do it, and never, with all due respect to our Jewish mothers, because someone else told us to.

That "someone else," by the way, could include yours truly. I'm fully aligned with what the late, great, writer Robert Greenleaf said in his classic, *Servant Leadership:* "What I am saying now is said with the intent that it will not mean much to you unless you respond with your own thinking as if this were a dialogue in which you have responsibility at least equal to mine. Your response is what is important to you, not what I say." I say, "Right on!" The anarchist in me always believes that it's up to you whether you accept, adapt, or totally ignore all the stuff I've been talking about. While the ideas may seem like "secrets," truthfully they're just tools. Use 'em, or lose 'em, as you'd like.

Sincerely though, I hope that the essays enclosed here have some relevance for the world in which you're working. That if you're just starting a business (or a non-profit, or, for that matter, a country), that these thoughts on writing a mission statement, creating a vision of greatness, and agreeing on guiding principles will help you build something special. That if you've already got a good thing going, that you can use these ideas to make it just a bit better. Perhaps you'll be a touch more appreciative, or better prepared to get through hard times. While I'm not striving to bring down the status quo quite as abruptly as many of my anarchist "insipiritors" (i.e., "those who conspired to inspire me") wanted to do a century ago, I do hope we can change the world by building businesses that operate in caring and sustainable ways that really work for you as the owner or leader, as well as for your crew, customers, investors, bankers, and the community at large.

In *How the Irish Saved Civilization,* Thomas Cahill wrote that, "the great gift-givers (of history), arriving in the moment of crisis, provided for transition, for transformation, even for transfiguration, leaving us a world more varied and complex, more awesome and delightful, more beautiful and strong than the one they had found." I would hardly presume that Zingerman's is a great gift-giver of history. But even if we're just bringing a small, smartly wrapped stocking stuffer, maybe what we do can sow the seeds for new ways of working that will help make the business world freer, more creative, more effective, and a bit more fun, to boot. It would be a fitting repayment (hopefully with, and of, interest) for all the great assistance, support, insight, and service that has been shared with us over the years. The work, after all, really isn't ever done. To quote Daniel Pink, "You can approach (mastery). You can home in on it. You can get really, really, really close to it. But . . . you can *never* touch it. Mastery is impossible to realize fully." But going after it every day really is a good way to go.

Thinking, then, again, about this idea of bookmarking, while I was researching at the Labadie Collection at the U of M Library, I came across a 1930s essay by Harry Kelly, an American anarchist I'd never heard of. I think it's safe to say his work isn't on anyone's top 10 reading lists this year. It might ought to be—I thought it was pretty powerful stuff. Mr. Kelly wrote, in full advance support of Mr. Pink's more modern points above, that, "Sincerity of purpose always expresses itself in action. Such sincerity," he said, "never fails to capture attention. So long as you merely talk about your ideals, they will remain mere ideals. But if your talk is no mere lip service, if you feel your convictions, if they permeate your being, they will inevitably express themselves in your daily life, in your attitude toward things, in your every action. They will then shape your life; they will make you different from other people, in proportion as your ideal is different from theirs. Then your ideal will cease to be merely an ideal. It will have become a part of yourself, and to that extent, materialized. Thus, and only thus, are ideals propagated and transmitted into life." Sounds a lot like running a sustainable 21st-century business to me.

As I start to close up my literary leadership shop here, let me quote from a couple of other authors whose work has bookmarked my business learning over the years. First up is Paul Hawken, who wrote one my favorite books, *Growing a Business,* back in 1988. "People," he wrote, "intuitively understand that a good business enhances the lives of all who work within it, and enriches the lives of all those who are touched by it. . . . Being in business is not about making money." And, in synch with Mr. Kelly's statement above, he added, "It is a way to become who you are. . . . Being a good human being is good *business.*"

The next note is from the late, and very great, Peter Drucker, who wrote in *Management Challenges for the 21st Century,* "Leadership is the courage to admit mistakes, the vision to welcome change, the enthusiasm to motivate others, and the confidence to stay out of step when everyone else is marching to the wrong tune." The fact that some folks will say this stuff is silly makes me a little nervous. But it's my freely taken decision to put it out there and share it and I choose the problem of vulnerability that that brings. Knowing that it's my call is the key—as Sam Keen (one of my other most favorite authors) said in *Hymns to an Unknown God,* "The most important decision we ever make is about whether we can make decisions."

I hardly think that Paul Hawken, Daniel Pink, Peter Drucker, or Sam Keen considered themselves anarchists, lapsed or otherwise. But really the positive part of anarchism is all about this idea that each of us can make decisions for ourselves. And that, when we're intrinsically driven toward a common, positive purpose, we'll willingly collaborate to achieve some really special things, out of which ever-better businesses will be built.

While all this sounds great, there will, of course, always be the bad days. Despite everyone's best efforts there are moments when being in business still basically just sucks. I say that with a smile because I freely and willingly choose to accept that challenge in exchange for the chance to lovingly do what I do every day. Being in business gives us a special opportunity—we get to bring people together to make meaningful things happen. But when the days do seem dim, I go back to a quote from Emma Goldman that I found in Paul Avrich's *Anarchist Voices:* "When things are bad," she said, "scrub floors." It's actually a good idea—if you want to build a great business, you have to be willing and able to do the scut work. But, hey, if you stick with it, you might just have fun . . . and make a difference while you're at it.

Almost-last lines here go to Julius Seltzer, an anarchist who briefly owned a little-known restaurant in Ann Arbor in 1911. (For those of you who've been here, it was located at 1114 South University, and was called Seltzer and Chatterton.) "The ideal [of anarchism]," Seltzer said, "is still floating all over the world. I have never been disillusioned. I am always optimistic."

I couldn't agree more. Here's to more fun, more free thinking, more learning, and more good business building to come!

working the sauté station on the line at the roadhouse

Time to Eat

Ten Recipes to Cook in Your Own Kitchen

To really get into our approach to food in far greater depth, pick up a copy of Zingerman's Guide to Good Eating—"Eating" sounds a lot like "Leading," I know, but it's about working in the kitchen, not consensus building or creating a compelling organizational vision. What follows are a handful of recipes to share just because . . . because it just doesn't feel right to me to do a Zingerman's book—even a business book—and not have any recipes in it! Seriously, even Emma Goldman, radical anarchist that she was, very much liked to eat good food, and was, according to many of her cohorts, quite a cook. In fact the potato latke recipe below is a tribute to her and my grandmother, Belle Perlis. Both were born in Lithuania, both came here as kids, and, while their politics couldn't have been further apart, they both loved latkes.

Beyond the need to pass on my grandmother's method of making potato pancakes, I actually spent a fair bit of time struggling to figure out some coherent pretext for which recipes to include. After a couple of months of not coming up with anything totally terrific, I decided to run with one recipe for each of the Zingerman's businesses. It made sense to my sometimes overly logical brain, and it also made for enough recipes to be interesting without turning this thing into a cookbook. Given that most of you bought the book to learn about business, not bacon, bakin', or barbecue, I decided to keep my selections on the simple side. Not that you can't do something more complex, but I figured you already own at least a couple of full-fledged cookbooks if you're in the mood for more serious cooking.

So, all that said, here are a few fairly easy-to-prepare, good-to-eat recipes. I hope they might help give you a little culinary lift while you're reading, thinking on, or discussing all this business stuff. Each has, in its own way, played a special little part in making Zingerman's what it is. Enjoy!

BELLE AND EMMA'S POTATO LATKES

So . . . let's start with those latkes. Taken together, my grandmother, Belle Perlis (née Levin), and Emma Goldman, Queen of the Anarchists, prove that the love for cooking and especially for potato latkes transcends politics. And for good reason—they're delicious. If there's one food I remember lovingly from my childhood, this is it. My grandmother made them every year at Chanukah; my mother took over the task when my grandmother got older. Other than the occasional grilled cheese it's really the only dish I can remember getting excited about helping to make. If a lot of relatives were coming over we'd have a couple of frying pans going at once—I'd flip five or six latkes, eat one, pour batter in for a few more, eat another one, make a few more.

My grandmother used to fry them in simple vegetable oil. Emma Goldman is said to have liked hers cooked in goose fat. That's a bit harder to find, but chicken fat would be the closest, at least moderately accessible way to go. And if you think about Jews coming originally from the Mediterranean, they work great in (extra virgin) olive oil, too.

The latkes should be soft, fairly thin, and about the size of silver dollar pancakes. They're at their best when the oil is plenty hot so you get little lacy bits around the edges. Serve 'em with sour cream, applesauce, or just on their own with a sprinkling of salt.

> 2 pounds potatoes (I like Yukon Golds, German Butterballs, or
> others of that ilk)
>
> 1/3 cup chopped onion
>
> 2 teaspoons coarse sea salt
>
> Pinch freshly ground Tellicherry black pepper
>
> 4 teaspoons flour
>
> 2 eggs
>
> Extra virgin olive oil for frying

Puree all ingredients, except for the olive oil, in a food processor or blender into a thin batter.

Heat the olive oil in a large skillet over fairly high heat. You're not deep-frying, but you'll want more than a thin film—probably a good 1/8 inch of oil in the pan so that the batter is almost floating in it. When the oil is hot, drop in 1 to 2 tablespoons of batter for each latke. You can cook several at a time, but don't crowd them. Cook until the bottoms are golden brown, about 2 minutes. Flip the latkes over and fry a few minutes more until golden. If you're impatient, eat them right out of the pan. Or, if you can hold off for a few minutes, remove and drain on a paper towel-lined plate. Serve immediately.

Zingerman's
DELICATESSEN

SANDWICH #23: THE MARY'S COMMUTE

This sandwich seems an excellent philosophical fit for this book on almost every level. For openers it's been a big-selling standard at the Deli ever since we opened. Second, the quality of the finished sandwich really depends wholly on the quality of the ingredients you use. To make the chicken salad we roast whole Amish-raised, free-running chickens, chop fresh vegetables, and mix with Hellmann's mayonnaise. Author Jim Harrison still talks about visiting the Deli 20-plus years ago and being stunned to find the prep crew picking the meat off of whole roasted chickens, rather than relying on the more efficient but far less flavorful pre-cooked and boned stuff. We finish off the sandwich with strips of Nueske's applewood-smoked bacon and thick slices of challah from the Bakehouse.

The sandwich is also a good fit here because Mary Economou, for whom it's named (and who used to work with me and Paul in restaurants years ago), was one of the most detail- and training-oriented managers I've ever worked with. And last because . . . well, thinking back to Natural Law #7—"Successful businesses do the things that others know they should . . . but generally don't"— the sandwich got its name because when we first opened Mary was riding the Amtrak train into Detroit every morning. In order to get a shot at picking up that "on the way to the train" business like hers, we decided to open earlier than anyone else, at 7 a.m. While that may not seem extreme today, it was hardly the norm at the time. And remember, too, we had to drive to Detroit to get the bread, so opening at 7 meant hitting the highway at about 5 a.m.

Regular commuter train service stopped years ago, but we're still opening every day at 7, and customers stopping for pre-commute coffee are a significant part of our morning sales.

For the chicken salad:
   2 pounds roasted chicken (both dark and white meat)
   2/3 cup diced onion
   2/3 cup diced celery
   2 cups Hellmann's mayonnaise

Sea salt to taste

Freshly ground Tellicherry black pepper to taste

Dice the cooked chicken and place in a large bowl. Add the remaining ingredients and combine well. Set aside.

For six large sandwiches:
12 slices challah bread

1 cup plus 2 tablespoons Hellmann's mayonnaise

Chicken salad (above)

12 slices bacon, cooked (we use Nueske's applewood-smoked at the Deli)

A mess of good lettuce

Spread a tablespoon of mayonnaise on each slice of bread. Put 6 1/2 ounces (about a rounded cup) of chicken salad on one slice, then add the bacon and lettuce. Top with the other slice of bread and cut the sandwich on whatever angle your heart desires. Serve!

RED FETA SPREAD

This is an easy hors d'oeuvre or sandwich spread, great for putting out with a loaf of good bread or crackers for folks to snack on during big meetings. It only takes about eight minutes to make and keeps for days. You really need to use the Marash red pepper (which we do mail order since you probably won't see it in most local shops) because it melts so nicely into a soft paste with the cheese. It comes from the city of Kahramanmaras (in southeastern Turkey, in case you're over that way), and it really is delicious. Here we get to use the traditionally made, no-vegetable gum cream cheese from Zingerman's Creamery, but you can make do with high quality commercial offerings. Also, the better the feta, the better the flavor of the finished spread. I swear by barrel-aged feta from Greece.

    2 teaspoons fresh lemon juice

    1 teaspoon Marash red pepper flakes

    1/2 pound Greek feta cheese, coarsely crumbled

    1/2 pound cream cheese

    1 tablespoon extra virgin olive oil, preferably Greek

Combine the lemon juice and Marash pepper flakes in a small bowl. Let stand until a smooth paste forms, about 10 minutes.

In a large bowl, mash the pepper mixture with the feta, cream cheese and olive oil until smooth. If you like the spread spicy, add additional Marash pepper. If you like it mellower, increase the cream cheese.

ALEX'S RED RAGE BARBECUE SAUCE

This is THE sauce at the Roadhouse for ribs, brisket, chicken, and a host of other good dishes (it's great for dipping fries, too). Alex Young, managing partner and chef, started working on the recipe when he was all of 13. He's now 43, and he and the sauce have matured beautifully together. Thanks to Alex's cooking skills and leadership, the Roadhouse has developed steadily into an ever-better restaurant (see Natural Law #11 on page 56). It's seven years and counting of steady improvement in food, service, energy, and leadership, all of which gradually came together to help win recognition from the James Beard Awards committee, Food Network, *Esquire*, *Bon Appetit*, and a host of others.

Decades down the road, Alex still makes occasional minor adjustments to improve on an already great sauce. Like the restaurant, it's about slowly simmering and steady stirring so that a host of diverse ingredients come together into a unique, complex, wonderful, still-appreciated-long-after-it's–over, eating experience.

   3 cups ketchup

   1/2 cup Muscovado (or other natural dark) brown sugar

   1/2 cup finely diced onion

   1/2 cup cider vinegar (we use the oak-barrel-aged vinegar from
      Pierre Gingras in Quebec)

   1/2 cup Pilsner beer

   2 tablespoons raw honey

   2 tablespoons dark molasses

   1 tablespoon minced garlic

   1 1/2 teaspoons freshly ground Tellicherry black pepper

   1 1/2 teaspoons ground coffee (we use Zingerman's
      Roadhouse Joe)

1 1/2 teaspoons Urfa pepper (another exotic red pepper
from Turkey)

1 1/2 teaspoons ground dried chipotle chiles

1 1/2 teaspoons dried pequin chile flakes

3/4 teaspoon sea salt

Combine all of the ingredients in a heavy-bottomed stockpot and mix thoroughly. Bring to a boil, then reduce to a simmer. Allow the sauce to gently simmer for 30 minutes or so, stirring occasionally.

P.S. If you want to do up a classic but little-known American recipe, use the sauce on pasta to make what folks in Memphis know as "barbecue spaghetti," or what we call at the Roadhouse, "Memphis Mac." You may want to toss a little bit of pulled pork barbecue on top, as well.

A SPICY BLT

I picked this dish to fill the ZingTrain slot in this recipe lineup because of the acronym—BLT is of course, Bacon, Lettuce, and Tomato, but at ZingTrain it also stands for their signature product, "Bottom Line Training." You can read more about what that means at zingtrain.com, but for the moment I'll stick to this really tasty, spicy, super-good sandwich! And, in one of those funny-the-way-the-world-works things, I actually first tasted a version of this sandwich at a (highly recommended) restaurant called 112 Eatery while Maggie Bayless, one of the managing partners of ZingTrain (and the woman who developed our approach to Bottom Line Training), and I were out doing ZingTrain work in Minneapolis.

For this sandwich I like a big bold smoky bacon like Allan Benton's dry-cured artisan offering from eastern Tennessee. Harissa is the spicy hot sauce of North Africa. My harissa of choice is the hand-made version we get from the Moulins Mahjoub in Tunisia (more about them later). If you can't get good tomatoes, skip 'em; you can sub in roasted peppers if you're in the mood. Grill the bread in the pan right alongside the egg if you like, or toast it separately while the egg is sizzling. The sandwich is sort of a mess to eat, but it sure is good!

    2 to 3 slices bacon

    4 tablespoons Hellmann's mayonnaise

    3/4 teaspoon Mahjoub's hot harissa

    1 egg

    2 slices crusty country bread

    2 slices ripe tomato

    Handful of fresh arugula

Cook the bacon in a frying pan until done. Meanwhile, combine the mayonnaise and harissa and set aside.

Remove the bacon from the pan, but leave the pan on the heat. Add the egg and fry to your liking. Remove the egg from the pan when done.

Meanwhile, toast the bread. Spread plenty of the harissa mixture on both slices of toast. Add the tomato, bacon, egg, and arugula.

Slice the sandwich in half on an angle and eat it while it's hot!

? *Zingerman's* ? Café Memmi

TO BE, OR LABLABI?

I'm putting this one in even though the Zingerman's business at which it might actually be served doesn't exist yet. Thus the pun in the dish's name: "To be, or Lablabi?"

Actually, I'm forecasting positive results for both. There's risk, of course, in putting this in here—now everyone will know that we're considering opening a Zingerman's Tunisian restaurant even though, as of this writing, I can't be sure it'll actually happen. But . . . I wanted to put the recipe in anyway, because this book is all about building a business, taking chances, going after what you believe, sharing passions and, in our case, flavors with those around you.

The dish is delicious and not hard to make, and it'll taste equally good whether or not our little southern Mediterranean model of a restaurant actually comes into being.

I include the recipe here, too, because Majid Mahjoub, from whom we buy a number of the key ingredients in the dish, is a model of almost every-thing I've written about in this book. He's part of the third generation (seven siblings total) to manage his family business. And his commitment to quality, to watching the details, to delivering exceptional products he believes in with great passion, and to building a sustainable business—both environmentally and economically—is inspiring. All of their products are hand-made according to traditional family recipes, most are organic, and, seriously, all of them are outstandingly good.

While less than 1/80th of the American population has yet to eat lablabi, it's essentially the national dish of Tunisia. Lablabi stands are to Tunis what taco trucks are to L.A., barbecue joints to Birmingham, or hot dog stands to Chicago—you can't go more than two blocks in the heart of Tunis without running into one.

Once again, the quality of the dish is dependent on getting good ingredients. We're fortunate that the Mahjoub's harissa, olive oil, preserved lemons, etc., are all available in jars. We ship lots of the stuff through our Mail Order and would be glad to send some your way. In fact, just for fun, if you mention this book when you order we'll gladly give you 10 percent off your Tunisian purchase.

You can certainly make lablabi with comparable offerings from other brands—I just think that the Mahjoub's stuff is pretty amazing.

- 2 (15-ounce) cans chickpeas, drained and rinsed (or 3 cups cooked chickpeas)
- 8 cups plus 2 teaspoons water
- 4 teaspoons Mahjoub sun-dried garlic or 3 teaspoons fresh minced fresh garlic
- 2 teaspoons coarse sea salt, plus additional to taste
- 2 tablespoons Mahjoub hot harissa
- 3/4 cup plus 2 teaspoons extra virgin olive oil
- 6 slices day-old crusty country bread, broken into small pieces
- 2 Mahjoub preserved lemons, seeded, cut into small wedges and sliced
- 3 Mahjoub sun-dried tomato pieces, halved and sliced
- 3 teaspoons ground cumin, toasted
- 2 tablespoons capers, rinsed and finely chopped (the Mahjoub sun-dried, sea-salted capers are, not surprisingly, really good too)

In a large soup pot, cover the chickpeas with 8 cups of the water. Add 1 1/2 teaspoons of the garlic and bring to a boil. Add the sea salt, reduce heat, cover, and simmer 20 minutes or so, until the chickpeas are tender. Be sure the broth is very hot since the other ingredients are going in at room temperature.

In a small bowl, combine the harissa, 2 teaspoons water (optional), and 2 teaspoons olive oil. Set aside. Meanwhile, warm 6 soup bowls in the oven. When they're warm, remove them from the oven and crumble bits of bread into the bottom of each one. Adjust the quantity up or down as you wish, but it's more than just a garnish, so don't skimp.

Ladle the broth and chickpeas over the bread. Add a generous spoonful of the preserved lemon, some sliced sun-dried tomato, a bit more sun-dried garlic, a nice sprinkle of ground cumin, a ribbon of extra virgin olive oil, a few capers, and finally a generous amount of the harissa and olive oil mixture. The bowl will look beautiful with all the colors at the top.

Before they eat, many Tunisians take a couple of soup spoons and "toss" the stew in the bowl to mix all the ingredients together.

ZINGERMAN'S MAGIC BROWNIES

These are the brownies Zingerman's fans have been feasting on for decades and are probably our most popular sweet. The truth is they *could* actually be our secret—you'll have to eat a few to find out. They have a soft, chewy interior dotted with toasted walnuts, and a thin chocolate crust.

13 tablespoons butter

6 1/2 ounces unsweetened chocolate, coarsely chopped

1 1/2 cups sifted flour

3/4 teaspoon baking powder

1/2 teaspoon fine sea salt

4 eggs

2 cups sugar

1 1/4 teaspoons pure vanilla extract

1 1/4 cups coarsely chopped walnuts, toasted

Preheat oven to 325°.

Grease a 13 x 9 baking pan; set aside.

Heat the butter and chocolate over low heat in a heavy-bottomed small saucepan, stirring constantly, until the chocolate is melted and smooth. Set aside to cool.

In a small bowl, stir together the flour, baking powder, and salt; set aside.

Beat the eggs and sugar in an electric mixer on high speed for 5 minutes, or until lemon-colored and fluffy, scraping the sides of the bowl occasionally. Add the cooled chocolate mixture and vanilla and beat on low speed until combined. Add the flour mixture. Beat on low until combined, scraping the sides of the bowl. Stir in the walnuts.

Spread the batter in the prepared pan. Bake for 30 minutes, or until brownies appear set. Cool in pan on wire rack. Cut into bars.

Makes 15 brownies.

Zingerman's
maiL order.

HOT COCOA CAKE

Bakehouse coffee cakes are our biggest selling Mail Order item. The original sour cream coffee cake is actually the top seller, but the cocoa cake is coming up fast. When we first worked on it about 10 years ago our goal was a cake that would work at any time of the day—chocolatey like a nice cup of hot cocoa, but not like a super-intense dark truffle. As with so much of our stuff it wasn't something people were asking for, but once they had it . . .

1 3/4 cup flour

1/2 cup plus 2 tablespoons unsweetened cocoa powder

1/4 teaspoon baking powder

1/4 teaspoon baking soda

1/2 teaspoon fine sea salt

2 tablespoons brewed espresso or very strong coffee (you can use instant espresso if necessary)

1 1/2 teaspoons pure vanilla extract

2/3 cup butter, room temperature

2 eggs, room temperature

3 egg whites, room temperature

2 1/3 cups granulated sugar

1/2 cup plus 1 tablespoon plus 1 teaspoon sour cream

5 1/2 ounces bittersweet chocolate, chopped

Sifted powdered sugar (optional)

Preheat oven to 350°.

Grease and lightly flour two 6-cup fluted tube pans or one 10-inch fluted tube pan.

In a medium bowl, combine the flour, cocoa powder, baking powder, baking soda, and salt.

In a small bowl, combine the espresso and vanilla. Set aside.

Beat the butter with an electric mixer on medium-high for 30 seconds. Gradually add the granulated sugar until combined. Add the sour cream and again beat until combined. Add the eggs and egg whites, one at a time, beating well after each. Add the flour mixture and espresso mixture in alternating thirds, beating on low after each addition just until combined. Stir in the chopped chocolate.

Evenly pour the batter into the prepared pan(s) and bake 35–40 minutes for the small cakes or 50–55 minutes for the large cake, or until a wooden toothpick inserted near the center of the cake comes out clean.

Cool for 15 minutes on a wire rack. Remove from pan(s) and cool completely on the rack. Sprinkle with powdered sugar, if you like.

BROWN BUTTER CARAMEL SAUCE

I struggled at first with what recipe to give here. What we make every day in the Candy Manufactory kitchen are artisan candy bars. They're exceptionally good, for sure, but I think it's about 80 times easier to enjoy one by buying it than by working through a complex candy recipe on your own. Happily, there are other, easier opportunities to make—and eat—good sweet stuff at home.

To make sure our recipe was easily replicated, we tested it with Lynn Yates, the woman who deftly manages our community giving work through Zingerman's Foundation but who, when it comes to cooking . . . as she herself says, "only knows enough to be dangerous." I'm happy to report that Lynn loved the results, and gave the caramel a big thumbs up.

In terms of ingredients, as always (are you getting tired of hearing me say this? Think what it's like to actually have to work with me every day!), the better the butter and sugar, the better the caramel. We always use the old style Muscovado brown sugar, made the way it was a couple hundred years ago—it's amazing how much more flavor it has. No room here for a long discourse, but let's just say it's akin to the difference between great dark chocolate and a Hershey bar.

Although the recipe really isn't very complicated, you'll want to read the directions all the way through before you start. Like a lot of in-the-moment management maneuvers, you can't really stop caramel making part-way through. I guess the good news is that even if you move too slowly, your sugar will shift swiftly through the soft caramel stage into toffee. Not all that bad a problem to have!

8 tablespoons butter

1 cup Muscovado (or other dark brown) sugar

1/4 cup water

1/2 cup heavy whipping cream

Pinch fine sea salt

299

In a small, heavy-bottomed stainless steel saucepan, melt the butter over moderately high heat. Cook until the butter begins to foam and turns golden brown. (Watch the pan carefully, as the butter can go quickly from browned to burnt.) Pour the browned butter into a heatproof container and set aside. (It will continue to cook if you leave it in the hot pan.)

In a medium, heavy-bottomed saucepan, combine the sugar and water. Bring the mixture to a rapid simmer over moderately high heat, stirring often.

Clamp a candy thermometer to the side of the saucepan. Allow the mixture to cook until the temperature reaches 238°F, about 7 to 10 minutes. Monitor it closely so the sugar doesn't burn. To ensure even cooking, carefully stir to keep the bubbles down off the sides of the pan. (If sugar crystals form on the sides, you can wash them down with a wet, heatproof pastry brush.)

Remove the saucepan from the stove. Slowly stir in the cream—be careful, it may spatter—then the butter and salt. Return the pan to the heat and bring the sauce to a rapid simmer. Cook 3 to 5 minutes more, until the sauce takes on the consistency of a thick syrup. (Remember, it will thicken further as it cools.)

Serve warm over pancakes, waffles, or ice cream, or cool it a bit and use at room temperature for dipping fresh fruit or biscuits.

COFFEE GRANITA

I'm not sure why I like this stuff so much, but I do. It's a really easy, tasty, and "cool" way to get your coffee fix. It does take time, but if you need a bit of distraction every now and then while you're working, this is the way to go. Good excuse to leave a meeting for a few minutes every so often, and great for chilling out after a hard day of building a business!

2 cups very strong coffee

4 teaspoons sugar

2 vanilla beans, split, seeds scraped

1 cup heavy cream

1 tablespoon sugar

Combine the sugar and vanilla seeds in a medium glass or metal mixing bowl (choose one that's heat and freezer-proof).

Slowly stir the hot coffee into the sugar mixture, stirring well to dissolve.

Place the container in the freezer, uncovered, and stir every 45 minutes until the mixture has reached the consistency of chipped ice, about 3 hours.

Just before the granita's ready, make the whipped cream: in a medium mixing bowl, beat the heavy cream until soft peaks form. Sprinkle the sugar over the cream and beat just until soft peaks return.

Serve the granita in chilled glasses with a generous dollop of the softly whipped cream.

Packing gift crates at mail Order

Extra Bonus Stuff

Visions, Guiding Principles,
Notes from the Back Dock, Timeline,
Suggested Reading, Appreciations

Zingerman's

mission statement

we share the zingerman's experience
selling food that makes you happy
giving service that makes you smile
in passionate pursuit of our mission
showing love and care in all our actions
to enrich as many lives as we possibly can.

Zingerman's 2009

A Food Odyssey

[written in 1994]

What follows is our vision of the future at Zingerman's: a unique Community of Businesses—15–20 of them by the year 2009—all sharing the Zingerman's name, all working to attain greatness within their own area of speciality, while working together to build organizational success for the entire ZCoB. Each business within the ZCoB will have a managing partner who takes responsibility for the success of its day-to-day operations, and work with Ari and Paul to provide long-term vision and direction. Each business will be located within the greater Ann Arbor area. And each will live by and teach Zingerman's business philosophies and guiding principles.

How did we arrive at this vision? And why? Learn the answers to these and other interesting questions in . . .

Benchmarking

Most folks hardly notice the worn black wooden bench out in front of the Deli. Chained loosely to the wrought iron railing, it's played host to thousands of customers on their way in to the Deli, to hundreds of staff members waiting for rides home, and to more than a few people who just didn't want to pass up its inviting, if somewhat spartan, comforts. Over the years it's also been the site of many a memorable, usually unplanned, business discussion.

If benches could talk, ours could tell a lot of tales.

A few years ago, Paul and I ended a long day's work on that bench, watching the sun start its daily slide down over the houses along Kingsley street. I'm not quite sure just how the conversation got started, but I clearly remember Paul popping the big question:

"What do you want the business to look like in 10 or 15 years?"

It's such an obvious question, one that every business person would like to have an answer to. Unfortunately, at that particular moment I had a tough time coming up with one. My mouth opened, but nothing much came out.

Imagine driving down the highway for hours, when suddenly the person in the passenger seat turns, stares at you intently, and says "Where are we going again?" and you look at him like . . ." You know, that's a good question. Where *are* we going?" You know you ought to know. You want to know. You thought you knew. But now that the question's out in the open, you have to admit: you're not quite sure.

Initial Vision

We acquired the bench along with the rather oddly shaped Deli building that we bought from Art Carpenter in 1982. A bit of bent wood continuity in an ever-changing business world; other than its color the bench hasn't changed much in the last 12 years. Back then it was painted a dull version of park bench green. There wasn't any courtyard filled with picnic tables to relax on, nor a Next Door to escape to, so we used to take our breaks on the bench.

And back then I'd have been able to sit on that bench and answer Paul's question pretty easily.

When we first opened Zingerman's we set our sights on establishing a one-of-a-kind delicatessen, known throughout the area, and even nationally, for its quality and creativity. A business that was connected to its community, that cared about the people who were a part of its world, whether customers, staff, neighbors, or suppliers. A spot that served people great tasting food, that gave caring, considerate, and enjoyable service. A place that was fun to shop and enjoyable to work.

Over the years things changed. We learned, we lived, we developed, Zingerman's got busier and bigger. Around the time we added onto the original building, in 1986, the bench was repainted a brighter, shinier green. And then, in the late '80's (I really can't remember exactly when) it was painted black. With so many people's bottoms gracing its surface, the bench paint wears thin. If you stop to really look at it, you can see a flock of green flecks showing through its most recent black coat. If you look really closely you can still see a few spots of its original dull green, and a couple of places where the old bare wood is showing through.

Lasting change comes slowly, gradually. But you notice it suddenly, as if it had just happened. Nearly a dozen years after we opened, here we were, me and Paul, rooted to the bench, realizing that what had been an almost rote conversation had given rise to a difficult emotional and ethical question. A question we really weren't sure how to answer.

The bench wasn't moving, but the business was coming up to a crossroads. It was time to pick a point on the map—to figure out where we were, and where we were headed.

Vision Accomplished

Over the course of the summer, Paul and I sat out there on the bench more than a few times, carrying our conversation to new lengths. Slowly, like someone waking up from a really great nap, we started to rub years of sleep from our business eyes. New perspectives became clear, new ideas emerged, old ones showed their age.

We started to realized that our original vision, our drive to create the Deli of our dreams, had been attained. We'd reached that destination. We just hadn't stopped moving long enough to realize it.

Now this may sound crazy, but it's incredibly hard for me to really admit to an accomplishment of this sort. I can look around on any given day and find 52 things that aren't up to snuff and 52 more I think we can do better. So my immediate reaction was "How can we have fulfilled our vision when there's so much more we can do and do better?"

And yet, if I was honest with myself, in my heart, I knew it was true. We had done what we set out to do in 1982. Vision accomplished.

Mid-Life

Having agreed on a common version of the past, Paul and I continued to gravitate to the bench. We still had to figure out where we were headed in the future.

Ann Arbor's Art Fair—a citywide street fair in late July that draws hundreds of thousands of visitors every year, seemingly every one of whom has to visit Zingerman's as part of their itinerary—came and went. August arrived. The bench got hotter out in the sun. So did the conversation. We talked, argued, agreed some, disagreed more. We looked back, we looked forward, we looked inward, and all too often we looked at each other with more than a bit of bewilderment. Sometimes we looked at each other like we were just plain crazy.

Like any couple in a good long-term relationship, we had some difficult moments. But in our commitment to each other, to our partnership, to Zingerman's, we kept on looking until we came up with an answer we both liked.

In retrospect, all this strikes me as kind of the equivalent of a mid-life review for a business. Like, "Well, we had the kids, we got the good job, we bought the house, and now what do we do with the rest of our lives?" Accomplishment is great, but you have to keep going.

And keep going we did. Right through September and into October. Gradually we got more and more a sense of what we wanted, a picture of a plan we were both excited about. Our energy level grew. This was going to be good. Really good. At the end of October we went out to San Francisco for a business conference. Traveling allowed us hours and hours of sitting together, talking without interruption, fitting together the final pieces of the picture.

The bench was still out in front of the building when we got back. But somehow, things were starting to look a little different. For the first time in a long time we could answer Paul's question with confidence. We knew where we were going. We knew what we wanted the business to look like 15 years down the road. And we were ready to get to work.

Still Only One Deli

So, you want to know, what is this vision of the future?

Well, before I tell all, let me tell you what it isn't. It isn't about opening a chain of Zingerman's across the country. Lord knows we get asked about this often enough. And, granted, it's the standard formula for business growth. But after many hours of introspection we came to the conclusion that we weren't going to do it.

Why not? Because although it's physically doable, it just doesn't fit with our principles and our passions. I mean, we could certainly open many more stores and stick the Zingerman's name on 'em. Even buy some black wooden benches to stick out front. But in my gut, I know that it wouldn't be the same.

Such a big part of what makes the Deli the Deli is its personality, its soul. And the soul, as Thomas Moore says, is a pretty darned mysterious thing. The soul of a business can't be copied. It just is. Magical. Mysterious. Even magnetic. But not manufactured. Start plopping Zingerman's Deli-Clones down all over the country and we'd end up with just another chain of fairly interesting, fairly effective delis with black and white tile floors and blackboard menus. The signs out front would say "Zingerman's," but the insides would say "wooden." Forced. Lacking in life.

The Zingerman's Community of Businesses

So if the future holds no Deli-Clones, then what's in it? Instead of franchising a deli, we decided to build around our principles, our philosophies of people and food, our commitment to our community. To enhance uniqueness we had to create more uniqueness. So we set out to create other soul-ful, principled businesses, guided by other people who shared our passion for great tasting food and exceptional service.

We decided to do that by building a Zingerman's Community of Businesses.

We envision a Community in which *each member business shares with Zingerman's a common vision, a common road map toward the year 2009, a common set of guiding principles.* Each is committed to the success of the other, committed to working in the best interests of the entire organization, linked financially and emotionally. Each is committed to the success of its staff and, beyond all else, the satisfaction of our customers.

But, significantly, each of these businesses will be owned and managed by someone who has chosen to be our partner in that particular venture. A partner with a passion for a particular food or service. A passion for creating an exceptional business that has a personality of its own, yet is grounded in the principles that have been such an important part of making Zingerman's what it is.

Paul's and my commitment is to work with each of our new partners to share our experience, our systems, our ideas, our insights, our help, in working to help to make these new businesses effective parts of the Zingerman's family. Our role is to take a back (bench) seat; our job is to help, encourage, and support, not to steal the spotlight. The day-to-day operations, the endless stream of decisions, dramas, and dilemmas of the business are for our partners—the new owner-operators—to manage. It's their show.

> *"If there isn't a champion—somebody who says, 'this is my thing, this is what drives me,' then nothing happens."*
>
> GERI LARKIN, Manager of Emerging
> Business Services at Deloitte & Touche, good
> Zingerman's customer, and all-around good person

Why New Partners?

It's a fair enough question. Why take on new partners in new businesses rather than simply expanding our current business and adding more managers?

Quite simply, because it is our firm belief that for a business to bring the kind of energy, excitement, commitment to food, service, and staff that we are looking for, there absolutely must be an owner-operator on site. The personality of every business starts at the top, and the personality of absentee-owned businesses is often far too absent to create the kind of businesses we want to be associated with.

"New partners" is also about working to keep decision-making where we think it belongs—close to the customer and close to the food. We don't want an enormous bureacratic operation that loses touch with its roots. But we do want to grow. And we believe that creating more small businesses, with more leaders and less followers, is an effective way to do that.

In the end, Zingerman's 2009 isn't about expansion. It's about creating more effective businesses with more independence, more room to take chances and make changes, an opportunity to produce ever-greater passions for great tasting food.

What Will These Businesses Be?

Well, in truth, I can't tell you right now what they will be, because, quite simply, I don't know.

The motivation, the driving force, the creative energy for each new business must come from someone within the organization who has a passion to make it happen. Me, I've got a million ideas. But the point of this whole project is that the ideas must come from the people who are personally committed to doing the long, sometimes rewarding, often arduous, work that will take them from "just another good idea" to a very tangible and very enjoyable reality.

Why Grow?

That's another good question. Just because we've grown steadily for 12 years doesn't mean we have to keep doing so. Growth for growth's sake isn't a good enough motivation to embark on such a long-term project—2009 is a long, long way off.

What it comes down to is that we have made a conscious choice to continue to grow our organization because we believe it will allow Zingerman's to better serve its customers and its staff. We have sought out a path to the future that will enhance the quality of our food, create new opportunities for staff, new offerings to customers. We believe that the path we have chosen allows us to go after that growth in a way that is compatible with who we are, staying true to our principles and our passions.

Better Quality

While we take great pride in what we serve at the Deli, we have never stopped searching for more ways to bring you more flavorful, more enjoyable foods. It is our belief that by opening more—and smaller—businesses we can raise the quality of food throughout the Zingerman's Community of Businesses.

In the last two years we've already seen this work wonders with the opening of Zingerman's Bakehouse. In retrospect, the Bakehouse was sort of our first tentative step toward 2009. Our partner and head baker Frank Carollo's passion for great baking, the focus on mastering a single product area, is really the heart of what we are working to replicate as we bring new members into the Zingerman's Community of Businesses.

The commitment to quality, attention to detail, and love of learning that start with Frank extend through the entire Bakehouse staff. By focusing all their energies onto baking, they have brought us across-the-board better quality in all of our breads, cakes, cookies, and croissants. We are looking for similar leaps forward in quality with each new business we bring into the Community.

Career Opportunities

Over the last 12 years we've always told people who worked here that they could create a future of their choosing at Zingerman's. If they figured out where they wanted to go, we were committed to helping them get there. But in the last few years, as the business has matured, we realized that we could no longer make that promise in good faith. Managers stayed put. Space was limited. Possibilities for upward mobility in the organization became harder to find. Instead of the limitless opportunity we wanted to provide, we found ourselves with fewer and fewer options to offer.

We're confident that with this vision of Zingerman's 2009 we can again offer that opportunity in good faith. The list of options is long—from new departments to new management positions to new foods to learn about, and just about everything in between. And for the first time we are able to offer the kind of opportunity for people in our organization that Paul and I had in 1982—to open a business of their own. A business in which they can pursue their own passions, make a difference in the world, bring great food and great service to our community. A business where five or ten years from now they, too, will have the chance to sit out front on a bench of their own, savor their successes, and struggle with their future and their fears.

Where Do We Go from Here?

Upwards and onwards. Better food. Better service. Better workplace. More businesses.

I can't tell you exactly what the businesses of the future are going to be. Like I said, that depends on the people within the Zingerman's Community. Because the driving force for any new business we open must come from them. My job, and Paul's job, is to nurture them, to help them take their ideas and their interests and their passions and translate them into successful business ventures. Businesses that share the Zingerman's Mission to bring you, "food that makes you happy and service that makes you smile." Businesses that are committed to making our Guiding Principles into a way of living and working together.

Starting Over

It strikes me that what all this is really about is starting over. Kicking into the same startup, risk-taking, chance-breaking mode that goes with getting a new business off the ground.

Starting over is scary. The road to 2009 is filled with potholes and dotted with detours. Setting off on it exposes us to the risk of failure; to that inevitable seedlet of self-doubt that you might not be able to make it all work if you try it again.

But starting over also feels great. Energizing. Exciting. It's the opportunity to challenge ourselves and our people and our organization to rise to new levels of achievement, to find new and more effective ways to get great tasting food to more people. To grow while staying true to our roots. To return to the beginning, to put all our chips back out on the table and go for a more exciting, more rewarding, more interesting future.

Thanks

Thanks to everyone who has ever worked at Zingerman's, whose efforts have contributed to getting us to the point where we could say with a smile that we were ready to start over again. Thanks to our suppliers, whose support and commitment to making good food makes it easier for us to do our jobs for our guests.

Thanks to our new partners for choosing to dedicate a big part of their lives to bringing better food, contributing their creative energy to Ann Arbor and the Zingerman's Community of Businesses.

Thanks to everyone who is a part of Zingerman's for their patience and support over the last year, waiting for me and Paul to figure out where we wanted the business to be in 10 or 15 years, waiting for us to get off that black bench and get started.

Thanks to you, our guests, for sticking with us over the years, for supporting us through thick and thin. To bearing with us when we err, for letting us know when we're doing right by you and when we aren't. Thanks for listening to all this. Thanks for embracing Zingerman's into Ann Arbor with such open and loving arms.

Back on the Bench

What I've written about here is only a brief glimpse at where we're headed and why. If you'd like to learn more about Zingerman's, its food, its principles, or its people, please don't hesitate to give me or Paul a call. We'd be glad to talk. While the warm weather lasts you may well find us sitting out front on the bench, trying to sort out whatever the issue of the day may be. After all, success is just getting yourself a better set of problems. So many millions of unknowns still to uncover, so many discussions to have, so many questions to answer on the road to 2009.

One thing we do know though. We know where we want the business to be in 15 years. And we're looking forward to the adventure of trying to get there.

Thanks again for listening.

Zingerman's Vision for 2020

[written in 2006/7]

*"Learn to see, and then you'll know that there is
no end to the new worlds of our vision."*

—CARLOS CASTANEDA, The Teachings of Don Juan

*What follows is our vision for the ZCoB for the year 2020. It began in the winter of
2006. Written by all of the organization's managing partners, reviewed and com-
mented on by hundreds of ZCoB staff members, revised, rewritten, and improved
many times to make it ever-more inspiring and effective. It paints a picture of the
organization that we will create. This is Zingerman's in the year 2020.*

Thanks to all of you who helped make it a reality.

In the Zingerman's Community of Businesses, we live our mission. Our guiding
principles manage our day-to-day actions. People we work with and serve comment on our integrity. "You really do what you say you do. And when you don't,
you make it right." We have developed a radical model of responsible business
growth in concert with our guiding principles and inspired by a commitment
to our community. Our work leads to positive change around the country and
even across the world.

Radical (radík'l)
definition 1 (a) of or from the root or roots;
going to the foundation or source of something;
fundamental; basic

better tomorrow than today

Changing Our World

> *"Any invasion of armies can be resisted, but not an idea*
> *whose time has come."*
>
> —Victor Hugo

We've successfully applied the model of sustainability to all aspects of our work. Today in 2020 everyone and everything we engage with—in our personal and professional lives; our business and community; our customers and staff; our suppliers and environment—are better than they were when we embarked on this vision 15 years ago. We have created a community of businesses where people willingly bring their whole selves to work. We feel free to express ourselves and tap into our deepest creative potential. We believe in what we are doing and integrate our sense of purpose into who we are.

Our work is driven from our guiding principles and focused on caring and cooperation. We empower and support each other and our workforce is representative of our community and its racial diversity. We've built thousands of strong, sustainable relationships and they nurture our growth.

We have a strategy for growth that is about the long-term economic health of our Community of Businesses and our local economy. When we talk about "great service" we refer not only to our customers, our community, and each other, but also to our planet; we push ourselves to go beyond basic compliance on environmental issues.

We must be profitable in order to survive but our primary purpose is to contribute to a better life for everyone we touch. We do this by providing meaningful work, dignified employment, beneficial goods and services, and relationships of trust and caring that are the foundations of a healthy community. Through this work we have helped to create true prosperity, economic security, and democracy in our larger community.

We know that we are a small presence in the universe; we make and sell food. Rather than focusing on a few grand gestures, we take hundreds and thousands of small actions with great passion and great love. We are changing the world with every transaction. Everyone who comes in contact with our organization—employees, customers, and suppliers, people asking for donations, journalists and reporters, public officials—leaves with the perception that we exist in order to be of service. We invite you to join us.

growing locally

12–18 Vibrant Businesses

The Zingerman's Community of Businesses (ZCoB) is more vital than at any time in its history. All 12–18 unique, food-related businesses are located in the Ann Arbor area. We are strongly rooted in the local *terroir* and our growth provides opportunities to individuals and to our whole community. The ZCoB is driven by people who bring their outsider ideas inside our business, follow the Path to Partnership, and see their businesses flourish. Passionate managing partners are present in each unique ZCoB business, making a big organization like ours feel small, nimble, and close. People who shop with us know we listen and respond. While each business is world class in its approach to food and service, we feel like the corner store.

Each Zingerman's business is an exciting leader in its field and enhances the performance of the entire ZCoB. Each partner shares our organizational values and has a passion and drive to develop their skills so their business contributes positively to all three bottom lines in sustainable ways. We are innovative, creative, and set high standards for the industry and for ourselves.

Together we work as a single organization, successfully navigating the challenges of interdependency. We know that while we operate our businesses independently day to day, our fates are linked financially and emotionally. Businesses push each other to become better; employees trade ideas and best practices more than ever. We've built a diverse community in which each member business shares a common vision, a common road map, a common set of guiding principles. We are strongly committed to each other's success.

Everyone here has embraced the reality that we all have multiple—and sometimes conflicting—roles to play, that we often change "hats" several times in a single day. Everyone takes responsibility for successfully leading us toward the ZCoB's mission, principles, and bottom-line performance. We feel a sense of connectedness to people in work environments very different from ours and a responsibility to support them. We act as a Community of Businesses to make the lives of everyone around us better.

how does it taste?

Radically Better Food

The food we sell here in 2020 is better than we ever imagined it could be back when we wrote this. In the same way that the "new" Zingerman's Bakehouse radically elevated the quality of bread we offered in 1992, we've found a host of new ways to very significantly improve the flavor and authenticity of everything we serve.

Great food is everywhere you go at Zingerman's. Some changes have been large, some very small. Perhaps the hardest trick to pull off has been making every dish we serve fantastic. We're seeing guests do double-takes with every bite because they can't believe how good the food tastes. They're coming back again and again, often ordering the same dish because they just can't get enough of it.

We've achieved this level, in part, because we've never stopped asking, "How can it be better?" Meaningful improvements happen all the time, at all levels of the organization. We've been searching ever-more actively, tasting more critically, learning with more enthusiasm and fiercely championing food producers we've encouraged and nurtured. We take pride in connecting more diverse foods with greater numbers of guests in ways we never thought possible. The call to radically better food led us to build ever-stronger relationships with every player in our food chain. And we've influenced businesses beyond ours—there's better food everywhere in Ann Arbor and our customers care about eating well more than ever.

Our goal has never been to invent the next great dish, just serve food with great flavor. Zingerman's isn't tracking trends to keep up with the food fashions. We're looking far and wide and often back in time, to cultures and continents that might not be getting a lot of media attention but that have been producing incredible food for centuries. Many times that means rediscovering and reinvigorating historical classics; it's a thrill to find old memories, foods our grandparents ate, then bring them to our customers and create a new generation of memories. We find and promote great food with passion, a mission to educate and a down-to-earth attitude. We know radically better food can come from simple, local ingredients. Or it can come from a spice imported from across the world. Whatever its source, you really can taste the difference.

crazy for customers

Radically Better Service

Even though our Community of Businesses has almost doubled in size since 2006, walking into any business in 2020 is as intimate an experience as walking into Zingerman's Delicatessen in 1982. We're amazed that we've actually been able to increase the level of service while growing into a bigger business. We make it so natural and comfortable for everyone involved it doesn't seem like work at all. Great service happens everywhere: every element of Zingerman's is a great experience. We are as charming, selfless, and accurate in our opening acts of hospitality toward a guest as we are when we recover from a problem. Our customers, our suppliers, our community, our fellow employees—everyone considers Zingerman's the standard bearer. We do the things everyone says a business can't do. We define great service.

Our commitment to serving others is inspiring, and it finds its way into everything we do. We make it happen in small but meaningful ways. A free brownie finds its way into a get well soon package. An accountant interrupts her regular work flow to go take out the kitchen trash. There are also extraordinary acts of service that surprise even seasoned veterans who thought they'd seen it all. A server volunteers to make things right by delivering a forgotten product to a guest's home. The cook smiles and happily makes something that's not on the menu and brings it out to the table personally.

Each of us recognizes that our work here is more meaningful because of the service we give to our guests and to each other. We really do make a positive difference in people's lives. Servant Leadership attracts individuals who thrive on giving exceptional service to everyone they come in contact with—staff, guests, the organization overall, and the community—every day. Service here is so pervasive it's contagious. You can't help but be caught up in its challenge and thrill.

books wide open

Radically Better Finance

A rich, generous culture of responsible finance exists everywhere at Zingerman's. Inside all our meetings, from staff huddles to partner-level strategy sessions, we're successfully performing a difficult financial balancing act: to seek profit not for its own sake, but because it gives us the opportunity to make the world a better place. We achieve short-term profits that make us viable while building for a positive financial future. We use sound financial practices to make our businesses, our suppliers' businesses, our community, and our employees' lives richer not just now, but for the long term. If someone working in the ZCoB has a personal vision of financial success and if it can be done within the context of our vision and values, we're committed to helping that person achieve it. In fact, we use a measure of staff members' personal financial standing as one of the ways we measure our organizational success. The work that we do funds Zingerman's Community of Businesses Foundation, allowing us to give back more than ever to our community, making us a model for other businesses to learn how to increase their giving.

The results are all around us. We have balanced growth across the ZCoB. Mature businesses and startups, producers and sellers—all work together to make a diverse, financially sound organization. Financial institutions fight for our business. We're in a strong cash position so we can self-finance ventures when it makes sense and manage the rainy days when they come. There are more opportunities for promotion and partnership than ever before.

We've found a way to share the growth and financial opportunity of the ZCoB at an organizational level. While back in '07 none of us could have guessed what the creative solution was going to be, it has worked out amazingly well. It supported the already high level of commitment from members of the ZCoB that we had 15 years ago and enabled us to share big, company-wide wins.

Our culture of finance has helped every person in our organization realize that numbers can be fun and we consistently get great financial results. Outside visitors are blown away by the level of involvement and understanding that front-line people of all ages, job responsibilities, and seniority display in their work. They're also stunned that our open culture extends to folks outside the ZCoB—we share our "secrets" with other businesses and, in so doing, help others achieve financial success.

science! (for food folks)

Intentional Technology

We actively use technology to help support every part of Vision 2020. But let's be clear: "technology" in our world doesn't necessarily mean something fancy or high tech. It can be ancient stone milling methods—thousands of years old, but still the best technology out there to produce some foods.

We've successfully used technology wherever we could to enhance the Zingerman's Experience. It's been simple, proven ancient food technology that improves the quality of what we make. (If there's a tool that makes the food more flavorful, and more traditional in its taste, that's for us.) It's communication technology that helps us deepen and broaden supplier relationships and helps improve the quality of our ingredients. It's marketing technology that allows us to sell more without wasting resources. It's educational technology that makes training easier and more effective, and helps us connect more smoothly with our customers and community.

We're guided by Webster's unglamorous definition of technology as, "a technical method of achieving a practical purpose," and it has led to great improvements in all aspects of our work. We have developed practical, time-tested technology that helps front-line people provide better food and service, reduces menial tasks and mistakes, improves our financial contributions to the bottom line, and let's everyone participate more creatively and actively in improving our work and food. Technology is a web that links our efforts in finance with service, food with education, and so on. It's something we pursue intentionally and actively, but it's never technology just for technology's sake.

and now for a sidebar conversation

We Put the F U in Fun

We have successfully quantified fun, measured fun, and improved our fun factor by at least 380% since 2007. We actively teach people how to have fun at work. We have games to increase the volume of fun we experience and reward ourselves with added fun. Organizations from around the world come to visit us for seminars, to take notes, to see fun in the works, to bring new ideas and techniques back to their own businesses.

When we're tired of having so much fun at work we all have the opportunity to escape to the Zingerman's recreation property—a small tract of land the Zingerman's Community of Businesses purchased to give us all a place to let our hair down and ignore fun for as long as we can stand it. It's become a great benefit for all our staff, a place to learn, relax, and sometimes to even share spreadsheets.

Putting fun in everything we do—from packaging to presentations—keeps us sane and healthy, and our customers happy and engaged. We're joking far too much to be considered food snobs or "corporate." (We've even had at least two unfortunate minor injuries caused by excessive laughter in the workplace.)

Zingerman's **word search**

```
b  L  s  d  r  a  t  s  u  m  y  c
a  r  u  g  u  L  a  v  a  j  h  u
k  p  e  g  g  t  u  n  a  q  c  p
e  f  L  a  v  o  r  f  u  L  i  a
h  g  u  o  d  m  i  L  k  c  w  s
o  a  n  o  c  a  b  p  k  v  d  t
u  x  m  e  a  t  r  L  u  e  n  r
s  n  o  i  n  o  e  y  L  o  a  a
e  s  e  e  h  c  t  a  e  i  s  m
a  L  L  e  r  a  z  z  o  m  d  i
```

ham	mozzarella	cup	onion
milk	sandwich	cheese	egg
bread	pickle	pastrami	bacon
flavorful	tomato	tuna	dill
dough	arugula	mustard	java
bakehouse	meat	rye	

a place of higher learning

Zingerman's Is an Education Destination

People come from around the world to learn about almost everything we do: baking, cooking, cheese making, coffee roasting, service, open book finance, leadership, operations, marketing, facilitation, food-friendly technology, sustainable farming, community giving, and more. Weekdays and weekends in Ann Arbor are filled with visitors learning about what Zingerman's is up to in settings casual and formal.

We're inventing and rediscovering ways to work, constantly teaching them within and outside Zingerman's. We teach people to learn so they learn to teach. Many employees have come to work here especially to further their education, be it about food, people, or organizational development. There's a well-established internship program with local educational institutions and interested individuals who are passionate about learning and getting hands-on experience.

When employees move on it's with a sense of self-confidence and with experiences they can use to better the next organization they're part of. Zingerman's alumni—employees and students—have gone on to become successful leaders and teachers in their own settings. They've developed a strong network of support for each other, improving their respective organizations and sharing what they've learned at annual conferences, reunions, blogs, classrooms, and offices around the world.

Half a dozen Zingerman's staff members have become published authors. We've established regular scholarships in the community for people in need that get them successfully into food careers. We offer shared work arrangements for hourly staff and managers with other like-minded businesses. We pursue educational opportunities at every turn: short courses, advanced degrees, sabbaticals, externships, entertainment shows, you name it. When the press lists places around the country to learn food and business in an alternative but highly effective and fun setting, Zingerman's is always near the top.

Education is one of our passions. The more we teach; the more we learn. The more we teach, the more customers and staff are drawn to visit and shop with us. The more we teach and learn together, the more effectively we connect with each other, strengthen our culture, and improve the lives of everyone we interact with. We thrive on sharing information lavishly.

opportunity and responsibility for everyone

Committed to Success Across the Organization

We provide a wealth of opportunities for people at every level of the organization. No matter what position we hold, we all have both the opportunity and the responsibility to help create the organization that we want to be a part of. Similarly, we have the opportunity and responsibility to grow and prosper within it as individuals.

Opportunities abound, and we all take advantage of them. Many of us have visited suppliers around the country and the world to learn about our food and where it comes from. We have international exchange programs for staff, all developed by the people who want to experience them. Educational opportunities have multiplied. Hundreds of us at every level—from partners through to part timers—have gained U of Z degrees and we're teaching classes to each other and to the public left and right. Others have taken advantage of our scholarship program to further their learning outside of the organization. Financial opportunities abound in the form of gainsharing, performance bonuses, mini games, ZCoB-wide games, 401k plans, benefits, and more. Our training on personal financial management—supported by the money that flows from great bottom-line performance across the organization—has helped everyone enhance their personal financial health.

Each member of the ZCoB acts as an effective leader in his or her work. We take responsibility for ourselves, our actions, our feelings, and our careers, always mindful to include others in our success. We're entrepreneurial, always treating our work like we own it. Since 2009 more than a few of us have moved up in the organization to become managing partners. But no matter what the position, everyone is actively learning and expanding their knowledge of food, service, and finance, creating opportunities for themselves and others along the way as we build a better organization and more positive community.

A spirit of generosity infuses all that we do and all that we are. We have created something of significance that is inclusive, positive, and life affirming. We believe that we have been successful because we have a vision and a strategy that seeks to promote the human potential that surrounds us.

Zingerman's ®

Guiding Principles
(from the Staff Handbook)

How to Share the Zingerman's Experience

Great Food!

At Zingerman's we are committed to making and selling high-quality food. Great food at Zingerman's means:

WE ARE A FOOD DRIVEN BUSINESS.

While we engage in many activities at Zingerman's, first and foremost we are in business to sell food. Our other work—including accounting, design, and management—is done to support and advance the sales of our food.

FLAVOR IN OUR FOOD COMES FIRST.

We choose our products first and foremost on the basis of flavor. We sell food that tastes great. We want our food to be full-flavored, delicious, and enjoyable to eat.

TRADITIONALLY MADE AND GREAT-TASTING FOODS FROM AROUND THE WORLD.

We sell foods that have roots, a heritage, a history. We seek out traditionally made, frequently hand-crafted foods, which are primarily of peasant origin. These are foods that people have been eating for centuries and will continue to eat for centuries to come.

WE WORK TO SELL OUR FOOD AT THE PEAK OF ITS FLAVOR.

Traditionally made foods are alive and different every day. They are affected by weather, soil, climate, the skill and craft of the producer, and the care and handling by our staff. We regularly taste and evaluate our products in order to assure our guests of the most flavorful food possible.

GOOD FOOD MAKES LIFE MORE FUN.

We value the pleasure one gets from savoring a sliver of fine farmhouse cheddar, from the aroma of an aged Balsamic vinegar . . . Eating and appreciating good food makes life more enjoyable. We value the opportunity to sell and enjoy so many fine foods.

GOOD FOOD IS FOR EVERYONE, NOT JUST A SELECT, "GOURMET" FEW.

We make our food accessible to as many people as possible. We put our guests at ease with our food. No advanced degrees are needed to appreciate it—just a willingness to taste and experience the pleasure it provides. To that end, we will gladly offer a taste of any of our foods to any of our guests.

OUR FOODS LOOK GREAT DAY IN AND DAY OUT.

Our food always looks neat, fresh, appealing, eye-catching. A just-split wheel of Parmigiano Reggiano, a "just-off-the-grill" Georgia Reuben (#18) are sights to behold. We work to present them to our guests simply and effectively. We display our food in abundance to demonstrate both our commitment to the food, and to convey that at Zingerman's, our food comes first.

Great Service!

If great food is the lock, great service is the key. Great service at Zingerman's means:

WE GO THE EXTRA MILE FOR OUR GUESTS, GIVING EXCEPTIONAL SERVICE TO EACH OF THEM.

We are committed to giving great service—meeting the guests' expectations and then exceeding them. Great service like this is at the core of the Zingerman's experience. Our guests always leave with a sense of wonderment at how we have gone out of our way to make their experience at Zingerman's a rewarding one.

OUR BOTTOM LINE IS DERIVED FROM CUSTOMER SATISFACTION.

Customer satisfaction is the fuel that stokes the Zingerman's fire. If our guests aren't happy, we're not happy*. To this end we consistently go the extra mile—literally and figuratively—for our guests. The customer is never an interruption in our day. We welcome feedback of all sorts. We constantly reevaluate our performance to better accommodate our customers. Our guests leave happy or they don't leave. Each of us takes full responsibility for making our guest's experience an enjoyable one, before, during, and after the sale.

AT ZINGERMAN'S WE BELIEVE THAT GIVING GREAT SERVICE IS AN HONORABLE PROFESSION.

Quality service is a dignified and honorable pursuit. We take great pride in our ability to provide our guests and our staff with exceptional service. Service is about giving and caring for those around us.

WE GIVE GREAT SERVICE TO EACH OTHER AS WELL AS TO OUR GUESTS.

We provide the same level of service in our work with our peers as we do with our guests. We go the extra mile for each other. We are polite, supportive, considerate, superb listeners, working on the basis of mutual respect and care.

> ** 1 out of every 300,000 guests will not be happy no matter what. If you think you are serving this guest, please refer him or her to the Manager, to the Managing Partner, or to Paul or Ari.*

A Great Place to Shop and Eat!

Coming to Zingerman's is a positive and enjoyable experience for our guests.

WE SURROUND OUR GUESTS WITH GREAT FOOD, GREAT ENERGY, AND GREAT EXPERIENCES.

The guest's first exposure to Zingerman's is a breathtaking experience; food, energy, and excitement are everywhere. There is a palpable feeling of energy. The aromas of fine food waft through the air. Visually, incredible-looking food surrounds us.

WE PROVIDE A SPADAZZELING ENVIRONMENT FOR OUR CUSTOMERS AND STAFF.

It's neat! It's clean! It's Zingerman's! Floors are swept and mopped constantly, windows sparkle, employees fall to the floor, colliding with each other as they race to clear each table, before the guest has hardly moved away from it.

WE FOLLOW SAFE FOOD-HANDLING PROCEDURES.

Handling food carries with it responsibility for the health and well-being of our guests. We are well-informed on safe food-handling procedures and implement them consistently in every area of our work.

OUR POLICIES AND SYSTEMS ARE DESIGNED TO HELP THE BUSINESS RUN BETTER.

We understand that our actions have an impact on our customers. With this in mind, we retain the flexibility to make exceptions to our rules when it is in the best interests of our guests to do so. We do not hold our guests responsible for not being familiar with our systems.

Solid Profits!

Profits are the lifeblood of our business.

WE OPERATE AT A HEALTHY LEVEL OF PROFIT.

Profits provide us with security and growth potential—both for the business as a whole and for each of us as components of that business—in order to fulfill our mission. Attaining healthy profits requires a concerted and consistent contribution from everyone at Zingerman's. Toward that end we educate our entire staff about the financial workings of the business.

WE WANT TO MAKE THAT PROFIT WORK FOR OUR STAFF, OUR GROWTH, AND OUR COMMUNITY, AS WELL AS FOR THE BUSINESS.

We regularly reinvest our profits in the business. We share profits with the staff. We regularly give back to our community through donations of money, time, and products.

WE ARE COMMITTED TO BEING FISCALLY RESPONSIBLE IN OUR WORK.

We spend according to our means. We are willing to delay gratification in order to build long-term rewards.

WE ARE A GROWTH BUSINESS.

We are committed to healthy, productive expansion and growth of our sales, consistent with our mission and our principles.

A Great Place to Work!

Working at Zingerman's means taking an active part in running the business. Our work makes a difference.

WE ARE EMPOWERED BY THE CREATIVITY, HARD WORK, AND COMMITMENT OF OUR STAFF.

It is the energy, effort, and active involvement of our staff in the running of the business that helps make Zingerman's successful. We actively seek to build on the creativity and intelligence of everyone who works here.

WE ARE COMMITTED TO EACH OTHER'S SUCCESS.

Each of us is committed to the success of everyone else who works at Zingerman's. We go out of our way to support each other, to listen well, to facilitate and encourage each other's growth and advancement.

WE COMPENSATE OUR STAFF WELL.

We provide income, a benefits package, profit sharing, meaningful work, and a sense of community for our staff, which balances their needs with the resources of the business.

WE PROVIDE OPPORTUNITY FOR GROWTH AND ADVANCEMENT FOR OUR STAFF.

We actively work to provide for healthy growth of our business. In so doing, we provide opportunities for staff who wish to grow within Zingerman's.

WE INVOLVE AS MANY PEOPLE AS POSSIBLE IN THE RUNNING OF THE BUSINESS.

We regularly bring as many people as practical into the operation of the business. In so doing, Zingerman's runs more effectively, benefiting from everyone's abilities, creativity, experience, and intelligence.

Each of us is committed to being proactive in our work.

We aggressively work to tackle difficult issues without waiting to be asked. We work with the knowledge that each of us bears the responsibility for what goes on around us, and has the opportunity and ability to effect positive change within the business.

We work to improve in every area.

We constantly seek to improve our performance, individually and as a group, and work up to our fullest potential, through self-reflection, education, and cooperation. When something is not working, we look first at ourselves to find room for improvement before we look at the work of others. We do so both as individuals, as departments, and as a business.

We learn from our errors and work quickly to correct them.

When we make mistakes, we view them as opportunities for growth and change. When we make an error we do not seek to assign blame, only to avoid repeating the problem in the future.

We strive to create a safe workplace.

We work within the limits of our "differently abled" historic space to create a safe workplace. We continually reevaluate and act to improve our work space. We walk slowly and carefully on the stairs, we never leave knives unattended in the sink, pay close attention at all times when using slicers. We catch each other when we fall.

Zingerman's embraces diversity.

We go out of our way to build a diverse and well-balanced workplace. We like to work with people who are committed to making Zingerman's successful. We hire individuals regardless of race, religion, gender, or sexual preference.

We like to have fun.

And we take our fun very seriously. So don't mess with it.

Strong Relationships!

Successful working relationships are an essential component of our health and success as a business.

WE BUILD MUTUALLY REWARDING, LONG-TERM RELATIONSHIPS WITH OUR CUSTOMERS.

We are here for the long haul and work to carry our customers right along with us. The long-term relationship with our guests is more important to us than any short-term transaction or interaction. To that end, we go the extra mile to take care of our guests and their families; to learn their tastes, their favorite sandwiches, their shopping needs.

WE ARE COMMITTED TO LONG-TERM WORK RELATIONSHIPS WITH OUR STAFF.

We build mutually rewarding and long-term relationships with our staff, based on a commitment to each other's success, mutual respect, and shared values. We work to retain those positive relationships even after one of our staff has chosen to leave Zingerman's.

WE ESTABLISH MUTUALLY REWARDING RELATIONSHIPS WITH OUR SUPPLIERS.

We view our relationships with our suppliers as a partnership in which both sides benefit. Our dealings are based on courtesy and consideration.

WE WORK TO BUILD CONNECTIONS TO OTHER BUSINESSES WHO SHARE SIMILAR VALUES.

We seek out like-minded businesses to develop an effective support network for ourselves. We work with them to share information and ideas. We give back to our industry through seminars, articles, and participation in industry events.

WE CELEBRATE GROUP ACHIEVEMENT AND RECOGNIZE INDIVIDUAL SUCCESS.

We regularly go out of our way to enjoy and recognize our accomplishments as a business. When one of us is successful we are all successful. At the same time we also recognize our individual achievements, and overwhelm each other with a steady stream of positive reinforcement.

A Place to Learn!

Learning keeps us going, keeps us challenged, keeps us on track.

WE ACTIVELY EDUCATE OUR GUESTS, OUR STAFF, AND OURSELVES ABOUT THE FOOD WE SELL.

We constantly work to educate our guests, ourselves, and our community about good food. We believe that the more we learn about food (where it comes from, how it's made, how to use it) the more effectively and profitably the business will operate.

WE ACTIVELY EDUCATE OUR STAFF ABOUT THE WORKINGS OF THE BUSINESS.

We regularly share business information with our staff. The more we understand about the business the more productive we will be.

WE ACTIVELY EDUCATE OURSELVES ABOUT ALL ASPECTS OF OUR JOBS.

We consistently seek to improve our understanding of our own jobs by staying current in industry literature, regularly reading books and periodicals on subjects both directly and peripherally related to our work, and attending seminars, conferences, and trade shows.

An Active Part of Our Community!

We believe that a business has an obligation to give back to the community of which it is a part.

WE ACTIVELY PARTICIPATE IN IMPROVING LIFE IN OUR COMMUNITY.

We are committed to leaving a positive mark on our community. We actively work to make our community a better place to live by contributing time, food, money, energy, and information.

WE ENCOURAGE OUR STAFF TO PARTICIPATE IN COMMUNITY SERVICE.

We encourage our staff members to contribute to their community, to be active citizens, to work to better their environment.

WE'RE HERE TO STAY.

We're committed to building long-lasting, mutually beneficial relationships with our city, our neighborhood, and our community. We are committed to a long-term business strategy that will keep us in our community for many years to come.

Notes from the Back Dock

What follows are some comments from real live Zingerman's folks about what it's like to actually work here.

When I mention where I work most of the time people say "Wow, how great! That must be such a great place to work." It is, but I get the feeling that sometimes they mean it like, "Oh, it must be so nice and everyone is always having a great day." Kind of like a Disney movie. While it is an amazing place to work it is also hard, challenging, it can be frustrating just like anywhere else. We face stress and bad moods just like all employees everywhere. The difference is the principles that guide our work environment. Leaders are expected to get in there and help, to care, to have a vision of greatness for their workday. That makes all the difference. I know great service is expected as is great food and great finance. We do all we can to bring that about for our business. I know that the people I work with genuinely care about me. I also know they care about the job we do. It is such a huge difference. It's not that we miraculously hire only perfect people. It is just that it is really clear what our priorities should be. Lots of people work in stressful jobs but here we know that it is "good enough" doesn't cut it. You can really take pride in the work. So it is hard but at the end of the day, we all feel like what we do here matters. People feel good when they walk out our doors. Being the best part of someone's day isn't just talk and the cool thing is that frequently it becomes the best part of my day too.

Nancy Eubanks, Manager, Zingerman's Catering

I love that I work in a place where I'm free to implement my ideas. I have really enjoyed being able to grow and cultivate a segment of our business (at the Farmer's Markets) that now accounts for about 15 percent of our yearly sales.

I like that my boss accepts my ideas about how we can grow the markets. I appreciate that you and Paul seem genuinely interested in getting to know the people that work for you. I don't think you'll find that from too many CEOs (I know you don't refer to yourself as such, but you get what I'm saying).

Mike Broman, Farmer's Market Man, Zingerman's Creamery

I'd worked at several very different jobs (including the cheese counter at the Deli and the Product Planning Department at General Moters) before starting ZingTrain in 1994. Through ZingTrain I've had the opportunity and privilege to see inside many, many interesting and successful organizations from all over the world. Our ZCoB culture is very different and very special. Despite the fact that we are not even close to perfect and I can get frustrated with all the things I wish were better, I've yet to encounter anywhere else I'd rather spend my working (and lots of non-working) time. Within the ZCoB I feel a sense of teamwork and support, a commitment to doing what's right for the customer and for the organization, that makes me happy and proud to work here.

Maggie Bayless, Co-Managing Partner, ZingTrain

What's different about Zingerman's is its genuine desire to serve others (customers, community, and each other). I've always felt immense support from all of my co-workers, as a newcomer, and until the day I left. I've had tremendous learning opportunities to further my own personal growth, as well as learning more about the business. Furthermore, I've always felt that my ideas were valued, and people were always taking action to improve whatever they could. Zingerman's would never settle for just "good enough," but strives to continually improve every aspect of its product and environment. If I had to name the first three words that came to my mind about working at Zingerman's, they would be: passionate, supportive, and knowledgeable.

Becky Ng, Sandwich Sales and Service, Zingerman's Delicatessen

As you may know, I have only been with the Deli for about 5 weeks, but I think it's long enough to cultivate some thoughts on the Zing-difference. Unlike many of the new employees here I have several decades of work experience under my belt; I have been employed by Fortune 500 companies, family run operations, I have owned my own wine shop and everything in between it would seem. There are a few hallmarks of the work environment here that resonate almost immediately when you are "accepted into the family." The general positive attitude and communal dedication to giving good service, food, and finance are evident from the very beginning. On my first day of work a dishwasher took a moment to talk with me about overuse of bleach in the sanitation buckets and how it could damage flavor and was wasteful. That sort of blew me away, and is an anecdote I have told more than a few times. Indeed all along the way there has been support and well meaning advice about the culture of business within the Deli. From an operational standpoint, I think that our approach to Open Book Finance and the employee vetting process are truly unique, not only their design but in the results they achieve as is evident by the sense of ownership that seem to prevail in every aspect of the operation.

Paul Hannah, Retail Counterperson, Zingerman's Delicatessen

I could write and write but I'm going to try to be concise and really sum the feeling up. What I like most about Zingerman's is the never-ending optimism and possibility. Ideas are most generally not shot down, thoughts and feelings are encouraged and there is TRUE encouragement to grow (personally, professionally, and as an organization) and be involved. I am amazed that the majority of the people who become part of the "Zing's clan" are in fact dynamite people— interesting, smart, fun, kind. Coming to work every day is a pleasure!

Elin Walters, Next Door Supervisor, Zingerman's Delicatessen

I love my job! This is the first thing I tell people. I have worked here for 21 years over a period of 26. This work has provided never-ending inspiration, challenge, and opportunity. I actually envisioned the position I'm in years ago so I am, in fact, living my dream job. I'm empowered to meet unending challenges and these always lead down a path of further learning or a chance to exercise my vast experience gained on the job. We are all encouraged to grow, contribute, excel, participate, and engage fully. All of us. We are in this together and this is an inspiration in itself to share so much potential. My work every day contributes to the greater good of our community, by feeding the hungry, role modeling great business practices, creating opportunity, providing excellent food with history, flavor in a meaningful context that enriches the lives of so many. People come from around the world to visit us—sometimes it's like walking in a parade with the excitement. At the same time, I can still focus in, greet, connect with people in a place and context where everyone's taking the time to value and really appreciate what's here now on our plates! I love providing hospitality in the way my parents taught—it's natural for me. I work some pretty long days and sometimes it's because I've just taken the time to chat with folks or kiss a lot of babies that day. I'm a people person and it's not hard to make folks feel welcomed and special. We are empowered to engage, focus, teach what is truly important to our guests and co-workers. Leadership is relentless in pursuing excellence, in touch and generous with time and support enlisting us each to engage fully. We are always growing and improving—there is never a dull moment here. Honestly, not a day passes that I don't reflect on how wonderful my life is to have meaningful work that I love, especially in these hard times. Oh yeah it is. I'll be here tonight installing a new Ansil system!

Nancy Rucker, Facilities Manager, Zingerman's Delicatessen

Our approach to business and why I continue to work here. Great service to guests is only possible if we are providing great service to one another. We never compromise on ingredients if the quality of the product will be diminished. We value each and every staff person equally and are committed to learning and teaching on all levels. Honesty and integrity are more important than making a quick buck. Open book finance leads to open communication and problem solving. We acknowledge our problems (they're the same as any other biz in the world) and are committed to working on them openly.

Betty Gratopp, Production Manager, Zingerman's Mail Order

After being a cubicle-dwelling drone (sitting for 10 hours a day under fluorescent lights in a window-less office in front of a computer, a slave to email and prisoner of soulless bureaucrats) for nearly 15 years, working at Zingerman's Roadhouse is a truly liberating, if sometimes frustrating experience. It is great to be part of a dynamic team that is all committed to the common mission of sharing the Zingerman's Experience with guests and colleagues. I've been a fan of Zingerman's for nearly 8 years (the whole time I've lived in Michigan), and now that I am part of the ZCoB, I am happy to realize that it is as "Zingy" as I'd imagined. That said, as I am new to the restaurant world, I sometimes struggle to balance "getting it done" with "getting it done well." I know the 3 Steps to Giving Great Service are fairly straightforward, yet I find myself still questioning how well that process is working for me, my colleagues, and my guests and how I can improve the process for all sides (going the Extra Mile without going too far). While working as a server can be both physically and mentally exhausting, it is also invigorating to share the love of great food with others.

Ashini Harris, Server, Zingerman's Roadhouse

Working in the restaurant industry for 17 years, I thought taking a job at the Roadhouse would just be a quick way to make some money. It is so much more than that! Whether it is one of our many regulars that come in and we impress time and time again by continually exceeding their expectations, or a first time guest just stopping in for a quick meal, we really do care about our customers. Some days I take for granted driving the 12 miles to work to "sling some burgers," and then I hear about the couple who chose the Roadhouse to come eat at when the Icelandic ash prevented them to fly to Paris, France, for their anniversary trip. Or that we have the ability to overhear a guest talk about their grandmother's collard greens, and then we sneak them a complimentary sample, and tears come to their eyes because it reminds them of their grandmother. Or maybe it's the unexpected thing, that even if you asked someone in another restaurant to help you with that they would NEVER do in a million years. Like overhearing a guest from out of town say they needed something to do for five hours while their friend is at the hospital—giving them directions to the movie theatre and information on what's showing blows them out of the water. Or maybe it's the guests coming to one of our special monthly theme dinners, eating amazing food that went beyond their wildest culinary dreams, and also learning from our guest speakers who've come from around the country to share their knowledge about food, culture, and history. Or maybe it is having Ari swing by your table and refill your water glass and make you feel better just because he (and Paul) continue to care just as much today as they did 28 years ago. But overall, I love working here, because we can push the envelope of giving great service every day, that helps enrich our guests' lives, but also enriches our own lives and continually challenges us to do more, better, and continue finding new ways to impress our guests, because it is the right thing to do.

Sharon Kramer, Server, Zingerman's Roadhouse

For me, a huge difference is our dedication to "making things right" for our guests. The aspect of this that I'm really talking about is the fact that everyone here is authorized to make it right. Even if it's only your second day on the

337

job, you can make it right. We all have experience with businesses messing up; we know what it feels like. I think we often think about the big problems, places where we've really messed something up and need to fix it, but I love the small "make it rights"— the ones that really could probably go unnoticed, unattended—and perhaps would at a workplace where there's not such an emphasis on the guest having an overall great experience.

Just yesterday I noticed a woman trying to split a bagel in half; I asked if I could slice it for her, at which point she explained that her son had dropped it and she was just trying to tear off the part that hit the ground. I offered to grab her a new one at which point she told me again that her son had dropped it and it wasn't my fault. I assured her that there was no need for her son to eat the bagel that he had dropped and that I would love to run and grab a fresh one. She was ever so gracious! It's these little gestures that don't seem like much, but that I believe build repeat customers. The Zingerman's mission of providing a great experience encourages us to really care for our guests. It's great for the guest and, honestly, it's a great feeling for me.

Working here is empowering. The freedom we get has responsibilities, so does putting into your work: you get what you put into it. I've been other places where everyone has to just do what they're told and there is not a chance for contribution. I recommend Zingerman's as a place to work for anyone who has the guts (and an open mind) to move ahead and be a leader.

Margot Miller, Chocolate Lady, Zingerman's Delicatessen

The openness and sharing make it a very comfortable atmosphere to work in. You don't have the worry of who knows what or who is supposed to know— everyone is invited to learn as much as they can about their business and the ZCoB. But with knowledge, comes responsibility. It is a privilege to be included in discussions with partners, prospective partners, and the intimate details of each business. I highly recommend this approach to business. The energy that can be wasted on stress is re-focused into positive energy to further the growth and progress of the business.

Elaine Steig, Zingerman's Service Steward

Zingerman's spoiled me rotten. It's a good thing I love working here so much because I'd never be happy anywhere else. They got to me early. I was 18 when I worked my first shift at Zingerman's Deli and fell for the pace, energy, and people around me. I've never felt like a cog in all the years since. I've always felt like an important part of the world around me . . . an aspect of the Zingerman's Experience rather than a tool. The way we run our business (open book finance, visioning, etc) is a big reason why. Pride, perspective, pause. These are tenets of *ownership*, yet commonly held beliefs in every employee at Zingerman's from baker to busboy.

Pride in the work we do, the food we produce, our involvement and contribution to the community around us. Because we share and talk about "the numbers" each one of us sees the results of our work. We watch NOP (net operating profit) rise. We see the impact in our community. We know that the work we do matters.

Perspective on who we are and where we're going. Because we talk about the future of our business, I know where I can grow and learn and progress. I know that it's up to me to carve my own path in that future, wherever my passion leads me.

Pause when things *don't* go according to plan. The economy impacted us all. It took the breath out of a lot of folks. We made hard choices. We sacrificed, but we didn't panic. We knew the score and what it took to survive because we *all had the same information* and we believed in each other.

Besides the continued financial health of our business, that was the real reward: knowing that what we'd believed in and worked on for so many years was actually the right way for us to run our business. It made us stronger in our convictions and tighter in our connections. It really worked.

It's nice being spoiled.

Brad Hedeman, "Scribe," Zingerman's Mail Order

I think I stopped telling this story every time I teach the "M.O.R. Money" class here at Zingerman's because I almost always get teared up and it gets sort of embarrassing! When we started the first Zingerman's Money Club four or five years ago, we decided to start the year off with writing a vision of where each of us wanted to be by the end of our year together. At that time, I had terrible credit and huge credit card debt and really no idea of how I could get out of it. I wanted to buy a house, but knew I was in no position to even begin that process. My vision stated that by the end of the year, I'd have reduced my debt and increased my credit score so that I'd be able to start talking to someone about getting a mortgage. It felt weird to just write that down because I didn't really believe at that time that I could do it. But month after month, I plugged away at my goals and with the help of the group—who were the people I communicated my vision with—I did in fact get into a position to apply for a mortgage and right now, I'm sitting at the computer in my house that I've lived in for the past 3 years. I've paid the mortgage on time or early every month and now have more savings than I've ever had. Writing a vision, putting it down on paper, and sharing it with others . . . what can I say? It's life changing.

Carole Woods, Human Resources, Zingerman's Delicatessen

I hadn't done much visioning work before Zingerman's. I'd set goals, but had never written a vision. The experience makes you think more deeply about what you are trying to accomplish. There is something very personal about writing one. This may be at odds with some corporate cultures, but at Zingerman's I'm supported to keep moving toward a personally inspiring vision. The things that help me are keeping in mind that: the more detail the better (and more excited about it you will be), there is power in the word DRAFT, and don't agonize over getting every word right—just get it out there.

Chris Krause, Mistress of Mission Control, Zingerman's Delicatessen

"Why do you want to be a partner in the ZCoB?" That is usually the first question in interviews. Either that or, "Why do you want to work here?" Well it actually starts with the first resume that I ever published back at culinary school in the '90s. At the top they teach you to write your "goal." I figured I better make that the good part because with my experience now the rest of my CV was going to suck. So I wrote: "I want to gain the knowledge and skills necessary to own and run a successful restaurant business and become one of the next generation of chef/professionals to guide the future of food." I came up with that one-liner 17 years ago in culinary school and it seems to have stuck with me since. The day I wrote it I knew it was the path for me. True I haven't had to update my CV in a while but that is because I have found a place where I can do just what I wrote. I have been able to live that goal here at Zingerman's Deli. Becoming a managing partner will strengthen that goal and make it even more of a reality by taking it to the next level.

Rodger Bowser, Chef and Prospective Co-Managing Partner, Zingerman's Delicatessen

My personal and professional life have intersected and become one. Working at Zingerman's is an extension of who and what I am. I am fortunate to have found you! It's great to be part of a place that allows for self-expression! It's quite a symbiotic relationship!

Anne Good, Retail Counterperson, Zingerman's Bakehouse

I applied to work at Zingerman's simply because I needed a job that offered health care benefits. What I got in addition to the insurance and the paycheck was a host of opportunities to explore beyond the scope of my day-to-day work. I was encouraged to create new challenges in support of my own growth and that of the business. I am grateful for those chances, and the inherent belief that goes along with them that I am capable of achieving great and meaningful accomplishments. Sixteen years later I am still happy to be working at Zingerman's for my health insurance, but now I know that whatever project I take on—both the mighty and the mini—has the potential to make life for other people a little better and a little happier than it was before.

Lynn Yates, Director, Zingerman's Community Foundation

After getting my undergrad degree at Harvard, and then studying cooking and baking in Paris, I was one of the original bakers at the Bakehouse when it was just forming in 1992. In 1997 I left to go to Denmark when my husband got an academic position there, and then NYC where I got my MBA at Columbia. After a year of working in my cubicle high up in a Manhattan skyscraper, I came back to Ann Arbor as co-managing partner with Frank at the Bakehouse.

Why do you work at Zingerman's?

I've asked this question of myself many times since 1992 when I took a job at the newly forming Zingerman's Bakehouse. And I've been asked this question just as many times by often confused and disbelieving friends and acquaintances who wonder why a Harvard and Columbia graduate would choose to spend her life being a part of a relatively small food business in the middle of the country ("You said you were in banking?"—"No, baking").

I came back for ownership in the bakery and great food. I am staying because of my spiritual partnership in the ZCoB (I say spiritual because my actual ownership is still only on the bakery), my complete belief in the processes we use to manage our organization, and the values that guide us in our decisions.

What about the food? My dedication to great food remains unchanged and is the critical foundation to being here at all.

I honestly can't imagine working in any other way. After 10 years of making decisions by consensus, practicing open book finance, sharing information in every direction about everything, working in a collaborative style in cross-organization groups of all levels, I feel like a different person, a better person, and definitely a more effective leader. Our values—caring for our community, providing a stimulating, respectful, and rewarding work environment, supporting and encouraging personal development, and going for greatness—are interwoven into all of my daily activities. Working like this feels rich and hopeful and just plain right. I know that it allows us to make small, daily differences in each other's lives, the lives of our guests, and our community. It's joyful too! I feel lucky to be a part of it.

Amy Emberling, Co-Managing Partner, Zingerman's Bakehouse

Zingerman's Timeline

1902— The building now known as Zingerman's Delicatessen is built on the corner of Kingsley & Detroit streets in Ann Arbor, Michigan. It opens as Disderide's Grocery.

1975—Paul Saginaw leaves graduate school at the University of Michigan to work at a local seafood restaurant.

1978—Ari Weinzweig graduates from the University of Michigan and goes to work washing dishes at a local restaurant, Maude's, where he meets Paul Saginaw, Frank Carollo, and Maggie Bayless, his partners-to-be.

1979—Paul opens Monahan's fish market in Kerrytown with Mike Monahan (the fish market is still there and still one of the best in the country!)

1980—Ari and Paul begin a conversation about how Ann Arbor could use a traditional Jewish deli like the ones they grew up with in Detroit (Paul) and Chicago (Ari).

November 1981—Paul notices that the building on the corner of Kingsley and Detroit is available. He calls Ari to see if he's ready to open the deli that they had talked about.

March 7, 1982—Ari and Paul are making final plans to open "Greenberg's

Delicatessen" named in honor of Hannah Greenberg, one of Paul's regular customers at the fish market. Ari takes a call from another deli owner in Michigan who has already filed papers with the state to own the name "Greenberg's Deli." After being told they can't use the name, they have a quick brainstorming session to find a new name (since Weinzweig is unpronounceable and Saginaw, though derived from the Jewish name Sagin' Or—which means "seer of light"—has decidedly non-Jewish connotations in Michigan). They settle on Zingerman's (in part because it starts with Z and will be easy to spot at the end of a list).

March 15, 1982—Zingerman's opens its doors for the first time. Ari and Paul are behind the counter making sandwiches and cutting bread and cheeses, working with one full-time and one part-time staff member. There are five tables and four stools along the counter in the front window. We feature a small but meaningful selection of sandwiches, traditional Jewish foods like chopped liver and chicken soup, cheeses, smoked fish, cured and smoked meats and breads, and pastries from local bakeries.

1985—Steve Muno begins work on the retail line. His inventive sign making would come to exemplify the Deli's signature artistic style and his unique handwriting, eventually dubbed '**Muno**' (pronounced "mew-no") would become the standard font for all Zingerman's signs and posters. Steve is still a regular Zingerman's customer.

1986—The 700-square-foot addition to the original Zingerman's building is completed. The pie-shaped wedge houses the sandwich line and provides expanded room for dry goods.

1988—Zingerman's Magic Brownies are baked for the first time. The recipe was developed courtesy of Ms. Connie Prigg, a Zingerman's staff member at the time who now lives in Baltimore.

1988—Zingerman's begins a food rescue program to feed the hungry in our community. **Food Gatherers** collects nutritious food from shops, restaurants, & hotels and quickly delivers it to the people in need in our community.

1991—Ian Nagy begins work as Zingerman's first full-time illustrator (he's still here too!) and goes on to define the Zingerman's style that has become famous nationwide thanks to our mail order catalogs and websites.

Zingerman's Next Door opens up in a converted residence one door south of the Deli on Halloween.

1992—**April:** Frank Carollo, an old friend from Maude's, gets together with Ari and Paul, and the three of them meet up with Michael London, bread baker extraordinaire, at his bakery in upstate New York. Michael teaches his techniques to Frank and the seeds of **Zingerman's Bakehouse** are planted.

October: The first official loaves of bread emerge from the Zingerman's Bakehouse ovens and head to the Deli breadbox and sandwich line. Among the original Bakehouse staff of 8 is Amy Emberling who goes on to manage the Bakehouse bread department, then the pastry kitchen, and, after a hiatus to complete her MBA from Columbia, returns to Ann Arbor to join Frank as Bakehouse co-managing partner.

1993—We write our mission statement and Guiding Principles.

Zingerman's first mail order catalog is released. Deli staff members Maurice (Mo) Frechette and Jude Walton take the lead in shipping food to hungry guests looking to get their Zingerman's fix from afar. Four years later food writer Ed Behr describes Zingerman's mail order catalog as " . . . the most discriminating selection of foods that I am aware of."

1994—After years of pondering how to grow their business and still stay rooted in the local community (and after rejecting numerous offers to franchise), Ari and Paul release "Zingerman's 2009," a unique vision for organizational growth that plants the seed of the **Zingerman's Community of Businesses**.

Ann Arbor becomes a sweeter place to live when Zingerman's Bakehouse begins baking sweet stuff to go with bread. Big O's (oatmeal raisin cookies baked with real maple syrup), Funky Chunky Chocolate Cookies, and AmaZing Cheesecake start emerging from the Bakehouse's new ovens in addition to the already successful Magic Brownies.

In response to numerous requests from others in the business world to learn the "secrets" to Zingerman's success, **ZingTrain**—Zingerman's consulting and training business—is born under the aegis of Maggie Bayless (a friend from the old days at Maude's and an early Deli staffer). ZingTrain offers all sorts of interesting information on service, training systems and other tools and techniques used throughout the ZCoB.

1996— Zingerman's Catering, famous for extraordinary deli trays and for bringing "the Zingerman's experience" beyond the Deli's doors, and into Southeast Michigan, is launched. The Deli's catering department grows to provide everything from casual meals to planning and catering for 2,000-person events.

1997—The new bread bag from Zingerman's Bakehouse's earns national design recognition from *Print* Magazine. Zing artists become *Print* favorites, receiving similar recognition the next three years in a row for four other Zingerman's design projects.

1998—Food Gatherers delivers over 2,000,000 pounds of food to help feed those in need in Washtenaw County.

After three years of outstanding effort, Jude Walton and Mo Frechette make the jump to full-fledged Managing Partners of **Zingerman's Mail Order**. The push toward Zingerman's 2009 continues.

1999—Led by managing partners Tom Root and Toni Morell, **Zingermans.com** goes online.

2000—*USA Today* names Zingerman's one of the country's top 10 places to buy ". . . a genuine Jewish Nosh."

As demand for ZingTrain seminars and workshops continues to grow, Stas' Kazmierski joins ZingTrain as Maggie's co-managing partner.

2001—Zingerman's Creamery opens up and cheesemaker and managing partner John Loomis begins making fresh cheeses.

2002—Zingerman's Mail Order and zingermans.com merge to become one business headed by Tom, Toni, Mo, and Jude.

2003—*INC. Magazine* calls us "The Coolest Small Company in America."

Chef Alex Young becomes managing partner and executive chef as **Zingerman's Roadhouse** opens up in the old Bill Knapp's building at the corner of Jackson and Maple roads on Ann Arbor's far west side.

Zingerman's Coffee Company opens and roastmaster and managing partner Allen Leibowitz starts selling Zingerman's coffee throughout the Zingerman's Community of Businesses and to wholesale customers across the country.

Zingerman's Guide to Giving Great Service is published and details the steps we take to provide the Zingerman's Experience for our guests, our staff, our vendors, and our community.

Zingerman's Guide to Good Eating by Ari Weinzweig is published and written up in *Fine Cooking, Saveur,* the *Chicago Tribune,* the *New York Times,* and other national publications at the top of their holiday book gift lists!

2004—Deli retail manager Grace Singleton takes the reins as Deli Managing Partner.

Zingerman's Roadshow, Ann Arbor's hippest drive-up coffee counter, opens in the parking lot of Zingerman's Roadhouse.

Zingerman's Coffee Company is featured in *Travel & Leisure* as one of the country's top roasters.

2005—The birth of the Zingerman's candy bar. Zzang!® bars coming out of the Bakehouse are quickly named "the ultimate handmade candy bar" by *Chocolatier* magazine.

2006—BAKE!, Ann Arbor's hands-on teaching bakery and CAKE!, a showroom worthy of the imagination-defying creations from the Bakehouse cake designers, opens at Zingerman's Bakehouse.

For the first time, produce from Zingerman's **Cornman Farms** highlights the Roadhouse's annual Harvest Dinner.

2007—Deli restaurant manager Rick Strutz joins Grace as co-managing partner at the Deli.

On March 15, Zingerman's celebrates our 25th anniversary with a 6,000-person street fair on Detroit Street outside the Deli, featuring guests and friends from our first quarter century. We sold 3,044 reubens and 1,241 cappucinos!

The *New York Times* relaunches its Wednesday Small Business section with a feature on the Zingerman's Community of Businesses, "The Corner Deli That Dared to Break Out of the Neighborhood."

Zingerman's launches our 2020 Vision charting the course for the Zingerman's Community of Businesses for the next 13 years.

Bon Appetit bestows their Lifetime Achievement award on Ari and Paul (previous winners include such food luminaries as Alice Waters, Jacques Pepin, and Julia Child!).

2008—Zingerman's Coffee Company manager Steve Mangigian joins Allen as co-managing partner of the business.

Zingerman's is featured on Oprah's sandwich episode and #97 Lisa C.'s Boisterous Brisket is Oprah's favorite, rating an '11' on a scale of 1-5.

The ZCoB nets a long piece on NPR's *Weekend Edition Sunday* detailing our growth from a corner Deli into a nationally renowned community of businesses.

Travel & Leisure features the Roadhouse in a long piece (with lots of great photos) in their November issue.

2009—*Bon Appetit* names Zingerman's Roadhouse one of the top 10 best new barbecue restaurants in the U.S.

Charlie Frank, who managed the pastry kitchen at Zingerman's Bakehouse, says goodbye to pastry and hello to candy as he launches Zingerman's Candy Manufactory, the 8th business in Zingerman's Community.

Suggested Reading

I have way more books that I like and have learned from than I'm going to list here. But below are a few of my favorites—some are new, others are longtime classics that helped form my thinking many years ago but still seem just as relevant now as they were then. Happy to get your recommendations as well— send 'em my way at ari@zingermans.com.

Anarchist Reading List

Paul Avrich, *Anarchist Voices*

Paul Avrich, *An American Anarchist: The Life of Voltairine de Cleyre*

Alexander Berkman, *The ABC of Anarchism*

Exquisite Rebel: The Essays of Voltairine de Cleyre Edited by Sharon Presley and Crispin Sartwell

Candace Falk, *Love, Anarchy and Emma Goldman*

Emma Goldman, *Living My Life*

Emma Goldman, *Anarchism and Other Essays*

Tom Goyens, *Beer and Revolution: The German Anarchist Movement in New York City, 1880–1914*

Peter Kropotkin, *Fields, Factories and Workshops, The Conquest of Bread*

Peter Kropotkin, *Mutual Aid; A Factor of Evolution*

Peter Marshall, *Demanding the Impossible*

Benjamin Tucker, *Why I Am an Anarchist*

Business Reading List

Ichak Adizes, *Corporate Lifecycles*

James Autry, *Life and Work*

James Autry, *Love and Profit: The Art of Caring Leadership*

Peter Block, *The Empowered Manager*

Peter Block, *Stewardship*

Peter Block, *The Answer to How Is Yes: Acting on What Matters*

Marcus Buckingham and Curt Coffman, *First Break All the Rules*

Bo Burlingham, *Small Giants*

Bo Burlingham and Norm Brodsky, *The Knack*

Anese Cavanaugh, *The Little Book of Bootism*

Chip Conley, *Peak: How Great Companies Get Their Mojo from Maslow*

Stephen Covey, *Principle Centered Leadership*

Max DePree, *Leadership Is an Art*

Max DePree, *Leadership Jazz*

Peter Drucker, *The Effective Executive*

Peter Drucker, *Management*

Peter M. Senge, *The Fifth Discipline*

Robert Greenleaf, *Servant Leadership*

Paul Hawken, *Growing a Business*

Lawrence Lippitt, *Preferred Futuring*

Hugh MacLeod, *Ignore Everybody*

Rosabeth Moss Kanter, *Confidence*

Burt Nanus, *Visionary Leadership*

Tom Peters, *The Pursuit of WOW!*

Gifford and Elizabeth Pinchot, *The End of Bureaucracy*

Daniel Pink, *Drive*

Ricardo Semler, *Maverick*

Jack Stack and Bo Burlingham, *The Great Game of Business*

Jack Stack and Bo Burlingham, *A Stake in the Outcome*

Dean Tucker, *Using the Power of Purpose*

Bob Wall, Robert Solum, and Mark Sobel, *The Visionary Leader*

Appreciations

Here at Zingerman's we end every meeting with a few minutes of appreciations. Anyone who likes can appreciate anyone they like—it's totally unplanned and can include anyone from their latest hire to a customer, colleague, or cousin in California. While this hasn't exactly been a meeting in the usual sense of the word, if you made it this far in the book, you and I have been meeting for quite a few hours now. I appreciate you reading and thinking through all this stuff— books without readers are akin to food that—no matter how well prepared— goes uneaten.

Less directly, there are thousands of people to appreciate. I'm sure I'm going to forget someone, so I'll start here with just a general appreciation of everyone around me who's shared a story, eaten a sandwich, baked or bought a loaf of bread, offered constructive criticism or contributed positively to what we do at Zingerman's, or helped me learn and grow as I have over the years.

More formally, first and foremost I appreciate Paul— he's the one without whom none of this would exist. Collaborative, caring, generous, insightful, funny, and supportive to the max, he's stuck with all of this and with me for three decades now.

Thanks to everyone whose been a part of Zingerman's over all the years, from Marci Fribourg and Ricky Cohen who were there in the beginning, to Vanessa Reeves, who was the last person hired before this book went to press.

Thanks to everyone who's worked on making the book a book—Jim Reische for excellent editing and patient insight, Pete Sickman-Garner for leading all the design work. Thanks to Jillian Downey for everything she's done to make Zingerman's published books a reality, and Elph Morgan for general counsel on the same. Much appreciation to Jenny Tubbs, for all the great recipe testing work, insightful editing, proofing, trouble shooting, and her seeming ability to do just about anything needed with two minutes notice and do it all with high spirits, good taste, and a great sense of humor.

Thanks to all the Managing Partners at Zingerman's for building an organization great enough that I could even consider writing a book about it. Frank Carollo, Amy Emberling, Allen Leibowitz, Steve Mangigian, John Loomis, Alex Young, Charlie Frank, Grace Singleton, Rick Strutz, Rodger Bowser, Mo Frechette, Tom Root, Toni Morell, Stas' Kazmierski, and, last but not least, Maggie Bayless, without whose help, guidance, and insight into how to turn all the ideas the rest of us might have had into teachable, learnable material, this book would probably not be here. Thanks too to Ron Maurer, our one and only Vice President of Administration, whose arrival at Zingerman's in 2001 is certainly one of the best things that's ever happened to us.

Thanks to Jo Labadie, who passed away in 1933, and Jan Longone, who is still going strong in Ann Arbor today. These two individuals shared a love of learning, a passion for books and for making the world a better place, a spirit of generosity, and, oddly, the same initials. While I'll never have the latter, I hope that I can come close to what each of the two of them has contributed in all those other areas. If you spend time in Ann Arbor, consider visiting the Longone and Labadie collections at the University of Michigan Libraries.

Thanks to Drs. Jay Sandweiss, Stuart Winston, David Schteingart, Jeff Sanfield, Randy Descrochers, Steve Thiry, Tom Gravelyn, Ariel Barkan, William Chandler, Kim Eagle, Laurel Blakemore, Cheryl Perlis, and Les Zun for helping me get through the last two years.

Thanks to Richard Kempter and Marge Greene for much of the wisdom that underlies what's in here and for helping me to make my life far more fun and much more rewarding.

Thanks to Ian Nagy, Nicole Robichaud, Betsy Bruner, Ryan Stiner, Billie Lee, Raúl Peña, and Pete Sickman-Garner for all the Zingerman's graphic design and illustration. To Becky Winkler for the 3 C's and for everything else she's done here over all the years we've worked together. Special appreciation to Ian and Ryan for the illustrations in the book. Business and art aren't usually seen as one, and business books rarely have great art in them. I appreciate these two for contributing a bit more character and color to making the book something special.

Thanks to Anese Cavanaugh for Bootist insight, great energy, daring to engage, and good ideas. Patrick Hoban for all the good leadership dialogue and sharp elbows. Appreciation to Julie Herrada at the Labadie Collection for all her help in tracking down relevant anarchist writing. Thanks for friendship, advice, insight, and good emails to Molly Stevens, Randolph Hodgson, Lex Alexander, Daphne Zepos, Karen Pernick, and Marifer Calleja. Special appreciation to Meg Noori for ongoing great dialogue, late night poetry and impromptu but effective assistance with editing.

Let's see . . . thanks too to Doe Coover, Rob Pasick, Wayne Baker, Majid Mahjoub, Edgar Schein, Jack Stack, Chip Conley, John T. Edge, Marcie and Bill Ferris, Gauri Thergaonkar, Dan Gillote, Connie Savander, Liz Lester, Marcia Labrenz, and a fair few other folks who I'm sure I'm forgetting but can't recall right now.

Going back 30 years, thanks to professors William Rosenberg, Arthur Mendel, Roman Szporluk, and Carl Proffer, for teaching me history many years ago. Thanks to Professor Jesse Cohn in Indiana for sharing his work on the anarchists.

Thanks to Emma Goldman, Alexander Berkman, Mikhail Bakunin, Peter Kropotkin, Voltairine de Cleyre, Nestor Makhno, Rudolf Rocker, Paul Avrich, and all the other insightful anarchists who were writing about this stuff so long ago. Special appreciation to Bo Burlingham, another modern-day lapsed anarchist, for insight and inspiration.

And, again, thanks to you for reading!

Ari

COMING NEXT

in the *Zingerman's Guide to Good Leading Series*

Zingerman's
GUIDE TO GOOD LEADING, PART 2

A Lapsed Anarchist's Approach to

BEING A BETTER LEADER

ari weinzweig

ALSO AVAILABLE!

ZINGERMAN'S GUIDE TO GOOD EATING

A deeper discussion of good food.

Zingerman's co-founder Ari Weinzweig has collected stories, recipes and pearls of wisdom into this tome of culinary knowledge. A must for serious chefs and weekend cooks alike. Not only does the reader understand the ins and outs of formerly mysterious foods like balsamic vinegar and great olive oil but its approachable writing makes it easy to become an authority on practically all things artisan.

ZINGERMAN'S GUIDE TO BETTER BACON

Pork Bellies, Hush Puppies, Rock 'n' Roll, and Bacon Fat Mayonnaise.

Ari guides you on a personal tour of bacon's long and curious history. You'll head to the farm and learn about 19th-century drovers who were crucial to the hog trade. Ari's story shows how bacon moved from delicious farm staple to a huge-selling flavorless commodity—and how it's going back to its roots today.

There are loads of delicious, well-tested recipes, from chocolate gravy to cheddar bacon scones.

ZINGERMAN'S GUIDE TO GIVING GREAT SERVICE

"When it comes to service, few establishments can rival Zingerman's." —Saveur

Eighty percent of complaining customers are unhappier after they complain. Why? How do you deal with tough customers? Or really good ones? Here's our quick guide to treating customers like royalty. It details our recipes for giving great service and for effectively handling customer complaints. There are plenty of usable, teachable tips and tools that are applicable for service providers in organizations of any size, in any industry.

Customer Service Training DVDs

ZINGERMAN'S 3 STEPS TO GIVING GREAT SERVICE

ZINGERMAN'S 5 STEPS TO EFFECTIVELY HANDLING A COMPLAINT

Hands on training tools for forward thinking businesses.

Invest in ZingTrain's acclaimed training DVDs, and make the tools we've learned over 28 years work help your staff excel. We share our down-to-earth service approach in the Zingerman's 3 Steps to Giving Great Service Training DVD, which features actual Zingerman's employees and customers sharing real-life service scenarios.

On the flip side, the Zingerman's 5 Steps to Effectively Handling a Complaint Training DVD takes you step-by-step through a service recipe designed to help take the stress out of one of the most challenging encounters in customer service.

notes

notes

notes

notes

notes

notes

notes

1999

Led by managing partners tom root and toni morell, zingermans.com goes online.

2000

amy emberling, one of the original bakers and founder of the pastry kitchen, returns to zingerman's bakehouse as co-managing partner.

as demand for zingtrain seminars and workshops continues to grow, stas' kazmierski joins zingtrain as maggie's co-managing partner.

2001

zingerman's creamery opens up in manchester, mi and cheesemaker and managing partner, john loomis, begins making fresh cheeses.

2002

zingerman's mail order and zingermans.com merge to become one business headed by tom, toni, mo and jude.

2007

deli restaurant manager rick strutz joins grace as co-managing partner at the deli.

On march 15, zingerman's celebrates our 25th anniversary with a 6,000-person street fair on detroit street outside the deli, featuring guests and friends from our first quarter century. we sold 3,044 reubens and 1,241 cappuccinos!

zingerman's launches our 2020 vision charting the course for the zingerman's community of businesses for the next 13 years.

"bon appétit" bestows their lifetime achievement award on ari and paul (previous winners include such food luminaries as alice waters, jacques pépin, and julia child!)

> "[zingerman's is] a national treasure. it is the center of my gastrodeli universe."
> mario batali

2006

bake!, ann arbor's hands-on teaching bakery and cake!, a showroom worthy of the imagination-defying creations from the bakehouse cake designers, opens at zingerman's bakehouse.

for the first time, produce from our own cornman farms highlights the roadhouse's annual harvest dinner.

2008

zingerman's coffee company manager, steve mangigian, joins allen as co-managing partner of the business.

zingerman's is featured on oprah's sandwich episode and #97 lisa c.'s boisterous brisket is oprah's favorite, rating an "11" on a scale of 1-5.